The Postage Stamp Vegetable Garden

THE POSTAGE STAMP
VEGETABLE GARDEN

Grow Tons of Organic Vegetables
in Tiny Spaces and Containers

KAREN NEWCOMB

TEN SPEED PRESS
Berkeley

Contents

Introduction

It's a beautiful day. There's not a cloud in the sky. The temperature is in the mid-80s. And there you are in your backyard, picking loads of vegetables from your own small garden tucked away in the corner of your property. Tomatoes, onions, corn, beans, you've grown them all—in fact, more than you ever dreamed possible from such a small space.

Impossible?

Of course not. That's exactly what a postage stamp garden is intended to do and what you will learn to do in the next several chapters. The techniques outlined here allow you to double or triple the quantities of vegetables you might normally grow in any given space.

The history of this incredible gardening system began in the 1890s. Outside Paris, a few enterprising Frenchmen began raising crops using a new method they discovered. Over their land they spread an 18-inch layer of manure (plentiful in the day of the horse and buggy) and planted their vegetables so close together in this rich material that the leaves touched one another as the plants grew. Under this carpet of leaves, the ground remained moist, warm, and vigorous. During periods of frost, they set glass jars over the tiny plants to give them an early start. So good were the Frenchmen in devising fresh ways of growing things that they were able to produce nine crops a year. Such was the birth of the French Intensive method of gardening, an early form of what we now call intensive, or wide-row, gardening.

In the following two decades, another organic gardening movement developed. In Switzerland, a remarkable philosopher from Austria, Rudolf Steiner, and his followers invented a gardening method called biodynamic.

They emphasized the exclusive and balanced use of organic fertilizers—composted leaves, grass, manure, and so on. They investigated what is now called companion planting and found that certain plants, when grown together (like beans and cabbages), do better than others (like beans and onions). They also sought new ways of arranging crops. These biodynamic gardeners hit upon the idea of planting in mounded beds that permitted adequate drainage and that were narrow enough so that a person didn't have to walk over them.

Between the 1930s and the 1960s, an Englishman, Alan Chadwick, set out to combine the French Intensive and biodynamic methods and add to them various ideas of his own, such as planting by the phases of the moon. In the 1960s he brought his meld of techniques to America, to the 4-acre Garden Project at the University of California at Santa Cruz. The acreage that he was given had "impossible" soil, in which even weeds failed to grow. In one season, using simple hand tilling and organic materials, Chadwick and his students brought the acreage to fertility. In a few seasons they had the richest, most beautiful gardens around.

The intensive method that Chadwick and his students used produced four times as many vegetables as a conventional garden using standard rows. It also used half the water and took less time to maintain. And the vegetables were wonderfully plump, tasty, and nutritious.

Chadwick's method, which came to be known as French Intensive Biodynamic Gardening, has proved to be perfectly adapted to small-space gardening. Using intensive methods, you can, for instance, grow as many carrots in 1 square foot as you can in a 12-foot row in a conventional garden. Properly handled, a 25-square-foot bed (5 by 5 feet) will produce a minimum of 200 pounds of vegetables.

To accommodate today's lifestyles, a garden needs to fit easily into a very small plot, take as little time as possible to work, require a minimum amount of water, and still produce prolifically. By combining the intensive methods with small-space innovations like vertical gardening and other crop-stretching techniques, that's exactly what a postage stamp garden does.

Postage stamp gardens are small. The smallest beds I recommend are 4 by 4 feet, the largest, 10 by 10 feet. Regardless of which size you choose, your garden will produce a tremendous amount of vegetables and, after the initial preparation, require little extra work, even less if you let an automatic drip system do the watering. The principles of postage stamp gardening are:

1   Start with an initial super-boosting postage stamp soil mix. This allows you to produce a greater quantity of vegetables in a much smaller space.

2   Plant the vegetables very closely together to save space, reduce watering, eliminate weeds, and create a healthier microclimate for your plants.

3   Utilize "crop-stretching" techniques such as intercropping, succession planting, catch crops, and vertical gardening to pack in as many vegetables as possible in a limited space.

4   Water deeply and regularly, but infrequently.

5   Use organic methods, including companion planting, to keep your garden and the food you eat healthy and safe.

When this book was first published in 1975, these concepts were unusual and revolutionary in the home garden. Since that time, there have been many imitators and variations, but the postage stamp method has stood the test of time. With more than half a million copies sold, this book has helped people of all gardening levels successfully grow many more vegetables in very tiny spaces.

This new edition is fully revised and now contains information on heirloom seed varieties. Heirloom varieties not only produce excellent results, but you can also save the seeds for the next season to guarantee the same vegetable as the parent plant. Because heirloom vegetables are living artifacts of history, these old-time varieties offer a glimpse of earlier times when vegetables were known and grown for their flavor.

The Postage Stamp Vegetable Garden offers simple, easy techniques that work. I hope you will try the postage stamp methods in your garden, and then experiment on your own. Get ready to plant. Whether you plant hybrid varieties or grow heirlooms, you will soon be able to enjoy the fruits of your labor.

CHAPTER 1

Planning Your Postage Stamp Vegetable Garden

If you like growing vegetables, there are few things more fun than planning the garden for next season. The best wintertime garden dreamers draw up dozens of illustrations of what their next garden is going to look like. I suggest that you do it, too. After all, things always go better with a plan. A good plan keeps your mistakes to a minimum by giving you some idea in advance of where to put your garden, what to plant in it, how much space to allocate, and what shape it should be.

Where to Put Your Postage Stamp Garden

The first thing to do in planning your garden, of course, is to decide where to put it. Your plants don't really care where they grow as long as you give them a lot of tender loving care—that is, good fertile soil, enough water, and whatever heat and daylight they need.

The main rule to consider is this: Most vegetables need minimally about six hours of direct sunlight. As long as your garden receives this minimum amount of direct sunlight every day, you can put your garden almost anywhere. Warm-weather vegetables (tomatoes, squash, peppers) can never get too much sun. Cool-weather vegetables (lettuce, greens, cabbage) will tolerate a little shade.

In addition, there are a few other placement considerations. Keep your garden bed at least 20 feet away from shallow-rooted trees like elms, maples, and poplars. Not only will the foliage of these trees block out the sun, but also their roots will compete for water and nutrients. Generally, tree roots take food from the soil in a circle as wide as the tree's farthest-reaching branches, and plants usually do poorly within this circle.

Don't put your garden in a low area that will collect standing water or near a downspout, where the force from a sudden rain can wash out some of your plants. Yet do try to place your garden near a water outlet. By doing so, you will eliminate having to drag a hose long distances. Also, try to place your garden as near the tool storage area as possible.

If possible, locate your vegetable garden next to an existing fence at the north end of your property, so that you can grow vining vegetables such as peas and cucumbers up against it. If you have a very large patio, or all the sunniest spots in your garden are paved over or occupied by existing flower beds, never fear. You can still plant a container garden (see page 25) or a flower bed vegetable garden. Who says that you have to grow a formal vegetable garden? Nobody, right? Not only can you mix vegetables with flowers in any flower bed, but doing so can also produce great quantities of vegetables. Here is some advice for "vegetablizing" your flower beds:

1   Plant vines such as cucumbers and small melons against back fences or walls. Plant beanstalks against a wall or stake them. Plantings like this give your garden an especially lush look.

2   Use leaf lettuce and Swiss chard as flower bed edging or borders. Grow head lettuce just behind the edging.

3   Plant root crops in small groups scattered throughout the flower bed.

4   Plant cabbage in a conspicuous spot where you're looking for a show-off.

5   Plant corn in a sunny corner. A 4 by 6-foot plot with plants 10 inches apart will produce a good crop.

6   Use attractive vegetable plants such as peppers, rhubarb, and artichokes as ornamentals to complement other plants.

What to Plant in Your Postage Stamp Garden

Before you rush out and plant a garden, spend a little time thinking about how you cook and how your family eats. Do you like salads, pasta, or hearty chowders and stews? If you don't care much for turnips, yet love tomatoes and use them in almost everything, then eliminate all turnips in the planning stage, even if they are easy to grow. Try new recipes that call for unfamiliar vegetables, and use a notebook to keep track of the vegetable varieties you've enjoyed.

After you make your choices, you can then select the number of plants you need by checking the Number of Plants Per Person table. If you enjoy canning or freezing vegetables, you can increase the number of plants recommended in the table to produce extra for preserving.

NUMBER OF PLANTS PER PERSON

VEGETABLE	PLANTS PER PERSON	VEGETABLE	PLANTS PER PERSON
Artichoke	1	Lettuce, leaf	2–4
Asparagus	12*	Melon	2
Bean, shell	3–4	Mustard greens	4–6
Bean, snap (bush)	2–3	Okra	1–2
Bean, snap (pole)	1–2	Onion	10–30
Beet	10–20	Peas	3–4
Broccoli	1–2	Pepper	1–2
Brussels sprouts	1	Radish	20–60
Cabbage	2	Rhubarb	1
Carrot	30–50	Spinach	3–7
Cauliflower	6–10	Spinach, New Zealand	5
Corn	5–6	Squash, summer	1
Cucumber	1–2	Squash, winter	2
Eggplant	1	Swiss chard	1
Garlic	4	Tomato	2
Kale	2–3	Tomato, paste	3
Lettuce, head	3–4	Turnip	8–15

*Asparagus is a perennial that can take over a garden bed over time, so be careful where and how much you plant.

Other things that will influence your choice of plants are the size of your garden, the size of the plants, and how much you will use companion planting, intercropping, succession planting, and catch cropping techniques. These are covered in chapters 4, 6, and 7, but you can go ahead and make a preliminary garden plan now and then tweak it as necessary as you read along.

To decide which herbs you'll need, look at the jars of dried herbs you already have in your kitchen. These are probably the ones you'll eventually want in your garden. I do not recommend that you plant everything the first year. Start with two or three herbs in your first garden, and add to them as you go along. You will also need to decide whether you want to plant herbs in with the vegetables or to have separate beds for them. Many herbs are perennial and don't need to be replanted from year to year, and keeping them separate means that you won't have to dig around them when replanting your annual vegetables.

Finally, garden catalogs and websites are good inspiration for deciding what to plant. There are numerous vegetable, flower, and herb companies with unique personalities and a seed selection you'll never find on the seed racks. Many of the printed seed catalogs offer planting tips, and some even have recipes. Before you start your garden, I suggest you send for some of the catalogs listed in Appendix B. This is one of my favorite preplanning chores every year. It will give you a chance to find new and different varieties that you really want to try.

Other Plants to Consider

In addition to vegetables, it's always nice to plant flowers in your postage stamp garden. Edible flowers, for example, can be used to add color and taste to salads. Some flowers repel harmful insects and nematodes or provide other beneficial effects for vegetables (see pages 170–171), and some attract butterflies, hummingbirds, bees, and other helpful insects to the garden to pollinate and protect your vegetables.

Edible Flowers

Some edible flowers to consider are cornflower or bachelor's button, primrose, daisy, day lily, lavender, pansies and violas, rose, sunflower, and violet. Many herbs also produce edible flowers, including anise hyssop, borage, chervil, chives, orange bergamot, oregano, marjoram, sage, savory, and thyme. The edible flower petals of calendula are used in ales and for food coloring. These plants also make a colorful ornamental that brightens the corner of any garden. In warm areas, they will bloom and be available all winter long.

Many cooks feel that nasturtiums are an essential part of their garden. Nasturtiums are often used in salads to add a peppery taste and color. They are also used as a garnish on many other dishes. Fastidious cooks like them because of the variety of colors they can add. *Creamsicle* has petals with a swirled pastel that highlights a deep red throat. *Peach Melba* has yellow petals accented with raspberry, *Moonlight* has pale yellow blossoms, and *Sungold* has deep butter-yellow petals. You can select from 1-foot compact types to 6-foot climbing/trailing varieties. Plant after all danger of frost has passed. Nasturtiums thrive when their roots are cool and moist. Plants that get too much water have large leaves but few flowers.

Plants That Attract Butterflies

Butterflies seem to add magic to the garden, especially when a swallowtail or a painted lady lights on a nearby flower. Butterfly gardens need plenty of flowers for nectar and food plants for caterpillars. Most caterpillars confine themselves to one plant family or one specific plant. Some butterfly plants are bee balm, coreopsis, morning glory, verbena, and zinnia. Shrubs such as the butterfly bush, fruit trees, mock orange, and spirea also attract butterflies. Most seed catalogs have butterfly garden seeds.

Plants That Attract Hummingbirds

Birds make a garden come alive, but at certain times of the year, they can also eat everything as soon as it pops out of the ground. As a result, when you plant early in the spring—when birds seem to be the hungriest—you have to plant most crops under row covers. If you are a bird lover, concentrate on hummingbirds: they make for good natural insect control because they regularly pick off insects. They also gather nectar from flowers with their needlelike bills and long tongues. To attract them you might want to set out one or two hummingbird feeders or add their favorite plants to your garden. Some suggestions are columbine, coral bells, sage, fuchsia, monkey flower, gilia, honeysuckle, or butterfly bush.

Attracting Orchard Mason Bees

Presently, there is a pollination crisis due to colony collapse disorder (CDC), a serious and mysterious phenomenon that has caused the widespread death of honeybees. Orchard mason bees help fill the void. Unlike the honeybee, orchard mason bees are native to North America, do not dwell in hives, and are not affected by CDC. They are small black bees that do not harm humans or pets.

When the weather warms up in early spring, the orchard mason bees emerge from their holes. After they mate, the females begin to make their nests and gather pollen and nectar from the spring blossoms. Gardeners can attract orchard mason bees not only by planting flowers such as English lavender, aster, black-eyed Susan, sunflower, zinnia, purple coneflower, goldenrod, and flowering herbs, but also by making their own nesting blocks out of untreated pieces of ponderosa pine or Douglas fir measuring 1 or 2 feet long, 4 inches wide, and 6 inches deep. Simply drill a number of $1/2$-inch-deep holes $3/4$ inch apart in the blocks and hang them around the garden. Alternatively, mason bee nesting block kits are available through seed suppliers.

Attracting Beneficial Bugs to Your Garden

It is a good idea to attract insects to your garden that prey on vegetable pests, pollinate plants, and build soil. Ladybugs, for example, the age-old symbol of good luck, are familiar to most gardeners with their spotted bright orange-red hemispherical shell. A ladybug eats two-and-a-half times its own weight a day in aphids, mealybugs, moth eggs, and spider mites. Ladybugs can be found on most flowering vegetables and herbs. The adult praying mantis consumes huge quantities of beetles, caterpillars, and grasshoppers. The young praying mantis eats aphids, flies, and other small insects. They, too, are drawn to flowering herbs and flowers. There are some nectar-loving beneficial insects like lacewings (sometimes known as stinkbugs), which are fragile-looking light-green insects. The adult is mainly a nectar lover, but the larvae (known as aphid lions) have a gluttonous appetite for aphids, mealybugs, mites, leafhoppers, thrips, and other insects.

To help attract these and other useful bugs to your garden, start with a 10-gallon plastic tub, which you can find at hardware stores. If the tub does not already have a hole in the bottom, drill a few to provide drainage. Fill the tub with a mixture of planting soil and compost. Now, include six to eight of these plants, which are rich in pollen and nectar: nicotonia, autumn sage, lemon queen, catmint, blue daze, verbena, silver thyme, lavender, cosmos, nasturtium, and trailing rosemary. Water several times a week and feed with fish emulsion or any organic feed on a weekly basis. Place this tub next to your vegetable plot to invite the good bugs to visit and stay for a while.

What Size to Make Your Garden

Most people are short on time. If you have a job and children, you may only have an hour or two a week to spend in the garden. The less time you have to spend gardening, the smaller you need to make your garden. You may know someone who rushed out and planted the entire backyard in plants, then wound up spending every spare moment just keeping up with it. If you are concerned about time and don't know what a good size is to start with, a single 4 by 4-foot garden is ideal. Planting in containers is also an option for busy gardeners. The good news is that with the postage stamp method, even a 4 by 4-foot garden or a few containers can produce a large amount of food.

Also, consider that the larger the garden, the more expensive it will most likely be. Gardening can be extremely expensive, or it can cost practically nothing. You can, for instance, buy garden compost or make your own. You can buy $42 pruners or a pair for $6, pay $48 for pliant pants or garden in a pair of old jeans. You may want to splurge on kneeling pads, a garden vest, and other gardening accessories—the choice belongs to you.

It pays to start small, spend a modest amount the first year, and then decide how much you can afford and want to spend on your garden as you go along.

How to Arrange the Plants in Your Postage Stamp Garden

By proper placement of individual vegetables in your postage stamp garden, you can produce extremely large quantities of vegetables in an extremely small space. The following are postage stamp planning guidelines that will help you obtain maximum results.

1 If your plot is large—say 10 by 10 feet or even 8 by 8 feet—you can plant different types of vegetables in separate squares or rectangles. In plots more than 5 or 6 feet wide, you'll need pathways in order to reach all your plants. However, if the plot is narrow or small, simply block out irregular groups of vegetables and fill in the spaces any way you wish.

2 Plant tall vegetables on the north end of your garden to avoid shading the smaller crops, and plant the other vegetables in descending order of size down toward the south end of the garden.

3 Plant vines (cucumbers, melons, peas, squash) against a fence or support at the north end of your garden. Smaller vertical supports can be

used within the interior of the garden. Use the air space above your garden as much as possible. That is, train tomatoes, cucumbers, and other vines and trailing plants to grow up trellises, fences, or poles, so that they won't run all over your garden bed, crowding out the other plants. The better you get at vertical growing, the more things you'll be able to pack into your postage stamp garden. (Several methods of vertical growing are discussed in the detailed sections on each vining vegetable later in the book.)

4 Forget about planting in rows. In a postage stamp garden you scatter the seeds across the bed to use all the space in your garden, and then thin out the seedlings (the small plants) as they come up. If you set out seedlings rather than seeds, space them without concern for straight rows. The mature plants should just touch one another on all sides. Make sure you space all major plants properly on your plan. Winter squash, for instance, requires at least 12 inches between plant centers (if grown up a fence). This means that if you have a 5 by 5-foot garden, you can plant six squash across the north end to grow up the vertical support frame. (In chapter 4 I discuss seeds and seedlings, as well as the best plant spacing for postage stamp beds.)

5 For root vegetables (such as carrots and beets), leafy vegetables (such as lettuce and spinach), and corn you need a special plan. The areas chosen for each of these vegetables should be subdivided into thirds or fourths, and each subsection should be seeded or planted a week to ten days apart. In this way you get continual harvests—as one sub-section stops bearing mature vegetables, another begins. This is not so with, for example, tomatoes and cucumbers, which bear from the same plant over a long period of time. After you've harvested a subsection of leafy or root vegetables, you can replant that subsection. That way your garden will produce everywhere all the time.

6 Major vegetables such as tomatoes, peppers, and eggplants should be surrounded by secondary vegetables or herbs, such as green onions and bush beans. Plant vegetables that mature quickly between those that mature more slowly (see chapter 6 for maturity rates). For instance, plant radishes in the same space in which you have transplanted tomatoes. Harvest the radishes four to five weeks before the tomato vines take over the space. You can also use this same space underneath the grown

tomatoes as a microclimate for radishes in warm weather to ensure a continuous supply of radishes long after they stop growing in the regular garden.

7   Remember to include flowers and herbs in every garden. Certain plants can repel or attract insects (see chapter 7). Borage, for instance, can attract bees, while marigolds are said to keep bean beetles away from snap beans and to repel nematodes. Garlic and chives may repel aphids. I urge you to put herbs and flowers among the vegetables when you have the space.

Putting Your Postage Stamp Garden Plan on Paper

In the next few pages, various plans are given for some postage stamp gardens. The plans are intended as guidelines or possibilities only and should be modified by your own experience to fit your needs. For one thing, you needn't limit yourself to conventional rectangles. Choose almost any shape for your garden that you wish—square, rectangular, triangular, circular, kidney-shaped—you name it. Give vegetables water, the right amount of sun, and good soil, and away they grow. The shape of the garden generally doesn't mean a thing to them.

Begin by putting your garden plan on paper, even if it is a small garden. Some gardeners draw this plan to scale (for example, making 1/4 inch equal 1 foot), which allows them to allocate space accurately. Others simply draw a rough sketch and go from there. I like to use graph paper because it enables me to see at a glance how much space I have. I've also been known to go to my garden and start marking off the beds with string or chalk. With a 5-foot bed, I let each square equal 2 inches, and with a 10-foot bed, 4 inches. Graphing allows you to easily plant in small groups. You can count the number of plants, or even seeds, that you are going to use.

If you prefer to make your plan online, there is a website that allows you to design your garden: www.plangarden.com. In addition, some of the seed catalogs offer garden planners.

Postage Stamp Garden Plans You Can Use

On pages 14–24 are eleven postage stamp garden plans that you can use to design your own garden. Just adjust them to fit your own needs.

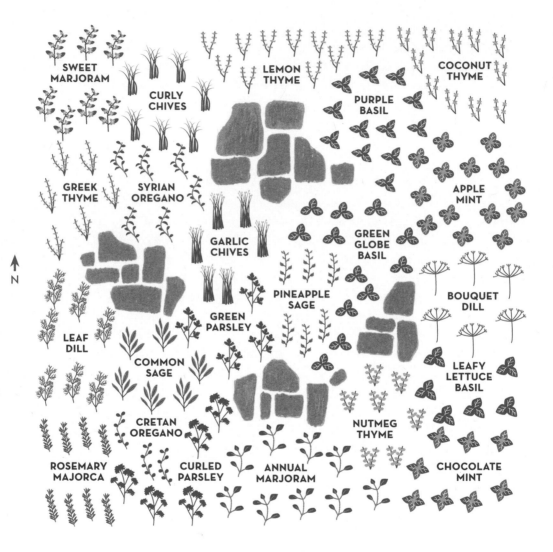

SWEET MARJORAM

CURLY CHIVES

LEMON THYME

PURPLE BASIL

COCONUT THYME

GREEK THYME

SYRIAN OREGANO

APPLE MINT

GARLIC CHIVES

GREEN GLOBE BASIL

N

PINEAPPLE SAGE

BOUQUET DILL

GREEN PARSLEY

LEAF DILL

COMMON SAGE

LEAFY LETTUCE BASIL

CRETAN OREGANO

NUTMEG THYME

ROSEMARY MAJORCA

CURLED PARSLEY

ANNUAL MARJORAM

CHOCOLATE MINT

Gourmet herb garden. Plant mint in a container to prevent spreading. 4' x 4' bed.

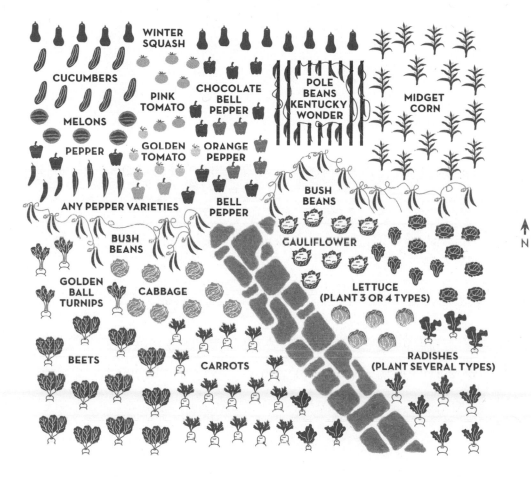

WINTER SQUASH

CUCUMBERS

PINK TOMATO

CHOCOLATE BELL PEPPER

POLE BEANS KENTUCKY WONDER

MIDGET CORN

MELONS

PEPPER

GOLDEN TOMATO

ORANGE PEPPER

ANY PEPPER VARIETIES

BELL PEPPER

BUSH BEANS

N

BUSH BEANS

CAULIFLOWER

GOLDEN BALL TURNIPS

CABBAGE

LETTUCE (PLANT 3 OR 4 TYPES)

BEETS

CARROTS

RADISHES (PLANT SEVERAL TYPES)

Plant peas before winter squash. Intercrop radishes, leaf lettuce, and green onion with larger plants. Plant spinach under the vertical frames used to support the melons and cucumbers. 4' x 4' bed.

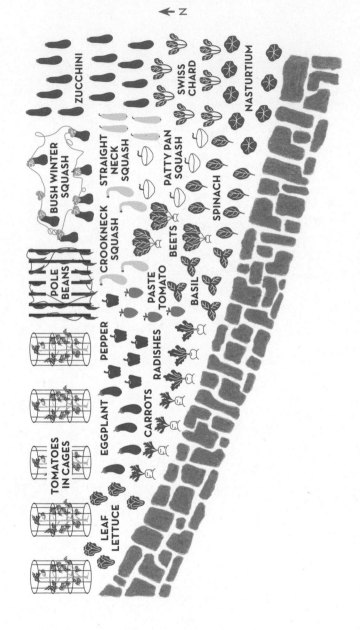

ZUCCHINI

SWISS CHARD

NASTURTIUM

BUSH WINTER SQUASH

STRAIGHT NECK SQUASH

PATTY PAN SQUASH

CROOKNECK SQUASH

BEETS

SPINACH

POLE BEANS

PASTE TOMATO

BASIL

PEPPER

RADISHES

EGGPLANT

CARROTS

TOMATOES IN CAGES

LEAF LETTUCE

Postage stamp garden along the border of a flower bed.

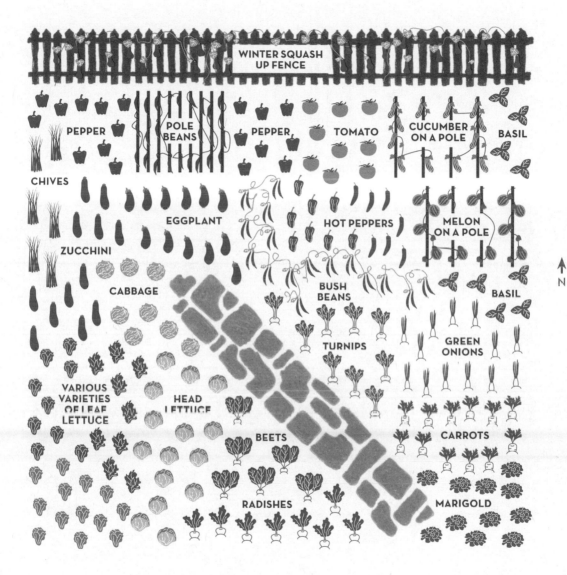

WINTER SQUASH UP FENCE

PEPPER

POLE BEANS

PEPPER

TOMATO

CUCUMBER ON A POLE

BASIL

CHIVES

EGGPLANT

HOT PEPPERS

MELON ON A POLE

N

ZUCCHINI

BASIL

CABBAGE

BUSH BEANS

TURNIPS

GREEN ONIONS

VARIOUS VARIETIES OF LEAF LETTUCE

HEAD LETTUCE

BEETS

CARROTS

RADISHES

MARIGOLD

General postage stamp garden. Plant and harvest peas before planting winter squash. Plant radishes at 2-week intervals. Intercrop radishes, leaf lettuce, and green onions with larger plants, and harvest before they take over the space. 5' x 5' bed.

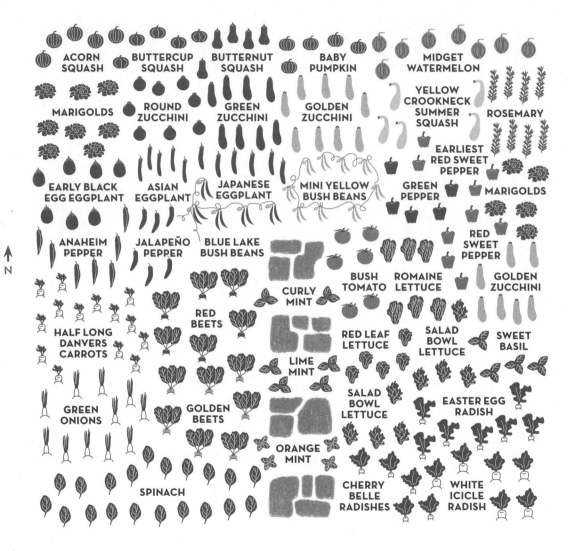

ACORN SQUASH

BUTTERCUP SQUASH

BUTTERNUT SQUASH

BABY PUMPKIN

MIDGET WATERMELON

MARIGOLDS

ROUND ZUCCHINI

GREEN ZUCCHINI

GOLDEN ZUCCHINI

YELLOW CROOKNECK SUMMER SQUASH

ROSEMARY

EARLIEST RED SWEET PEPPER

EARLY BLACK EGG EGGPLANT

ASIAN EGGPLANT

JAPANESE EGGPLANT

MINI YELLOW BUSH BEANS

GREEN PEPPER

MARIGOLDS

ANAHEIM PEPPER

JALAPEÑO PEPPER

BLUE LAKE BUSH BEANS

RED SWEET PEPPER

N

CURLY MINT

BUSH TOMATO

ROMAINE LETTUCE

GOLDEN ZUCCHINI

RED BEETS

RED LEAF LETTUCE

SALAD BOWL LETTUCE

SWEET BASIL

HALF LONG DANVERS CARROTS

LIME MINT

GREEN ONIONS

GOLDEN BEETS

SALAD BOWL LETTUCE

EASTER EGG RADISH

ORANGE MINT

SPINACH

CHERRY BELLE RADISHES

WHITE ICICLE RADISH

Postage stamp garden stressing winter and summer varieties. Keep mints trimmed with a weedeater. Replace spinach with carrots in the summer. 6' x 6' bed.

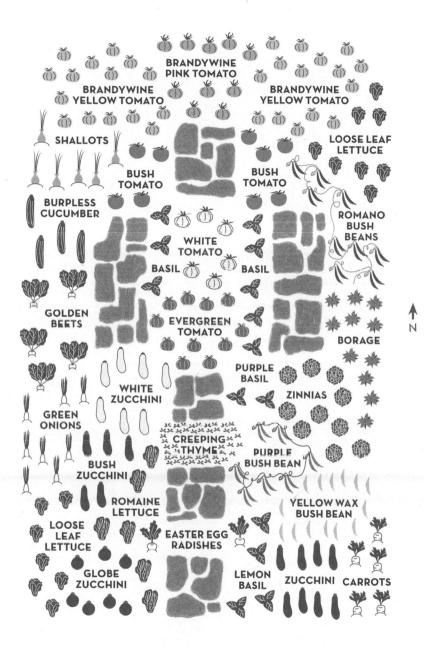

BRANDYWINE PINK TOMATO

BRANDYWINE YELLOW TOMATO

BRANDYWINE YELLOW TOMATO

SHALLOTS

LOOSE LEAF LETTUCE

BUSH TOMATO

BUSH TOMATO

BURPLESS CUCUMBER

ROMANO BUSH BEANS

WHITE TOMATO

BASIL

BASIL

GOLDEN BEETS

EVERGREEN TOMATO

BORAGE

N

PURPLE BASIL

ZINNIAS

WHITE ZUCCHINI

GREEN ONIONS

CREEPING THYME

PURPLE BUSH BEAN

BUSH ZUCCHINI

ROMAINE LETTUCE

YELLOW WAX BUSH BEAN

LOOSE LEAF LETTUCE

EASTER EGG RADISHES

GLOBE ZUCCHINI

LEMON BASIL

ZUCCHINI

CARROTS

Experimental postage stamp garden. 5' x 10' bed.

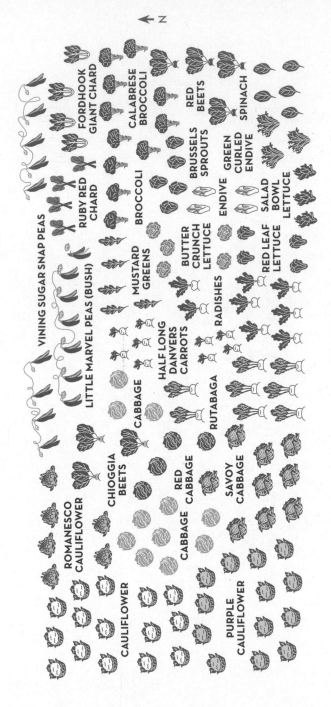

N

FORDHOOK GIANT CHARD

CALABRESE BROCCOLI

RED BEETS

SPINACH

BRUSSELS SPROUTS

GREEN CURLED ENDIVE

RUBY RED CHARD

BROCCOLI

ENDIVE

SALAD BOWL LETTUCE

VINING SUGAR SNAP PEAS

MUSTARD GREENS

BUTTER CRUNCH LETTUCE

RED LEAF LETTUCE

LITTLE MARVEL PEAS (BUSH)

HALF LONG DANVERS CARROTS

RADISHES

CABBAGE

RUTABAGA

CHIOGGIA BEETS

RED CABBAGE

SAVOY CABBAGE

ROMANESCO CAULIFLOWER

CABBAGE

CAULIFLOWER

PURPLE CAULIFLOWER

Fall/spring postage stamp garden. 10' x 4' bed.

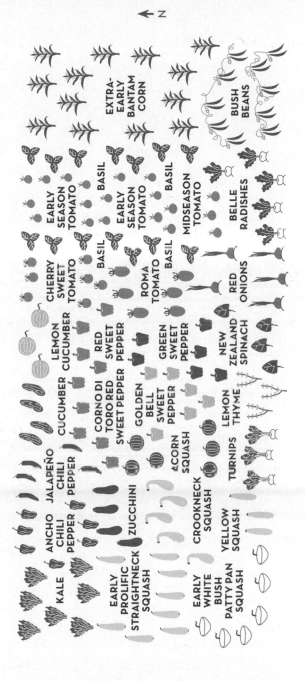

N

EXTRA-EARLY BANTAM CORN

BUSH BEANS

EARLY SEASON TOMATO

BASIL

EARLY SEASON TOMATO

BASIL

MIDSEASON TOMATO

BELLE RADISHES

CHERRY SWEET TOMATO

BASIL

ROMA TOMATO

BASIL

RED ONIONS

LEMON CUCUMBER

CUCUMBER

RED SWEET PEPPER

CORNO DI TORO RED SWEET PEPPER

GREEN SWEET PEPPER

GOLDEN BELL SWEET PEPPER

NEW ZEALAND SPINACH

ACORN SQUASH

LEMON THYME

TURNIPS

JALAPEÑO CHILI PEPPER

ANCHO CHILI PEPPER

ZUCCHINI

CROOKNECK SQUASH

YELLOW SQUASH

KALE

EARLY PROLIFIC STRAIGHTNECK SQUASH

EARLY WHITE BUSH PATTY PAN SQUASH

Summer postage stamp garden. 10' x 4' bed.

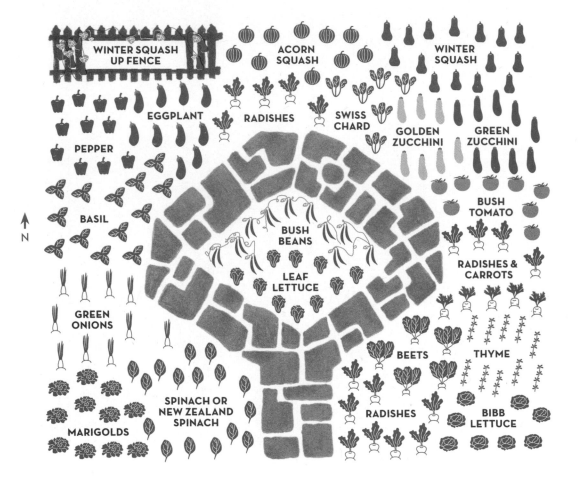

WINTER SQUASH UP FENCE

ACORN SQUASH

WINTER SQUASH

EGGPLANT

RADISHES

SWISS CHARD

GOLDEN ZUCCHINI

GREEN ZUCCHINI

PEPPER

N

BASIL

BUSH BEANS

LEAF LETTUCE

BUSH TOMATO

RADISHES & CARROTS

GREEN ONIONS

BEETS

THYME

MARIGOLDS

SPINACH OR NEW ZEALAND SPINACH

RADISHES

BIBB LETTUCE

10' x 7' bed.

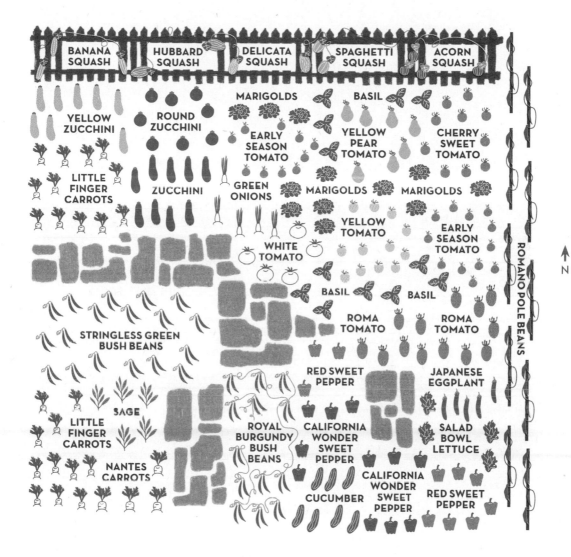

BANANA SQUASH · HUBBARD SQUASH · DELICATA SQUASH · SPAGHETTI SQUASH · ACORN SQUASH

YELLOW ZUCCHINI · ROUND ZUCCHINI · MARIGOLDS · BASIL

EARLY SEASON TOMATO · YELLOW PEAR TOMATO · CHERRY SWEET TOMATO

LITTLE FINGER CARROTS · ZUCCHINI · GREEN ONIONS · MARIGOLDS · MARIGOLDS

YELLOW TOMATO · EARLY SEASON TOMATO

WHITE TOMATO

BASIL · BASIL

ROMA TOMATO · ROMA TOMATO

STRINGLESS GREEN BUSH BEANS

RED SWEET PEPPER · JAPANESE EGGPLANT

SAGE

LITTLE FINGER CARROTS · ROYAL BURGUNDY BUSH BEANS · CALIFORNIA WONDER SWEET PEPPER · SALAD BOWL LETTUCE

NANTES CARROTS · CALIFORNIA WONDER SWEET PEPPER · RED SWEET PEPPER

CUCUMBER

ROMANO POLE BEANS

N

Large postage stamp garden. 9' x 9' bed.

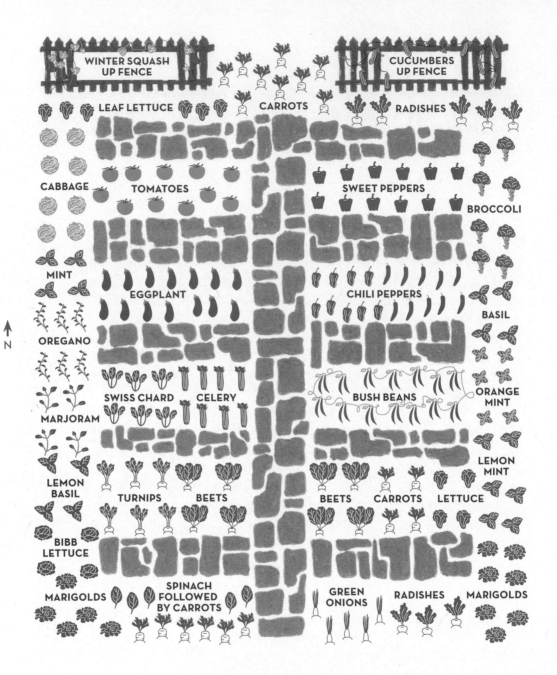

WINTER SQUASH UP FENCE

CUCUMBERS UP FENCE

LEAF LETTUCE

CARROTS

RADISHES

CABBAGE

TOMATOES

SWEET PEPPERS

BROCCOLI

MINT

EGGPLANT

CHILI PEPPERS

BASIL

OREGANO

MARJORAM

SWISS CHARD

CELERY

BUSH BEANS

ORANGE MINT

LEMON BASIL

TURNIPS

BEETS

BEETS

CARROTS

LETTUCE

LEMON MINT

BIBB LETTUCE

MARIGOLDS

SPINACH FOLLOWED BY CARROTS

GREEN ONIONS

RADISHES

MARIGOLDS

N

Large postage stamp garden. 8' x 10' bed.

What Kind of Garden?

You can choose to garden directly in the ground, in raised "boxed" gardening beds, or in containers. In the ground is the most simple, but boxed beds allow you to build up deeper levels of good soil and you don't have to bend down as far to take care of your garden. However, if you have hot summers and sandy soil, raised beds will heat up early and dry out quickly. Under these conditions, you will probably want to garden at ground level. Containers are helpful for growing on top of paved areas, such as patios or even indoors.

Boxed Gardens

For some reason, 4 by 4 foot boxed gardens spark the imagination of a lot of people. They're neat, clean, and easy to handle. You can walk all the way around them, you can thin the plants without getting dirty, and you can have as many as you want in any arrangement you like—one or two or a bunch.

Actually a boxed garden is not really a "box" with a bottom. It's more of a frame. To make one, all you have to do is measure out a 4 by 4-foot space, prepare the soil, and then frame the space with standard 2 by 4-inch planks set slightly into the soil to hold them in place. You can nail the corners for greater security if you wish.

Generally, you can plant one or two vegetables in each of these small box beds and corn in three separate beds about two weeks apart. Split most beds in two, planting a different vegetable in each section—half to spinach, half to carrots, or whatever. These sections can also be subdivided into thirds, which can be planted two weeks apart. Plant all root and leafy vegetables this way. Train cucumbers, cantaloupe, beans, and other vines and trailers to grow up stakes, trellises, or cages.

A lot of the seed catalogs sell raised-bed garden kits if you don't want to make your own. They also sell raised-bed corner joints if you want to make your own boxes.

Container Gardening

By planting vegetables in containers, you can grow your garden almost anywhere, indoors or out. Start by looking for places you might squeeze in a container or two.

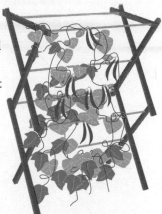

A drying rack can be a perfect frame for vertical gardening.

Now walk through your house looking for unused space where you might grow vegetables, either in a window space or under lights. Consider bedrooms, living rooms, closets, bathrooms, and any additional interior space. You can grow many vegetables under lights—the only limit is your imagination.

You can plant in standard containers that you buy from a garden center, or you can turn almost anything into a vegetable container—the sources are endless.

As a general rule, the larger and deeper the container, the better the yields. While you can grow small bush-type tomatoes in smaller containers, the larger varieties require up to 20 gallons (3 cubic feet) of soil to produce a good crop.

Windowsill and Window Box Gardens

With 12 feet of sunny windowsill, you can raise enough salad to feed a family of four for a year. You can "farm" twenty-five 4-inch pots in which you can grow:

- 5 to 6 kinds of herbs
- 20 to 30 carrots
- 30 to 35 beets
- All the radishes you can eat
- Even a few tomatoes

That windowsill space is a potential green mine. You can grow anything on a windowsill that requires a 1- or 2-inch spacing between plants, or single plants that keep producing an edible crop. This gives you a choice of four categories:

SPROUTS: radish seeds, alfalfa seeds, mung beans, soybeans, wheat, buckwheat, and cress

ROOT VEGETABLES: carrots, beets, green onions, and garlic

HERBS: chives, parsley, basil, dill, rosemary, sage, summer savory, tarragon, and sweet marjoram

TOMATOES: All seed catalogs have the tiny varieties for container tomatoes.

Outside, you can grow almost anything in window boxes. It's easiest to plant in pots and simply set the pots in the box. Most gardeners like to mix vegetables, herbs, and flowers.

CUCUMBERS
BEANS
PEPPERS
BEETS
ZUCCHINI
ONIONS
TOMATOES
CARROTS
LETTUCE

Planting Your Patio

For patios and balcony gardens, measure your space. A 9 by 15-foot balcony, for instance, contains 135 square feet. Estimate how much space you'll need for general living, lounging, barbecuing, and so on. Then subtract this amount from the total space available. If you feel you need about half the total space for general living, you still have more than 64 square feet left in which to cultivate your garden.

Whiskey barrel halves make great patio planters. They are 22 inches across, so they hold enough soil to support good vegetable growth. A single barrel will hold seven or eight corn plants, two or three zucchini plants, and two or three tomatoes. You can place them on wheels and roll them around the patio should you need to follow the sun or want to rearrange the containers. Wheels can be purchased at any hardware store or garden center. A wheelbarrow also works well as a planter.

Wooden boxes are also excellent for standard patio planting. Wood has a high insulation value and keeps the hot summer sun of most patio areas from rapidly drying out the soil and damaging the roots. You can buy these boxes from a garden center or make them. Boxes come in many sizes. Terra-cotta pots also come in many shapes and sizes, but they allow the water to evaporate faster than wood containers.

Some gardeners like paper pulp pots. They are easy to lift and fill with potting soil. I recommend using pots with either a 12-inch or an 18-inch inside diameter, depending on what you want to plant. You can plant carrots and lettuce in 12-inch pots and eggplant, tomatoes, peppers, and other larger plants in 18-inch pots. Hanging wire baskets and containers also enhance any patio garden.

Eight Easy Steps

Follow these steps for planting your container vegetables.

1 Select an attractive container with drainage holes. If the container you select doesn't have holes, drill them.

2 Add commercial potting soil to within 1 inch of the top of the container.

3 Moisten the soil before planting.

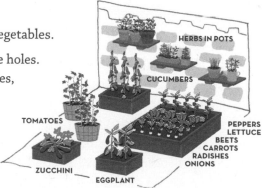

4   You can plant both herbs and vegetables in the same container. When you plant them together, you can crowd them a little bit. An 18-inch pot, for instance, will easily hold as many as ten herbs.

5   If you are planting several vegetables and herbs together in the same container, set the taller varieties in the center.

6   Water to settle the soil around the roots.

7   Add more soil if it's needed after watering.

8   Keep the container moist and fertilized.

Container Soil Mixes

Container soil is a combination of organic materials (bark, compost, peat moss) and minerals. Any container mix must also provide the right nutrients for vegetable growth and enough air space (despite compacting) to allow for good air and water movement. You can also grow vegetables in the commercial soilless mixes (such as Supersoil), because many of them contain all the ingredients necessary for good plant growth.

Planting Seeds and Seedlings in Containers

When planting seeds in a container, you don't have to space them any particular distance apart. Simply scatter the seeds across the entire container. Later, however, you will have to thin the seedlings. Carrots, for instance, are thinned first to 3/4 inch apart, then to 1 to 2 inches apart. You can throw the small carrots you're thinning into a soup or stew, and you won't feel as if you're wasting anything. The 8-inch containers of carrots planted at a 1-inch spacing will produce the equivalent of a 5-foot row grown in an outdoor garden.

If you plant young seedlings in outdoor containers, you should get them used to outdoor conditions by taking them out in the morning and back inside at night. Gradually expose the seedlings to low temperatures and more sunlight for about two weeks, or until you can leave them out without damage from frost.

No-Mess Watering Techniques

Watering your indoor containers shouldn't be any problem. Pots less than 8 inches in diameter should be watered from above with a 1-quart kitchen measuring cup. Another technique is to submerge the bottom half of the pot in a pail of water (or fill a kitchen sink). When the air bubbles stop coming up from the soil, take the pot out and let it drain. Large containers should be watered from above with a plastic pail, or a gentle stream from a hose, until the soil is completely saturated.

Don't water again until the soil is dry to a depth of 1 inch. To find out how dry the soil is, poke a finger into the soil or take some soil from this depth and rub it between your thumb and index finger. If it's dry, water. If the soil is mud-coated or feels wet, it won't need water for at least twenty-four hours.

You should not let your containers dry out because vegetables must grow rapidly to maturity. If the plant is overwatered, the soil becomes waterlogged, forcing air from the soil and suffocating the plant. If at all possible, connect your containers with a drip system, put the whole thing on an automatic timer, and water each container with an emitter.

You can also buy large self-watering pots. They come in a number of shapes and sizes. These contain a built-in reservoir that gets filled through a slot in the side of the pot. During warm, dry weather, you need to refill these reservoirs once or twice a week. You can also fertilize these pots by adding fish emulsion or any organic fertilizer directly to the water. Dump the water when it turns brackish.

Midget Vegetables

I sometimes wonder whether plant breeders developed the whole range of midget vegetables just for container gardeners. Seed catalogs have entire sections dedicated to these small vegetables. A number of vegetables have been developed that are only half, even a fifth, the size of regular ones. The ones listed below have both generic descriptions as well as information on varieties. The seed source codes listed throughout this book correspond with the codes in Appendix B (page 195).

My recommendation is to browse the seed catalogs and select the varieties you want to try. Unfortunately, most baby vegetables are hybrids. To avoid hybrids you can plant heirloom varieties and pick the fruit while it's still in the baby stage.

BABY BEETS

To grow baby beets, scatter the seeds across an entire container. Cover with about ¹/₄ inch of planter mix. Thin to stand 1 to 2 inches apart.

KESTREL 53 days. A hybrid baby beet with dark-red roots that have a small crown. 8–10" tall tops are green with contrasting red veins. Seed source: HAR • TER • THO

BABY CABBAGE

Start the midget cabbages from seeds indoors in aluminum pans or peat pots about six to eight weeks before you intend to plant them in containers. For outdoor containers, plant small cabbage about 4 inches apart. For windowsills or under lights, plant in 6-inch pots. Keep the temperature between 60°F and 70°F.

CARAFLEX 68 days. Hybrid. Pointed heads are sweet with succulent texture. Small, 1¹/₂-pound heads are well protected by tight outer leaves. Heads hold up to 8 weeks. Seed source: JOH • JOHN • NIC • PAR

EXPRESS 55 days. Hybrid. A baby savoy cabbage designed to be harvested no larger than 6", at around 1 pound. Yellow-green exterior and buttery-yellow interior. Ideal for short growing season or in a container. Seed source: BURG • JOHN

GONZALES 55–60 days. Hybrid. Softball-size, aqua-green heads are suited to tight compact plantings and small gardens. Seed source: JOH • JOHN • PAR

PRIMERO 72 days. Hybrid. Dark red cabbage has compact, upright habit making it an excellent choice for small-space gardens. Round 2- to 3-pound heads. Seed source: TER

BABY CARROTS

Plant baby carrots in the spring, and continue the planting throughout the summer. Plant six to ten per 4-inch pot. You can grow carrots in windowsill pots, under lights, or in large containers outdoors.

ADELAIDE BABY CARROTS 67–70 days. Hybrid. Adelaide is a miniature Nantes type, with straight sides, shaped like a baby finger. Harvest this bright orange carrot when it is no larger than 3", the smaller the better. Seed source: JOHN

BAMBINA 60 days. Heirloom. A baby carrot with slender, cylindrical blunt roots and a very small core. Smooth skin and deep orange. Adaptable to a variety of soils. Good container variety. Seed source: TERR

LITTLE FINGER 55 days. French heirloom. Deep orange baby-type carrot. Sweet 3" carrots. Seed source: ANN • BAK • BOT • BURP • GOU • IRI • PAR • SHU • TERR

PARIS MARKET 50–68 days. Heirloom. 1–2" long round, red-orange, very sweet carrots. Good container variety. Seed source: ANN • GOU • SEED

PARMEX 60 days. Heirloom. Round, smooth 1–1½", small cored. Thin to 1–2" apart. Seed source: JOHN • NIC

BABY CAULIFLOWER

Start from seed indoors about six to eight weeks before you intend to plant in containers. For outdoor containers, plant midget cauliflower about 5 inches apart. Though I haven't found any miniature varieties, you might want to try these.

BROCCOVERDE 69 days. Heirloom. 1-pound chartreuse green heads retain color when cooked. Upright plant. Seed source: NIC

CHEDDAR 80–100 days. Hybrid. Deep yellow-orange curds. 4–7" heads. Easy to grow. Seed source: BURG • GOU • JOH • JOHN • NIC • PAR • SHU • STO • TER • TOT

CLOUD 75 days. Hybrid. Pure white heads with tightly packed beads. 5–7" heads. Strong upright plants. Seed source: TER

BABY CORN

Plant midget corn 5 inches apart in 12-inch or larger pots. Midget corn grows especially well in 5-gallon cans. Plant in the spring after your patio has warmed up. Make additional plantings every few weeks for continuous harvest. You can also grow 5-gallon containers of midget corn behind a south-facing window. Or you can select the container-bred variety below.

ON DECK 61–63 days. Hybrid. The first sweet corn bred for containers. 4–5' tall, produces 2 or 3, 7–8" long ears per stalk. Simply plant 9 seeds per 24" container and harvest in about 2 months. Seed source: BURP

BABY CUCUMBERS

Plant these midget cucumbers in 6- to 8-inch pots, and cover with 1 inch of soil. You can plant in larger containers with 4-inch spacing between the plants. Place the containers out on the balcony or patio after the weather has warmed up in the spring.

MINIATURE WHITE 50–55 days. Heirloom. Dual-purpose cucumber. 3" long, yellow-white, lightly spined, bitter-free cukes. Slightly compact habit. Great variety for small-space gardens and containers. Seed source: SEED • TER

SALAD BUSH 57 days. Hybrid. All-American Selections Winner. Very tasty slicers that are 8" long, with smooth, dark green skin. High yields in small spaces. Very compact, disease-tolerant. Seed source: BURP

SPACEMASTER 52–75 days. 2–3' vines. 7^1/$_2$" long green cucumbers. Widely adapted. Ideal for small gardens and containers. Seed source: BOT • BURP • NIC • SHU • SOU

BABY EGGPLANT

Plant seeds ^{1}/$_2$ inch deep in compressed peat pots. Plant pots and all in a 12-inch or larger container. Place in full sun, and don't move outdoors until the weather warms up in the spring.

BLACK BEAUTY 73 days. Heirloom. Uniformly large-fruited eggplant 1 to 3 pounds. Very deep purple-black color. 18–24" tall plant. Seed source: ANN • BAK • BOT • BOU • BURG • BURP • COM • COO • GOU • IRI • PAR • SHU • STO

CALLIOPE 75 days. Hybrid. Baby 2" oval, cream-streaked purple eggplant. Perfect for containers or small-space gardens. Seed source: JOH • THO

DIAMOND 70 days. Heirloom. 2' tall plant sets fruits in clusters of 4–6. 9" x 3" dark purple eggplant that is rarely bitter. Seed source: ANN • BAK • SEED

HANSEL 55 days. Hybrid. All-American Selections Winner. Nonbitter, tender, smooth, and miniature in size. Begin picking at 2–3" long and leave the rest until they reach 4–5" long. 18" tall plant. Seed source: HAR • JOH

INDIA PAINT 65–70 days. Hybrid. 18–20" tall plants bear small 4" neon purple-and-white streaked eggplant. Good for containers and small-space gardens. Seed source: COO

MORDEN MIDGET (MORDEN MINE) 65 days. Hybrid. 12–16" tall plants bear 3–4" purple oval fruit. A good variety for containers or small-spaces. Seed source: SOU

BABY LETTUCE

There is no need to buy "baby lettuce," although there are such varieties. Lettuce is a cut-and-come-again vegetable that will keep you supplied throughout the growing season and requires little space. Plant lettuce directly in a container 4 to 5 inches apart. Make outdoor plantings every two weeks in separate small containers. Start two to four weeks before the last killing frost in the spring. Inside, plant anytime. You can easily grow lettuce on a windowsill or under lights.

BABY MELONS/PUMPKINS

Plant three seeds per 5-gallon container. When about 5 inches high, cut two of them out with a pair of scissors. Let the remaining plant grow to maturity.

DELICE DE LA TABLE 85–90 days. French heirloom cantaloupe whose name translates as "Delight of the Table." Ribbed dessert melon that has sweet orange flesh. 1–2 pounds. Seed source: SEED

HONEY BUN 73 days. Hybrid. True bush cantaloupe for container or small-space gardens. 3 pounds. 5" melon is perfect for two servings. 3–4 fruits per plant. Seed source: BURP

LIL' LOUPE 70 days. Hybrid. Single-serving-size cantaloupe. Bright orange flesh. 2 pounds. Seed source: HAR • TER

ORANGE SHERBET 85 days. Hybrid. Compact variety perfect for small spaces. Slightly oval Charentais-type fruits. 1 pound. Seed source: THO

LIL' PUMP-KE-MON 100 days. Hybrid. Mini pumpkin features orange and green stripes on a white background. 1–2 pound fruits, flattened shape with slight to medium netting. Compact space-saving vine. Seed source: HAR • PAR • STO • TER

SNACKFACE 95 days. Hybrid. Light orange pumpkin weighs 1–2 pounds and is packed with seeds that are hull-less. Semi-bush habit makes it perfect for small gardens or containers. Seed source: SHU

BABY TOMATOES

Start indoors six to eight weeks before you intend to plant in your containers. If you're planting on a patio, don't move the seedlings outside until the weather has warmed up. These tomatoes will grow in 8- to 10-inch pots.

BUSH EARLY GIRL 65 days. Hybrid. 4" across red tomato. Compact, space-saving 18" tall plant. Very productive. Determinate. Seed source: BURP

MICRO TOM 88 days. Hybrid. 6–8" tall plant bears loads of 1-ounce, deep red tomatoes. Ideal for windowsill and patio containers. Determinate. Seed source: TOT

SILVERY FIR TREE 58 days. Russian heirloom. Round, slightly flattened, 3–3$^1/_2$" red tomatoes. Does well in hanging baskets. 24" compact plant with carrot-like silvery-gray foliage. Determinate. Seed source: SEED • TER • TERR • TOT

TINY TIM 60 days. Hybrid. Tree-like, dwarf type for containers. 15" tall plants produce $^3/_4$" red tomatoes. Determinate. Seed source: STO • TOT

TUMBLING TOM YELLOW 70–80 days. Hybrid. 18" cascade of 1–2" yellow, ever-so-sweet cherry tomatoes. Plants are 6" wide. You can plant several in a 10–12" pot. Determinate. Seed source: BURP • PAR • STO • TOT

BABY ZUCCHINI

Plant two or three plants in a 10-gallon container. You may want to wrap your container with a wire cage to help support the plant.

BUSH BABY 59 days. Fruit have light and dark green stripes. Bred to produce smaller fruit and are in their prime when they are 2" x 6". Compact bush plant. Seed source: JOH • TER

PATIO STAR 50 days. Bred specifically for container cultivation. Attractive, compact plants and sharply green fruits. Produces full-size zucchini. Seed source: TER

CHAPTER 2

The Postage Stamp Soil Mix

The condition of the soil can actually make or break the productiveness of your garden. It is, in effect, the motor; if you expect to grow a lot of vegetables in a small space, it's extremely important to build the very best motor possible.

Look at it this way. Suppose you buy a Porsche, and after you get it home you remove its engine and install one from a Volkswagen. Then you go on a trip. You wouldn't expect to rip up the road getting to your destination, because you know that a Volkswagen engine can't handle a Porsche.

On the other hand, imagine that you take the Porsche engine out and put it in a Volkswagen body. Chances are you'll be able to beat anything in sight . . . and then some.

You want to squeeze every last bit of productivity out of the soil in your postage stamp garden. Like the Porsche engine in a Volkswagen body, you're going to make the soil in your garden super productive.

If you take the time in the beginning to build your soil right, your postage stamp garden will reward you with some of the greatest vegetables you've ever seen. Now, as a starter, let's take a peek at what's under the ground in your backyard.

How Soil Works

Most people look at their soil and see a bunch of dirt. It's the stuff that comes in on the kids' clothes, that has to be swept off the back porch, or that has to be cleaned up off the kitchen floor. Actually, soil is a lot more than that.

Every square foot of soil swarms with millions of bacteria and other microorganisms. The organic material that's in the soil or the raw material that you deposit there—leaves, grass clippings, garbage, and so forth—contains essential elements that plants use to grow. These elements are tied up in such a way that vegetables need help to reach them—the soil bacteria break them down and convert them into forms that plants can build with. How fast the soil bacteria act on this raw material depends on the nature of the material itself, the temperature, the amount of air available, and the moistness of the soil.

In the spring, when the soil warms up, the number of bacteria in the soil and the bacterial action increase tremendously. When you add fresh organic material, the bacteria immediately attack it, breaking it down into food for your plants. The bacterial organisms themselves need nitrogen to grow. And if you don't have nitrogen in the material that you put in the garden, then the bacteria will steal it from the vegetables you're trying to grow.

You can get around this problem by building a compost pile of organic material. This pile lets the initial bacterial decomposition take place outside the soil. Then when you turn the material into your soil, the nutrients are in a form that plants can use immediately.

How Soil Is Structured

Basically, there are three kinds of soil: clay, sand, and loam. Clay soil has particles so small that you can't see them without a microscope. They are extremely close together and take in water slowly. Once the clay particles absorb water, they hold it so tightly that it's almost impossible for plants to utilize it, and air can't get in. When clay dries, it's even worse. Plant roots have difficulty penetrating it, and the soil itself contains little air and water.

Sand, on the other hand, has particles many times larger than clay. Air penetrates deeply, and water moves through it too rapidly, dissolving away many of the nutrients.

Loam is somewhere between these two extremes. Loam has clay, sand, and a good supply of decomposed organic material called humus. The grains have good structure. The soil drains well, yet retains enough water for plant growth. Air can circulate, and the soil provides plenty of room for roots to grow easily.

Don't worry if your backyard isn't loam. We completely renovate the soil so that it doesn't really matter what you start with.

I might also mention here something that some gardeners seem to worry about a great deal: the pH of their soil. This is the measure of whether your soil is sweet (alkaline) or sour (acid). The pH scale runs from 0 for extremely acid to 7 for neutral to 14 for extremely alkaline. Most vegetables prefer soils that are neutral or slightly acid, that is, with a pH of 6.5 to 7.0. There's no doubt that pH is important. Generally, however, when you make up postage stamp garden beds you will automatically make them just right for vegetables. Unless you have a really unusual problem, like trying to garden near alkali flats or salt marshes (alkaline soil) or in a peat bog (acid soil), just forget about the pH problem and simply make up your garden according to the instructions given in this book. If you do have one of those problems contact your local nursery and ask how other gardeners in the area have handled it. Once you've answered that question then you can proceed to make up your postage stamp garden in the regular manner.

Getting the Ingredients for Your Postage Stamp Soil Mix

I don't have to tell you that plants need to eat just like you do. That's not technically correct, of course, but plants need certain soil conditions and nutrients—sixteen of them—in order to be healthy and vigorous. There are three major nutrients—nitrogen (N), phosphorus (P), and potassium (K)—and a number of minor and trace elements, including calcium, zinc, iron, manganese, copper, sulfur, and magnesium, among others. To provide these nutrients and organic material in our postage stamp soil mix, we create a base of compost and manure, plus a fertilizing blend of blood meal, bonemeal, and wood ash (or similar substitutes, as discussed later in this chapter). After planting, I sometimes supplement with a sixth ingredient, fish emulsion or liquid seaweed. With the postage stamp method, you are using only organic fertilizers and avoiding all chemical fertilizers. Because you are going to be eating the plants that you grow, you don't want them full of chemicals!

Compost

Probably the most important ingredient that you can add to your postage stamp bed is compost—the mixture of decayed leaves, grass clippings, garbage, and other organic matter that you prepare yourself in piles and then add to the soil. In composting, the organic matter is broken down by bacterial action into food that your vegetable plants can use immediately. Without it (or some good substitute), you'll get only mediocre vegetables. With it, the ground seems to come alive. Also, it helps to give the soil a lighter texture, letting the soil breathe.

You can prepare compost very easily. Detailed instructions for different types of composting are given in Appendix A. Most composting, though, takes time. It can take a few weeks or even a few months for the raw organic material in a compost pile to break down into compounds that vegetables can use. For this reason, you should begin as soon as possible to build a compost pile for your garden.

If you are not able to make your own, don't let a lack of compost stop you from preparing a postage stamp garden. Simply buy some and work it into your garden. You can buy compost in large quantities from a landscape firm, and many nurseries sell bagged compost.

Animal Manures

Animal manures are a must in your garden, for they add many needed nutrients, especially nitrogen. And just to make the matter more complicated, every type of manure has different properties and varying amounts of nitrogen, phosphorus, and potassium.

Generally, you should use rotted manure, not fresh. The bacteria in the soil needs extra nitrogen to break down fresh manure, and this process can use up some of the nitrogen that would otherwise go to the plants. Moreover—as with organic materials that have been composted—plants can easily use rotted or decomposed manure.

Dried manure, which you can buy from a nursery or a landscape material firm, is also usually just right. It can be worked into your garden soil directly from the sack.

Do not buy steer manure, however, because its high salt content offsets any benefit that it might have. Although the salts can be leached out by watering, leaching also washes out the nitrogen.

Hen, horse, and sheep manures are known as "hot" manures because of their high nitrogen content. Cow manure is called "cold" manure because it is low in nitrogen and breaks down fairly slowly. I always prefer horse manure, because I think it gives the best results. You can also buy compost or soil with manure in it directly from a landscape materials supplier.

I suggest you start out by using whatever you have available (given the cautions mentioned) and then later experiment to see what gives you the best results in your particular garden. If you prefer not to haul your own manure, I suggest you call a landscape materials supplier and see what they have available. Most of these firms deliver.

NATURAL PLANT FOODS

TYPE	SOURCE	COMPOSITION (%)		
		N	P	K
Animal manures (fresh)	Cattle	0.53	0.29	0.48
	Chicken	0.89	0.48	0.83
	Horse	0.55	0.27	0.57
	Sheep	0.89	0.48	0.83
Animal manures (dried)	Cattle	2.00	1.80	3.00
	Horse	0.80	0.20	0.60
	Sheep	1.40	1.00	3.00
Organic nutrients	Dried blood meal	9–14		
	Bonemeal	1.6–2.5	23–25	
	Fish emulsion	5–10	2.0	2.0
Pulverized rock powders	Rock phosphate		38–41	
	Greensand		1.35	4.1–9.5
Vegetables	Cottonseed meal	6.7–7.4	2–3	1.5–2.0
	Seaweed	1.7	0.8	5.0
	Soybean meal	6.0	1.0	2.0
	Oak leaves	0.8	0.4	0.2
	Wood ash		1.5	7.0

Blood Meal

Blood meal, which you can buy at nurseries, contains up to 14 percent nitrogen and sometimes some phosphorus and potassium, and is my favorite method for adding nitrogen to the soil. However, some alternatives include cottonseed meal, fish emulsion, and bat guano.

MAJOR NATURAL SOURCES OF NITROGEN

MATERIAL	NITROGEN (%)	APPLY PER 100 SQUARE FEET
Blood meal	9–14	5–10 pounds
Cottonseed meal	6.7–7.4	10 pounds
Fish emulsion	5–10	5–10 pounds
Bat guano	10	5 pounds

Bonemeal

Generally I supply phosphorus (one of the major nutrients) to my plants by adding bonemeal. Bonemeal has a whopping amount of phosphoric acid—20 to 25 percent or more—as well as 1 to 2 percent nitrogen, and vegetables love it. You can buy steamed bonemeal where garden products are sold. If you like, you can substitute rock phosphate, a finely ground rock powder, for bonemeal.

MAJOR NATURAL SOURCES OF PHOSPHORUS

MATERIAL	PHOSPHORUS (%)	APPLY PER 100 SQUARE FEET
Rock phosphate	38–41	5 pounds
Bonemeal, steamed	11	5 pounds

Wood Ash

Wood ash supplies the potassium needed by your plants. Most wood ash contains about 7 percent potassium and can be obtained simply by burning wood outdoors or in a fireplace. (Wood ash should not be allowed to stand in the rain, because most of the potassium will be leached away.)

If you have trouble getting wood ash, it's possible to substitute greensand and granite dust, which you can buy at many nurseries. Both of these materials contain about 4.1 to 9.5 percent potassium. Both also contain a number of minor and trace mineral nutrients.

MAJOR NATURAL SOURCES OF POTASSIUM (POTASH)

MATERIAL	POTASH (%)	APPLY PER 100 SQUARE FEET
Wood ash	7	5 pounds
Greensand	4.1–9.5	5 pounds
Granite dust	5	5 pounds

If you find the idea of buying and mixing blood meal, bonemeal, and wood ash yourself too difficult, you can buy commercial organic fertilizers containing these ingredients (already mixed for you) from most nurseries. Many gardeners start out this way rather than trying to handle the individual ingredients. It will add extra cost to starting up a garden, but save on time.

Fish Emulsion

Fish emulsion generally has 5 to 10 percent nitrogen and sometimes phosphorus and potassium, although many brands are marked on the bottle 5-0-0, which in nursery language means 5 percent nitrogen, no phosphorus, and no potassium, respectively. You can use fish emulsion about every two weeks to add nitrogen to those plants that are pretty heavy feeders, such as leafy vegetables (cabbage, lettuce, spinach, collards).

Some gardeners prefer to use liquid seaweed in place of fish emulsion. It contains nitrogen, phosphorus, and a number of minerals. Any of these fertilizers can be added to your soil to give your feeding plants an extra boost.

The Earthworm

Earthworms, like bacteria, are great for the soil; they are extremely helpful in keeping your postage stamp bed in good shape. By burrowing, feeding, and excreting, earthworms let air and moisture in and break up the soil particles. They usually don't burrow very deep, but when the plant roots start going deeper, the earthworms go with them, making the soil even better.

The grayish pink ones (*Helodrilus caliginosus* and *Helodrilus caliginosus trapezoides*) are important to your garden. The red one (*Eisenia fetida*), the fish worm, is not as good, because it stays in damp spongy places instead of getting down to work in garden soils. You'll find *Eisenia fetida* works great in compost piles, however, and you may want to buy a few to add when you make your own compost.

The earthworm takes in the soil, grinds it up, mixes it with calcium carbonate, pulverizes it, sends it on through its intestine to be digested by enzymes, and then excretes it in the form of castings. These final earthworm castings contain nitrogen, phosphorus, and potassium, all elements that vegetables need. And when the earthworm dies, its body adds a good nitrogen fertilizer to the soil.

It is important to note that chemicals and earthworms don't mix, at least not well. Chemical fertilizers seem to decrease the number of earthworms in the soil, killing them or driving them off; ammonium sulfate is particularly harmful. Many insect sprays also are toxic to earthworms and will cause the population in the soil to dwindle.

Earthworms actually are a little finicky about the soil in general. You can't put them in infertile or hard, clay soils and expect good results. They like rich soil, and if they don't have it, they just take off.

Earthworms make a good soil even better. So, when possible, dig up earthworms from other parts of the yard (or anywhere else) and deposit them in your future vegetable garden. You may have to keep turning dirt over with a shovel until you find them—generally there are fewer of them in most flower beds. Or you can order earthworms through many seed catalogs.

Creating the kind of soil that bristles with the right organic nutrients is the most important thing that you can do in your garden. And your vegetables will love you for it.

Now that you know the components that make up a great soil mix, the next chapter will show you how to combine them and get your ground ready to plant.

CHAPTER 3

Getting Your Ground Ready

Postage stamp gardens, in general, aren't very difficult to grow, nor do they take very much work. Getting the soil ready in the first place takes more effort than anything else you'll do.

In a conventional garden, you must dig up the soil and then, throughout the season, cultivate and weed. In the postage stamp garden, you dig up the ground—the big push, but a fairly easy one—but after that, except for watering, you more or less coast. And, believe me, that's the kind of gardening I really like.

Methods for Preparing the Soil

As stated in chapter 2, the whole purpose of the postage stamp garden is to create a super fertile, well-textured soil that will support the growth of a large quantity of vegetables in a small space. To accomplish this goal you can choose from two ways of preparing the soil.

Method #1 uses a rototiller and is therefore faster and easier. You can plow a small bed in about ten minutes; after that, you simply spade in your compost, manure, and other nutrients and rake over the soil. It has only one general drawback. Because the rototiller breaks down everything in the soil to about the same consistency, it does tend to destroy some of the soil structure and the layering effect that helps create soil fertility.

Method #2, on the other hand, employs hand tools only, so it is more labor-intensive but it structures the soil in a special way that is better for the plants.

It is a good way to achieve super fertilization because it allows you to control soil texture. It helps condition the soil so that water comes up automatically. This method also gives you a slight mound. It generally produces the best results because it stimulates root growth by providing different nutrients at different levels.

If you intend to garden in an area where the soil is hard and clayey and, therefore, difficult to dig, it may be an especially good idea to use method #1 (rototill) the first year. In subsequent years the soil will be looser, and you can use method #2 (shovel) if you like.

Method #1

Here is the procedure:

1 Rototill your bed at least 1 foot deep.

2 If you have clay soil, use a spade or spading fork to turn sand and compost into the soil until your bed consists of one-third compost, one-third sand, and one-third original soil. You can purchase sand from most building supply or garden centers. If you have sandy soil, do not add any sand, but add plenty of organic compost to the soil until your bed consists of one-third to one-half compost and the rest original soil. For in-between soils, just estimate how much you'll need of one thing or another in order to end up with a mixture that contains at least one-third compost and whose texture is loose and fairly fine, has good air space, and is easy to dig.

3 Level the bed with a rake.

4 Spread a 2-inch layer of rotted manure over the entire bed. Add blood meal (4 pounds per 50 square feet), a sprinkling of bonemeal (4 pounds per 50 square feet), and a small dose of wood ash (3 pounds per 50 square feet)—or any of the substitutes mentioned in chapter 2. Using a rake, turn this into the top portion of the soil, and then rake the topsoil to a light texture. Most garden centers also sell an organic fertilizer that contains these ingredients, making the job easier. Just buy this fertilizer and spread it in your garden.

Method #2

Here is the procedure:

1 For heavy clay soils, cover the entire bed with 2 to 3 inches of sand. Adjust the amount of sand to meet the needs of your own soil, whether clayey, sandy, or something in between. When this stage is finished, you should come out with soil that is roughly half sand and half original soil.

2 Start at one end of the bed, and with a shovel dig a trench along the entire side. Make the trench one spade (about 9 to 10 inches) wide and deep. Put the excavated topsoil (along with the sand) where you can get it later. (Fig. 1, page 46)

3 Loosen the subsoil in the trench that you've just created—again, one spade wide and deep—to about 18 to 20 inches below the original surface. Make sure that this subsoil is nice and loose, but not too fine. The soil should grade from a fairly coarse texture at the bottom to a fairly fine texture at the top.

4 Remove topsoil to the depth and width of one spade (including the sand) from the strip of bed directly beside the trench that you've just opened, and fill in your trench. Make sure that you mix the sand and soil well in the trench that you're now filling up. (Fig. 2, page 46)

5 You now have a new trench next to the first one that you filled up. In this new trench, loosen the subsoil in the same manner as before. Again, fill in the trench with topsoil (and sand) from the adjacent strip.

6 Dig one trench after another across the width of the bed, always loosening the subsoil and mixing the topsoil and sand, until you've finished the entire bed. Into the very last trench put the topsoil (and sand) that you laid aside originally from the first trench. (Fig. 3, page 46)

7 Leave the garden rough for a few days.

8 Now go back and excavate the topsoil from each strip again, one by one. As you then return the topsoil to each trench, you will be adding different nutrients at different levels. First, spread a small amount of blood meal (4 pounds per 50 square feet) and bonemeal (4 pounds per

50 square feet) at the bottom of the topsoil. Add some topsoil. Second, spread a 4-inch layer of compost. Add more topsoil. Third, add about 2 inches of rotted manure. Add some more topsoil. Fourth, add a small amount of wood ash (3 pounds per 50 square feet). Spread over the remaining topsoil. If you prefer, use the substitute nutrients cited in chapter 2.

9   Rake the soil at the top (don't disturb the strata) until it has a very fine texture.

Fig. 1. Dig the first trench, putting the soil to one side.

Fig. 2. Fill first trench with soil from the second.

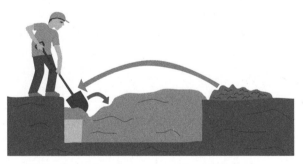

Fig. 3. Repeat process across the entire bed.

Putting Moisture into the Soil

After you've dug up the soil and added the nutrients, soak the soil for a day or two before sowing your seeds or setting out your seedlings. You want to get moisture down to a depth of at least 10 inches, so if it hasn't rained recently, you may have to water for a long while to reach that level. After that, you can begin planting any time.

Maintaining the Soil

Once you've prepared your garden soil the first year, the hardest part is done. However, you can improve your soil throughout the growing season and in subsequent years through refeeding and crop rotation.

Refeeding and Retilling

In the course of a growing season, every time you take out a crop you should refeed the soil before planting anything new. It's very easy. To revitalize the soil, simply spread a couple of inches of rotted manure and a couple of inches of compost on top of the garden bed and work it in as thoroughly as possible. Because you really worked up the bed the first time, you won't have much trouble now. Also add small amounts of blood meal (4 pounds per 50 square feet), bonemeal (4 pounds per 50 square feet), and wood ash (3 pounds per 50 square feet)—or the substitutes.

Every new year in the spring, completely spade or rototill your beds again, according to the methods described in this chapter.

Crop Rotation

In addition to adding compost and other ingredients each growing season, you should rotate the crops to keep the soil healthy. Some vegetables make heavy demands on the soil (heavy feeders); others take out very little (light feeders); and a few (the legumes) restore soil fertility. By moving these various kinds of vegetables around in your postage stamp beds, you can keep the soil in good shape throughout the years and even add vigor to it as you go along.

When possible, heavy feeders should be followed by legumes (beans and peas), which restore the soil fertility. After the legumes, you then plant the light feeders. In a postage stamp garden, this rotation is a little difficult because taller vegetables are planted to the north and smaller ones to the south. But if you want to give the soil a break, you must restore the balance whenever possible.

In sum, as you continue gardening the postage stamp way, your soil will get better and better. If there's a secret to turning brown thumbs into bright green ones, the postage stamp method is it. When you create the right soil conditions and continue to add compost and other nutrients each growing season, your soil will continually produce vigorous, healthy vegetables with only a minimum of additional effort.

SOIL NUTRIENT DEFICIENCY

SYMPTOM	CAUSE	NUTRIENT SOLUTION
Yellow leaves starting with the lower leaves; stunted growth	Nitrogen deficiency	Apply blood meal at the rate of 10 ounces per 100 square feet
Bluish green leaves followed by bronzing or purpling, drying to a greenish brown or black	Phosphorus deficiency	Apply phosphate rock at the rate of 4 ounces per 100 square feet, or test soil and follow recommendations
Dry or scorched leaves; dead areas along margins; plants stunted; rusty appearance	Potash (potassium) deficiency	Apply wood ash or greensand at the rate of $1\frac{1}{4}$ to $1\frac{1}{2}$ pounds per 100 square feet, or test soil and follow recommendations
Mottling of lower leaves, margins, or tips, or between veins; leaves wilt from bottom up	Magnesium deficiency	Use 1 pound of Epsom salts per 1,000 square feet, or test soil and follow recommendations

SYMPTOM	CAUSE	NUTRIENT SOLUTION
Mottled yellowing leaves; stunted growth	Manganese deficiency	Use manganese sulfate, or test soil and follow recommendations
Dark green, olive gray leaf edges; edges curl upward	Copper deficiency	Use 6 ounces of copper sulfate per 1,000 square feet, or test soil and follow recommendations
Mottling, yellowing, or scorching of the tissues between veins	Zinc deficiency	Use 8 ounces of zinc sulfate per 1,000 square feet, or test soil and follow recommendations
Yellow leaves; green veins	Iron deficiency	Use a soluble iron complex, iron sulfate, or chelated iron, or test soil and follow recommendations
Young leaves turn pale green to yellow; older leaves remain green	Sulfur deficiency	Most soils contain adequate amounts of sulfur; if not, test soil and follow recommendations
Stem tips die; distortion of young stems	Calcium deficiency	Spray plants with calcium nitrate or add calcium sulfate (gypsum), or test soil and follow recommendations
Leaves turn pale green or yellow; leaves crinkled; stunted	Molybdenum	Use about 1 teaspoon of sodium or ammonium molybdate per 1,000 square feet, or test soil and follow recommendations

CHAPTER 4

When and How to Plant

Just how do you know when to plant so that everything comes up rapidly and keeps right on going to maturity? I really become frustrated when I turn a seed package over to read the planting instructions and they merely say, "Plant after all danger of frost has passed." Unfortunately, although this advice is good as far as it goes, it is inadequate because different classes of vegetables need different amounts of growing heat. Let's begin by looking at the question of warm and cool seasons.

Mother Nature's Time Clock

Vegetables are divided into warm-season and cool-season crops. Generally, plants that we harvest for their fruit—such as tomatoes, squash, peppers, eggplant, melons, and lima beans—need a lot of heat and long days to grow well. If there isn't enough heat during the day to satisfy a plant's heat requirements, it will just sit there and do nothing. I've planted tomatoes in April, for instance, and wondered why they weren't growing. Then suddenly the days started to turn warm and the plants took off. Since then, I've experimented with planting tomatoes at one-week intervals starting in March. The early plants never seem to reach maturity any faster than the plants set out later, because their development is held back by cool weather.

Cool-season plants, on the other hand, do quite well when the weather is on the cool side. These are generally the leafy and root vegetables: carrots, beets, spinach, cabbage, and lettuce. You also have to include peas as a cool-season plant, even though you harvest the fruit. When the weather is cool and the days short, these plants put all their effort into forming leafy or root materials, but when the days begin to warm up, they stop producing leafy material and eventually go to seed. As a result, you generally have to plant cool-season vegetables early so that they can achieve the right size before the weather becomes too hot. You can also plant them late so that they mature in the cooler days of fall.

WARM- AND COOL-SEASON CROPS

COOL SEASON*	WARM SEASON**	INTOLERANT OF FROST AT MATURITY
Artichokes	Beans	Carrots
Asparagus	Corn	Cauliflower
Beets	Cucumbers	Endive
Broccoli	Eggplant	Lettuce
Brussels sprouts	Melons	Peas
Cabbage	Okra	Rhubarb
Kale	Peppers	Swiss Chard
Mustard greens	Squash	
Onions	Tomatoes	
Radishes		
Rutabaga		
Spinach		
Spinach, New Zealand		
Turnips		

*Adapted to 55°F–70°F. Will tolerate some frost.
**Requires 65°F–80°F. Readily damaged by frost.

Besides warm-season and cool-season vegetables, we also have early and late varieties of most vegetables. The early varieties require less heat to mature than the late. If you want to start your vegetables early, start with one of the early varieties, then follow through with a late variety for that particular type of vegetable. Or, if you live in an area that is continually cool throughout the summer, never rising above temperatures in the 70s, you might plant only an early variety, because it requires less heat to mature than the late variety.

VEGETABLES BY GROWING SEASON

SPRING	SUMMER	FALL
Beets	Beans	Beets
Broccoli	Corn	Broccoli
Brussels sprouts	Cucumbers	Carrots
Cabbage	Eggplant	Lettuce and endive
Carrots	Melons	Radishes
Cauliflower	Peppers	Spinach
Onions	Squash, summer	Turnips and rutabagas
Radishes	Tomatoes	
Turnips and rutabagas		

All of this means that you have to watch the heat requirements of particular plants to know when to plant in your area. Experienced gardeners know exactly when to plant for best results. For the rest of us, nature provides a guide that we can use effectively to know when to plant. This guide relies on the blooming of fairly common plants, and because Mother Nature does all the juggling herself, the system is far more accurate than arbitrary planting rules or a good guess. Here's what to watch for.

MOTHER NATURE'S PLANTING GUIDE

CONDITION	PLANT
Development of color in flowers from spring bulbs, such as tulips or narcissus	Beets, carrots, leaf lettuce, onions, peas, radishes, and spinach
Appearance of plum and cherry blossoms	Head lettuce
Appearance of apple, cherry, quince, and strawberry blossoms	Everything else—cucumbers, melons, squash, tomatoes, and so on

Planting with a Zone Map

The only problem with referring to a zone map (and you can find this map in every seed catalog and online at http://planthardiness.ars.usda.gov/PHZMWeb) is that it's impossible to group the entire country into clearly defined climatic regions. Within each region you'll find many different microclimates, where the average date of the last killing frost varies. Spring nighttime temperatures, for instance, are warmer near the ocean, cooler in inland valleys, and still cooler at higher elevations inland. Geographical points only a few miles apart may have radically different temperatures. This means that you can only generalize. A zone map can be helpful, however, in determining approximately when to plant in the spring.

To use a zone map, look up your zone on the map to determine the average date of the last killing frost. The vegetable planting list below will then tell you approximately on what date to plant particular vegetables. For instance, if you live in Zone 3, the average dates of the last killing frost fall between May 1 and May 15. Referring to the vegetable planting list, you will find that you can plant kale sometime between April 1 and April 15, carrots between May 1 and May 15, and tomatoes after May 15, when the ground has warmed up.

LAST FROST DATES		
Zone 1: June 15	Zone 5: April 1–15	Zone 9: January 15–31
Zone 2: May 15–31	Zone 6: March 15–31	Zone 10: January 1–14
Zone 3: May 1–15	Zone 7: March 1–15	Zones 11–13: Frost-free
Zone 4: April 15–30	Zone 8: February 1–28	

VEGETABLE PLANTING LIST
- In Zones 6, 7, 8, and 9, plant these vegetables from fall to early spring. In all other zones plant these vegetables 2 to 4 weeks before the last killing frost in spring: broccoli, brussels sprouts, kale, lettuce, mustard greens, onions, peas, radishes, rutabagas, turnips.
- Plant these vegetables on approximately the date of the last frost. They tolerate cool weather and very light frost: beets, cabbage, carrots, cauliflower, spinach, Swiss chard.
- Plant these vegetables after the ground has warmed up: beans, corn, cucumbers, eggplant, melons, okra, peppers, rhubarb, squash, tomatoes.

Planting by Moon Cycles

Planting by moon cycles sounds like an old superstition, doesn't it? Yet we know, for instance, that both the moon and the sun affect the tides and that the pull is greater at certain times than at others. If you watch the growth of your garden a while in relation to various phases of the moon, you'll see some startling things. There seem to be noticeable sprouts of growth in the garden that coincide with the new moon and the full moon. Some gardeners swear by this and will plant only at times when they feel that the gravitational effect is best.

MOON CYCLES

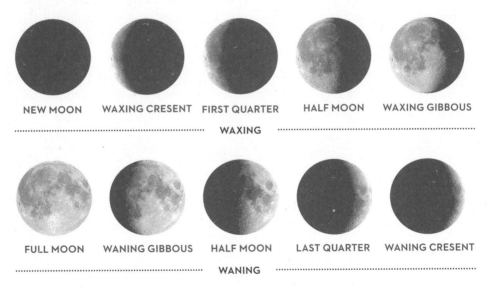

NEW MOON   WAXING CRESENT   FIRST QUARTER   HALF MOON   WAXING GIBBOUS

WAXING

FULL MOON   WANING GIBBOUS   HALF MOON   LAST QUARTER   WANING CRESENT

WANING

For anybody who'd like to give this method a try, here are some rules:

1   Plant vegetables that grow above ground (such as tomatoes, squash, and lettuce) two nights before the new moon or in the first quarter of the new moon (look at your calendar for the exact dates). You can also sow when the moon is waxing from half to full. When you sow during the waning moon (from full to smaller size), the seeds won't germinate at all but will wait until the next period.

2   Plant root crops (such as carrots, beets, radishes, and onions) in the third quarter of the moon, when it is waning.

3   Transplant on the waning moon. That way the root will take immediately.

How Far Apart to Set Plants

No matter where the moon may be, you had better know where your plants are. Spacing is very important in the postage stamp bed. The object is to set out the plants so that their outer leaves just touch one another when the plants are about three-fourths mature and so that the leaves virtually carpet the bed when fully mature. The plants shade their own root zones, allowing the bed to retain moisture (calling for less watering) and ensuring that almost no weeds come through. This area beneath the leaves also creates its own fertile microclimate. At maturity there's virtually a little greenhouse under those leaves. Wind bounces off the foliage, and sunshine glances off. The area doesn't become too hot or too cold or dried out by the wind. The microclimate is extremely important to good garden beds.

When planting vegetables in the postage stamp garden, space the plants a little closer than generally recommended on seed packets or on instructions for seedlings. Corn, for instance, does quite well planted 8 inches apart in postage stamp gardens (as opposed to the 12 inches usually recommended for conventional gardens).

POSTAGE STAMP PLANT SPACING

VEGETABLE	SPACING (IN INCHES)	VEGETABLE	SPACING (IN INCHES)
Artichoke	36*	Cabbage	14
Asparagus	12	Carrot	2
Bean, fava	4	Cauliflower	15
Bean, lima (bush)	8	Corn	8
Bean, lima (pole)	10	Cucumbers	6
Bean, snap (bush)	4	Eggplant	24
Bean, snap (pole)	6	Garlic	3
Beets	3	Kale	8
Broccoli	15	Lettuce, head	10
Brussels sprouts	14	Lettuce, leaf	6

continued

VEGETABLE	SPACING (IN INCHES)	VEGETABLE	SPACING (IN INCHES)
Melon	12	Rutabaga	6
Mustard greens	4–6	Shallot	2
Okra	16	Spinach	4
Onions	3–4	Spinach, New Zealand	10
Onions, bunching	2	Squash, summer	12
Peas	2–3	Squash, winter	12–24
Peppers	12–24	Swiss chard	6
Radishes	2	Tomatoes	18
Rhubarb	12	Turnips	3

*Because artichokes require so much space, you might want to consider planting them outside your vegetable bed, elsewhere in your garden.

How to Start the Vegetables

You have a choice as to how you can start your vegetables:

1   For some vegetables, such as carrots, beets, and other roots, you should sow seeds directly in the ground.

2   For broccoli, cabbage, cauliflower, lettuce, onions, tomatoes, and several other vegetables, you can buy seedlings from the nursery and transplant them directly into your garden.

3   For most vegetables, you can plant seeds in containers indoors and then later transplant the resultant seedlings outdoors, when the weather warms up.

Now let's take a closer look at each of these methods to see how they can work into your own gardening plans.

Sowing Seeds Directly

Where do seeds come from? For most of us, they come from the seed racks found in hardware stores, nurseries, grocery stores, and elsewhere. The varieties found on racks in your area are generally fine for your particular climate.

There are other places to find seeds. Some of us are incurable seed catalog fans. Seed catalogs are good dream material. (In Appendix B, page 195, you'll find the addresses and websites of companies that will mail you seed catalogs.) These same catalogs have tons of garden suggestions and advice.

To get good results with certain plants, you must start with seeds. Such plants as bush beans, beets, carrots, dwarf peas, radishes, rutabagas, spinach, and turnips don't transplant very well, so you'll want to sow their seeds directly into the garden bed. Here's how to do it:

1   Soak the soil the day before planting.

2   Scatter the seeds evenly across the bed (or a portion of it), and try not to miss the corners. Try to space the seeds roughly according to the spacing table. The bigger seeds—such as those for radishes and spinach—won't be a problem. You can see exactly where they are, and if you get too many in one spot, just move them around. With tiny seeds—such as those for carrots—you'll have more of a problem, but you can get the hang of it by practicing with coffee grounds over a piece of paper.

3   Cover the seeds with fine soil. Different vegetable seeds require different depths below the soil surface (consult the instructions in chapter 6).

4   Later, if too many plants come up, crowding one another, don't worry about it. Just thin them out a bit, pulling up a number of the plants so that the ones that are left are more evenly distributed according to the desired spacing. (You'll get a dividend here: The small beets and carrots that you pull up can be extra tender and delicious.)

Not all the seeds will come up. Germination is never 100 percent—a few seeds in any collection will be sterile. Even the germination of fertile seeds is affected by soil moisture, depth of planting, and other conditions that are rarely perfect.

Unused seeds, by the way, can be saved for the next year. The germination rate will drop only slightly from year to year. Simply seal the seed packets airtight with tape, and store them in a very cool place.

SEED GERMINATION

VEGETABLE	MINIMUM FEDERAL STANDARD GERMINATION (%)	SEEDS PER OUNCE (AVERAGE)	RELATIVE LONGEVITY (YEARS)
Asparagus	60	1,400	3
Bean, lima	70	20–70	3
Bean, snap	75	100	3
Beets	65	2,000	4
Broccoli	75	8,100	3
Brussels sprouts	70	8,500	4
Cabbage	75	7,700	4
Carrots	55	22,000	3
Cauliflower	75	8,600	4
Corn	75	140	2
Cucumbers	80	1,100	5
Eggplant	60	7,000	4
Endive	70	17,000	5
Kale	75	10,000	4
Lettuce	80	26,000	6
Melon	75	1,100	5
Mustard greens	60	10,000	4
Okra	50	500	2
Onions	70	8,500	1
Peas	80	50–230	3
Peppers	55	4,500	2
Radishes	75	3,100	4
Rutabaga	75	11,000	4
Spinach	60	2,900	3
Spinach, New Zealand	40	430	3
Squash	75	180–380	4

VEGETABLE	MINIMUM FEDERAL STANDARD GERMINATION (%)	SEEDS PER OUNCE (AVERAGE)	RELATIVE LONGEVITY (YEARS)
Swiss chard	65	1,500	4
Tomatoes	75	10,000	4
Turnips	80	14,000	4

Buying Seedlings and Transplanting

Some vegetables—such as broccoli, brussels sprouts, cabbage, cauliflower, eggplant, peppers, and tomatoes—seem to get off to a better start if they are first grown from seeds indoors and then later transplanted into the garden as seedlings. Lettuce, melons, and onions seem to develop well either way—from seeds sown directly in the garden or from transplants. In general, transplanting gives you a head start because you have little plants already developed by the time that it's warm enough outdoors to plant. Also, you avoid having to thin plants, because you space the seedlings directly. If you decide to buy vegetables as small plants, you can generally find most of the popular varieties at your local nursery or garden center.

When planting seedlings, dig a hole in your postage stamp bed large enough to avoid bending or squeezing the root mass. Try not to disturb the roots any more than possible when transferring to the ground, and once the plant is in, make sure that the soil is firm but not packed around the roots.

For transplanting, you can probably get by with a small trowel, but there are other tools that can be useful. One of the best is a pointed stick, just a small dowel with a rounded point. Use it in your left hand to poke in the soil. With your right hand hold the seedling in the hole, and then, with the stick, fill in around the roots and push the soil back.

Starting Seeds Indoors in Containers

Why bother to start your own seeds indoors at all when it's a lot easier to just go down to the nursery, pick out what seedlings you need, and come back and plunk them in your garden? The reasons for developing your own seedlings are both psychological and practical. The psychological reason is purely the joy and feeling of accomplishment of having grown something entirely yourself.

WHEN TO START SEEDLINGS INDOORS, FROM SEED

1 MONTH BEFORE PLANTING IN GARDEN	2 MONTHS BEFORE PLANTING IN GARDEN	3 MONTHS BEFORE PLANTING IN GARDEN
Corn	Broccoli	Lettuce
Cucumber	Cabbage	Squash
Eggplant	Cauliflower	
Onions	Melons	
Peppers	Tomatoes	

The practical reasons are several. First, buying seeds is cheaper than buying seedlings. Second, only a relatively small selection of vegetable varieties are sold at nurseries; if you want to experiment with new or unusual varieties, you must grow your plants from seeds. And third, seedlings (whether you grow them yourself or purchase them from a nursery) are a great advantage for such warm-weather crops as cucumbers, melons, squash, and tomatoes. These crops don't do well until the weather warms up and outdoor temperatures stay in the 60s or above. So, by planting them indoors early and transplanting them later, you can get a head start on the weather.

Here are some methods for starting vegetables indoors.

Metal Foil Pans

1 Purchase metal foil pans at a variety or grocery store. To fill them, make up a soil mix of equal parts sand, loam (soil with a lot of organic material), and compost or peat moss. Screen this mixture so that the particles are fairly small. You can also buy prepared planting mixes at any nursery and save yourself the mess of blending your own.

2 Plant the seeds 1 or 2 inches apart, and cover them with soil or vermiculite. Vermiculite—light mineral granules that can be bought packaged at any nursery—is best because it holds moisture well. There are prepackaged planting mixes in which this is included.

3 Place the containers in a warm place (above 60°F to 70°F), where they will be in full sun or under a fluorescent full-spectrum light for about twelve hours a day, if possible (just do the best you can). For fast germination of the seeds of eggplant, peppers, and tomatoes, you'll need

a soil temperature of 75°F to 85°F. Within a couple of weeks, in any event, most plants will have begun to poke through the soil.

4   When the second pair of leaves opens, move each plant to a separate small pot or to a small paper cup, or space the plants 3 inches apart in another foil pan.

5   Transplant the seedlings outside according to the dates given earlier in this chapter in the vegetable planting list.

Starter Kits

If using foil pans seems too hard, you can buy starter kits for tomatoes and other vegetables—the kits come with a container, soil, and seeds—already put together. All you have to do is take the lid off the container and water the soil. (Sometimes, though, you'll find the seeds in a separate packet that you sow yourself.)

Flats

You can also start seeds in a flat: A good size is a 14 by 24-inch box about 3 inches deep. Again, use the soil mix of sand, loam, and compost or peat moss, or buy big packages of planting soil. Soak the soil in the flat thoroughly. For small seeds, sow gently over the surface, then press in. For larger seeds, make furrows with a pencil—2 inches apart and at the depth required for particular vegetables. Then drop in your seeds, and cover them with planting mix or vermiculite. Place the flat in a warm, light spot like that described for metal foil pans. When the first two sets of leaves have developed, transplant the seedlings individually to small pots or to other flats, spacing them 3 inches apart. When transferring seedlings, always be careful to disturb the roots as little as possible.

Hardening the Transplants

Before actually planting the young seedlings in the soil outdoors, you should get them used to outdoor conditions. Adjust the young plants to outdoor temperatures by putting them outdoors (in their containers) when it's sunny. Bring them indoors whenever frost seems likely, especially overnight. In one way or another, expose them to the lower temperatures for about two weeks before setting them out in your garden bed.

There are, of course, more complicated methods of growing young seedlings for transplanting. But this book is dedicated to giving you the easiest, most hassle-free ways possible.

Other Seeding Methods

By making coverings that intensify heat, it's possible to plant outdoors before the weather really gets warm enough to expose particular plants fully to the elements. For melons, for instance, you can make small frames or boxes, each 1 by 1 foot and 3 or 4 inches high, with a clear vinyl plastic cover, and place them on your prepared garden bed. Plant eight to ten seeds within each frame. Remove the plastic cover on warm days; replace it on cold nights or days. Remove the cover entirely when the danger of frost has passed.

Another idea is to make "jug houses" for your plants. You do this by cutting off the bottoms of 1-gallon plastic bottles and setting the bottomless jugs (with the lids still on) over your planted seeds. Or you can simply buy commercially made wax-paper plant protectors (often called hot caps) from a nursery. All of these methods will give your seedlings a faster start. Just make sure that you remove the hot caps, jugs, or plastic sheets on warm days or your plants are liable to burn.

How to Stretch Your Crops

You probably know gardeners who produce so many vegetables out of their small gardens that you wonder whether they aren't hauling them in from the country. They aren't. They've just mastered those little tricks that make Mother Nature work over time. These miracle "crop stretchers" are intercropping, succession planting, and catch cropping. More detail on how to apply these methods to specific vegetables is provided in chapter 6, but here is an overview.

Intercropping

Intercropping simply means planting quick-maturing crops between slower maturing crops. With intercropping you can plant quick-maturing radishes, green onions, or leaf lettuce between rows of corn or tomatoes. Because you plant corn and tomatoes far apart—8 inches for corn and 18 inches for tomatoes—you will harvest the intercrops before the corn and tomato plants have become big enough to crowd the smaller plants out. That's getting double duty out of your postage stamp bed.

Succession Planting

In succession planting, later crops are planted as soon as you take out early ones (make sure that you add compost and additional organic fertilizer before you replant). For instance, harvest spinach and then plant beans, or take out broccoli and then plant corn. Or plant early, midseason, and late-maturing varieties of the same kind of vegetable. Any combination of early and late varieties stretch the productivity of your garden. Here are some suggestions for succession planting:

- Beets followed by brussels sprouts
- Snap beans followed by cabbage, cauliflower, kale, lettuce, or spinach
- Peas followed by beans

Catch Cropping

In catch cropping, quick-maturing plants are planted in places from which you've just harvested larger, slower growing vegetables. For instance, let's say you've just harvested a couple of slow-growing broccoli plants in late summer. It's too late to plant more broccoli, but you can still grow quick maturing radishes or green onions in the very same space.

The basic rule here is simple: Don't leave bare ground unplanted.

FAST-GROWING VEGETABLES
Bush beans, carrots, green onions, lettuce, kale, radish, spinach

SLOW-GROWING VEGETABLES
Broccoli, brussels sprouts, cabbage, cauliflower, corn, eggplant, tomatoes

---

CHAPTER 5

Watering Your Postage Stamp Vegetable Garden

Watering your postage stamp garden, like doing everything else recommended in this book, should be simple and easy. In fact, it is simple and easy, but it is also absolutely crucial to the success of your garden. The truth is that water—or the lack of it—can sometimes create tremendous garden problems.

Without enough water, bean pods produce only a few seeds and the rest of the pods shrivel, beets become stringy, radishes get pithy, cucumbers stop growing well, and more. Once started, vegetables must grow rapidly, without interruptions or slowdowns. Stop growth by checking the water supply, and you really set your vegetables back. Agronomists tell us that when a plant isn't getting enough water, it's under "water stress." And although this may be useful for flowers, because water stress can induce blooming, it nearly always sets vegetables back. Once you do this, they never seem to recover.

How Much to Water and When

You've heard that old saying, "Damned if you do, and damned if you don't." Well, watering is like that in a vegetable garden. It's absolutely essential, but it can also create problems. Water itself is a nutrient used directly by the plants, and it also dissolves and carries other nutrients to the roots. That's the good part. The roots of plants also need air just like we do. Oxygen must reach the roots, and carbon dioxide must be given off by the roots to return to the air.

Most soil has enough air space for this exchange to take place. If you eliminate the oxygen by filling all the soil space continually with water, however, root growth stops, and if this condition continues long enough, the plant dies. That's the bad part.

An ideal soil for plant growth contains 50 percent solid matter and 50 percent pore space (that's what our postage stamp soil has). About half this pore space should be occupied by water, and that's the object of your watering program.

The general rule for watering postage stamp gardens is this: Water thoroughly, regularly, and infrequently. When you soak the soil thoroughly, you add water until it reaches "field capacity"—that is, roughly all the water that the air spaces of the soil can hold. And you want to keep your garden between this condition and the point at which moisture is so scarce that plant roots can no longer take water from the soil.

Whenever you water your postage stamp beds, you must water them thoroughly to a depth of about 3 feet. The length of time that it takes to water this deep will depend on the type of soil under the bed, but it will usually take at least an hour or two. A good rule is to simply water until you can easily sink a stick about 3 feet deep. If there are a lot of rocks below your postage stamp subsoil, you may not be able to do this; if so, then just estimate. After thoroughly watering your beds, don't water again until the soil has almost dried out to a depth of 10 inches. Just take a trowel and dig down to see how moist the soil is. If the soil is almost dry to this depth, water deeply again—and then don't water until the moisture has receded to 10 inches again.

At some times of the year, such as when it's cool or rainy, this interval between watering may extend two weeks or more, but when it's hot and dry, you may have to water every two to six days. It generally doesn't matter one bit whether or not it rains. You simply don't water until your 10-inch trowel test shows that watering is necessary. By letting the soil almost dry out this way, you give it a chance to take in a good supply of air as the water supply is removed.

After a few years of vegetable gardening, you'll have acquired enough experience to sense whenever watering is necessary and how much to water. You'll have adjusted to the special needs of your climate and seasonal rainfall.

Which Way to Water

Some gardeners insist that the only way to water is with a drip system or a hose lying on the ground. Others simply set up a sprinkler in the middle of their bed and turn it on when it's time to water.

What should you do? I personally feel that you should do whatever is easiest, as long as you water thoroughly until the soil reaches field capacity. Then don't water again until the soil is almost dried out.

In my own garden I originally set up a sprinkler and turned it on at regular intervals. This is easy and simple. There's no doubt that cool-season root crops take well to this method. But overhead watering like this can damage hot-weather crops like squash and tomatoes (tomatoes will crack). You can prevent tomato cracking and other problems by watering overhead until the plants start to produce fruit, and then use a ground hose after that.

If you live in an area where the humidity is high, overhead sprinkling can encourage mildew. Generally, you can overcome this by watering in the morning so that the plants are dry by evening. As a rule, though, you should water in the morning during the spring and fall (that is, in cool weather) and in the evening during the summer heat.

If you find that the leaves of your vegetables wilt somewhat during the hot summer, don't panic. Actually, some plants deliberately let their leaves droop in order to prevent the hot sun from drawing moisture from their exposed flat surfaces. A squash vine, for instance, that looks quite wilted in the afternoon will snap back the next morning crisp and fresh.

Besides watering the garden with a hose or a sprinkler, you can lay out two or three pieces of perforated plastic pipe or hose just under the vegetable leaves in your garden. When you're ready to water, just attach a hose and allow the water to trickle out. For deep-rooted plants like tomatoes, you can push a piece of 2-inch hollow pipe 6 to 12 inches into the soil and then send water down the pipe to those deep roots.

Drip systems, however, currently provide the best way to water postage stamp gardens. Eventually, I changed my watering to an automatic drip system in my beds. A drip-watering system supplies water to plants at ground level through emitters. It uses a $1/2$-inch polyethylene hose that runs throughout the garden or an ooze hose and a $1/2$-inch perforated plastic line that delivers water along its length.

The controls consist of a shutoff valve (manual or electric), a filter to catch sand and foreign material, and a pressure regulator that keeps your drip system from getting too much pressure. You can also use an automatic time clock that turns the system off and on at the same time each day. The clock can be set to run several layouts at the same time. This takes the guesswork out of when to water and allows you to leave for several days at a time, confident that the garden will be watered while you are gone.

For widely spaced plants like squash, eggplant, and tomatoes you will want at least one 1-gallon-per-minute emitter at each plant. For root and leaf crops that are close together, use an ooze hose or a perforated plastic hose that will water across the entire space.

You can buy drip kits and all the necessary supplies, such as rolls of plastic tubing and automatic timers, at any garden supply store. Or purchase them through most of the seed catalogs listed in Appendix B (page 195).

In sum, that's the watering system for the postage stamp beds. Water deeply, and then don't water again until the soil is almost dry. Do this and your garden will work its heart out growing big healthy, tender vegetables for your dinner table; it also could produce so much extra that you'll wind up having to beg the neighbors to take the surplus off your hands. If this happens, you can pat yourself on the back: It means you mastered the techniques of growing lots of vegetables in a very small space and are well on your way to becoming a wise and enlightened harvester of the fruits of nature.

Now Get Growing!

Okay, so now you know how to grow postage stamp gardens and produce all you can eat in a very small space. I hope that as you garden from here on out, you'll try as many of the suggested garden combinations as possible.

The best thing about postage stamp gardening, of course, is that it's simple, easy, and in balance with nature, making the soil better and more productive each and every season. And if in the beginning you started out with a brown thumb, like a lot of gardeners, somewhere along the way you're bound to discover that it isn't brown at all anymore but has turned a very satisfying green.

CHAPTER 6

Heirloom Vegetables and Herbs You'll Love to Grow

Which vegetables and herbs should you grow in your postage stamp garden? When selecting, consider what you like to eat, as mentioned in chapter 1. It's also important to select varieties that grow well in your geographical area. You can do this by contacting your local nursery or by ordering seed catalogs specifically for your growing area. Generally, anything purchased from local seed racks in nurseries, home centers, or any store that carries seed packets will do reasonably well because they are selected specifically to grow in your area.

Vegetables

In a postage stamp garden you must consider how much ground the vegetables take up and just how long they will tie up that space. Most pumpkins and winter squash, for instance, have large vines that run all over the place. For example, if you're planting a 6 by 6-foot garden, a pumpkin vine or a large squash vine just won't do. Potatoes take up only about a square foot per plant, but they tie up the ground for a good four months. Potato grow bags or potato barrels (found in seed catalogs and online) can come in handy if you still really want to grow potatoes, but it might be better to just buy potatoes at the supermarket. The same is true of parsnips (four months), celery (four to six months), and a few others. They are all great vegetables in their own right, but they are just not suitable for the type of high-yield gardening that we're discussing here.

One popular fad has been to grow so-called midget vegetables. The midget vegetables, whose size is half to one-third of regular vegetables, are space-savers all right, and there are now quite a few of them available. The only problem is that if you're looking for quantity, you'll have to grow twice or three times as many of these midgets to obtain the same production that you would get from regular-size plants.

In this chapter I include all vegetables that grow well in postage stamp gardens as well as a few that are just marginally acceptable. Each vegetable is rated from one stamp (▓ = marginal) to four stamps (▓ ▓ ▓ ▓ = excellent) for postage stamp gardens. The marginal ones, like cabbage and asparagus, are here because they're old favorites; they can be grown if you're willing to put up with a few special considerations (which are discussed later).

All vegetables mentioned in this chapter are marked as either a cool-season crop (♦) or a warm-season crop (♦), as discussed on pages 50–53, and all vegetables have a source code next to them. The codes are for the seed catalogs that carry the seeds (see Appendix B: Seed Sources).

Crop Stretching

In most vegetable listings you'll find information on crop stretching. These are tips and tricks that will produce a bigger and better harvest, using the methods described on pages 62–63.

Heirloom Varieties

Not too many years ago, heirloom vegetable seeds were hard to find. Today, that's all changed. The trend of growing heirloom vegetables in gardens has been gaining popularity in the United States and Europe over the past decade. With the fall of the Iron Curtain, many Eastern European heirloom seeds have found their way out into the rest of the world. All seed suppliers now offer heirloom seeds. From their origin to today, these seeds have a genetic history that has been grown, savored, saved, and passed down through generations. Heirlooms are a living glimpse of our past yet connect us to a sustainable food future.

What's the difference between seeds labeled "hybrid," and those labeled "heirloom"? Hybrids are a cross between two parents of different types. Each parent imparts its own particular qualities. The seeds of hybrid varieties will not retain the varieties' characteristics. This means you can't save the seeds and produce the same plant next year. In contrast, heirlooms are old open-pollinated (OP) seeds that are a genetically stable pure line, which is suitable for seed-saving. Heirloom seeds are an OP line that is at least fifty years old.

Heirlooms invite passion in gardeners. There is something about all their wonderful shapes, sizes, colors, and flavors that spark a sense of history in us. Today, seed companies and seed savers offer literally hundreds, if not thousands, of heirloom varieties. You can actually grow eight different colors of tomatoes alone, not to mention a variety of sizes and shapes. Have fun growing these old-timers and expect flavors like never before.

Keeping Heirloom Lines Pure

If you intend to grow more than one heirloom variety of the same species at a time, it could result in cross-pollination. If you save the seeds from those plants to replant next year, they could produce something entirely different than what you were expecting. Let's face it: This is how the diversity of heirlooms started. However, if you plan to seed save and want your varieties to remain pure, take caution when planting your beds. There are several ways to keep cross-pollination from occurring.

1   **SPACING.** Plant only one variety together. If you plant in small beds, say 4 by 4-foot beds, and you want heirloom tomatoes, then plant one or two of your favorite slicing heirlooms of the same species and culti-var. Then plant any other heirloom vegetables you choose in the same bed (making sure they are the same species and cultivar). In a second bed plant your favorite paste tomato using the same criteria as above. In a third bed plant your tiny cherry or salad tomatoes. By planting in separate beds you'll lessen the risk of cross-pollinating and you'll more than triple your vegetable production.

2   **TIMING.** To reduce cross-pollination, you can also plant different varieties of the same species at different times so they don't flower at the same time. You can plant in a spring garden, and then again in the fall. Make sure there is enough time at the end of the season for a late planting.

3   **ISOLATION CAGES.** Insects are great at pollinating, so to prevent them from visiting one variety or another construct screen cages around the plants. This is easy to do with upright plants such as tomatoes, beans, okra, and peppers.

4 **HAND-POLLINATING.** This means you have to transfer the pollen from one flower to another using a paintbrush. With tomatoes all you have to do is give the plant a good shake.

If you are a serious heirloom gardener and want to save the seed from year to year or pass them along to family and friends, you'll need to take the above rules under consideration.

Harvesting

There is a right and a wrong time to pick vegetables. Many plants go through a chemical change, converting sugar to starch (this is especially true of corn). The trick is to catch them when the sugar (or flavor) content is highest. The general rule is to try to pick vegetables before they're completely mature and then cook them as soon as possible. Vegetables picked this way are far tastier than anything you can buy in the supermarket, because by the time vegetables travel from the commercial grower, to the wholesale market, to the store, and then to you, the best part of the flavor has already been lost.

In the list of "Recommended Varieties" under each vegetable in this chapter, I give the days to maturity—that is, the average length of time that it takes vegetables to ripen, from planting to maturity. The figures are averages only and are affected by sun, cloudiness, temperatures, and other climatic variables in different regions of the country. Moreover, seed catalogs aren't always clear on what the figures mean. For most vegetables, the maturity days denote the period of time from planting seeds outdoors to harvesting. But for some vegetables, such as tomatoes, peppers, and eggplant, the maturity days denote the period of time from planting seedlings outdoors to harvesting; this period has, of course, been preceded by four to eight weeks of indoor growing.

ARTICHOKE

Cool-season crop. Rated marginal for postage stamp gardens.

The huge, grayish, deeply cut leaves of the artichoke plant add a touch of class to any garden. Because it's such a big plant (it can spread to 4 feet across), you may want to try growing one plant in a flower bed or wine barrel where it can show off its foliage. Artichokes are harvested in summer, but are perennial plants and regrow every summer.

Planting

Plant root divisions or plants purchased from the nursery during the spring. Set them in a protected area with southern exposure. Artichokes bear one year after planting, sometimes the first summer. To fertilize, apply a fish emulsion at ten-day intervals during the summer.

Recommended Varieties

GREEN GLOBE 88 days. Globular heads with thick and succulent scales. Hard to grow in most parts of New England. Seed source: ANN • BAK • COM • GOU • IRI • TERR

ROMANESCO 85 days. An Italian heirloom. Very large and flavorful bronze and purple artichokes. Seed source: ANN • GOU

VIOLETTO DI CHIOGGIA 85 days. This is an old Italian heirloom and, typical of such an old variety, it is picked small when it has no choke. A spineless purple artichoke. Seed source: ANN • GOU • TERR

Typical Problems

Artichokes have very few problems.

Harvesting

To harvest, cut the unripened flower heads before the bracts begin to separate. Cut artichokes darken in color once they are exposed in the air. To slow the discoloration, drop them in water fortified with 2 or 3 tablespoons of lemon juice.

Storage

Artichokes can be stored in a refrigerator drawer for only a few days.

Growing Tips

Replant in cold-climates: Artichokes grow best as a prennial in areas of long mild winters and cool summers. They can be grown in hot summer areas, but where the ground freezes in winter they will have to be replanted yearly.

ASPARAGUS

Cool-season crop. Rated marginal for postage stamp gardens. ♩ ▦

Like the artichoke—and unlike most other vegetables, which are annuals—asparagus is a perennial plant; once it's planted and gets going, it just keeps right on pouring out a continuous food supply every season for the next fifteen years or so.

Planting

Asparagus is not the best plant for a postage stamp garden because it tends to take over and eat up space. But if you're an asparagus lover you'll find a way to sneak it in somewhere. You definitely, however, don't want your asparagus in a small postage stamp bed with other vegetables. I'd recommend a separate bed for asparagus so the roots won't spread among your other vegetables. You can successfully grow it alone in a 4 by 4-foot intensive postage stamp bed surrounded by a frame. Grown this way, it stays fairly well within boundaries. Asparagus also does extremely well in a flower bed because its ornamental fronds blend in nicely.

You can start asparagus from seed, but if you do, you'll throw away a whole year right there. Grown from seeds, it will not produce its first crop until the third year. Therefore, buy one-year-old roots from your local nursery and transplant them directly into the garden. Even using roots, you will not get a crop until the second year.

In some ways, asparagus and the postage stamp bed were made for each other—asparagus demands rich, loose soil that's nice and deep. In early spring, just plant the roots about 12 inches apart. That's pretty close for asparagus, but it seems to work out all right. For each plant, make a hole about 5 inches in diameter and 8 inches deep. At the bottom of the hole spread out the roots, crown side up, and cover with 2 inches of soil. As the plant grows, simply keep filling the hole with additional soil, but do not cover the crown tip. Two to three months after planting, the hole should have been filled to ground level.

Unfortunately, asparagus doesn't grow nearly as fast as other vegetables. Although you'll get some spears the first year, don't cut them, but let them go to foliage. When they turn brown in the fall, cut them to the ground. The second year, though, you can harvest spears for about four weeks. The year after, you can cut spears for eight to ten weeks.

Feed asparagus with fish emulsion, or other organic fertilizer, a couple of times a year (apply according to the instructions on the box or bottle).

Crop Stretching
Asparagus is extremely prolific without much help.

Recommended Varieties
Be sure to choose rust-resistant varieties of asparagus. These can be found in seed catalogs or at your local nursery.

GIANT PRECOCE D'ARGENTEUIL Delicious stems can be blanched white, rose-colored buds. Seed source: ANN • BAK • BOU • GOU

MARY WASHINGTON An all-time favorite. Medium green tips. Rust-resistant. Seed source: ANN • BURP • GOU • IRI • SEED • SHU

MARY WASHINGTON IMPROVED High-yielding with tighter tips than the original. Seed source: THO

Typical Problems
You'll have few problems with asparagus—except for insect pests (which I take up in chapter 8).

Harvesting
When the asparagus spears are 8 to 10 inches long and when the buds at the tips are still compressed, you can harvest by cutting the spears at ground level or a few inches below. You can also snap the spears off by bending them over sharply until they break.

Storage
To store, wrap the bottom ends in a damp paper towel and refrigerate. To freeze asparagus, use only the tender portions (the tops and smaller shoots) and prepare them immediately. Blanch them in boiling water for two to four minutes, cool rapidly, place in containers, and freeze.

Growing Tips
Better production: To grow more asparagus, strip off the green peppercorn-size berries as they appear on the fronds of the female plants. This increases the yield almost immediately.

BEANS

Warm-season crop. Rated good to excellent for postage stamp gardens. 🌡 ▤ ▤ ▤ ▤

Bean plants are literally small food factories that really give you your money's worth in the postage stamp garden. In addition, they do double duty, because they're one of the legumes (peas being the other major vegetable) that help improve the fertility of the soil. That is, bacteria living in the nodules on the roots of legumes take nitrogen from the soil and combine it with sugars to produce ammonia, a nitrogen compound that plants can use. Legumes thus actually conserve and restore the soil.

Planting

Beans are heat lovers, so plant the seeds after the ground has warmed up in the spring. Plant seeds of bush types 1 inch deep and about 4 inches apart and of pole beans 1 inch deep and about 10 inches apart. Make plantings every two weeks (until about sixty days before the first fall frost) in order to harvest beans all summer long. Beans need lots of water and shouldn't be allowed to dry out while they're still growing.

In a postage stamp garden the nutrients that you've already put in the soil will carry your beans through the season, but they'll do better if you give them some fish emulsion (or any organic fertilizer) just as the pods begin to form (apply according to the instructions on the label).

Crop Stretching

Although horizontal space in the garden is tight, you have almost unlimited vertical space. Therefore, the more you can get your plants up in the air, the more food your garden will crank out. Here are some methods that work well for beans:

1   Set up four 6-foot posts (preferably 2 x 2s) at the corners of one square foot of space. Plant two seeds per pole; let the vines twine up the pole. It's possible to place two or three of these setups around the garden.

2   Set up a 6-foot post (again, a 2 x 2), and at the top affix two 1-foot cross arms at right angles to each other. From the ends of these cross arms, run strings or wires to the bottoms of the post. Plant four to six seeds around the post. The vines twine up the strings or wires. (See illustration at right.)

3 Between two 6-foot posts (preferably 4 x 4s), spaced about 6 feet apart, run a sheet of chicken wire, creating a kind of trellis or fence. Along the fence, plant seeds about 8 inches apart, and train the vines up the chicken wire. (See tomato illustration, page 149.)

4 Beans go mad when properly supported by a bean tower. This tower of bean power grows up to 20 pounds of Kentucky Wonder string beans a season. Construct the tower from ³/₄-inch, 4-foot-tall PVC pipe. (See illustration at left.)

Recommended Varieties

Some of the many types of beans enjoyed by home gardeners are snap beans (also called string beans or green beans), flat podded Italian beans, soybeans (also called edamame), fava beans, lima beans, and shell beans. Snap beans are grown for their long, edible pods, and can include wax beans and French filet beans. Italian flat podded beans also have edible pods. Shell beans are typically dried and shelled to be cooked later (for example, in soups). Lima beans (sometimes called butter beans), soybeans, and fava beans are also shelled, but most gardeners enjoy cooking and eating them fresh, rather than dried. Many beans come in bush varieties, which grow 15 to 20 inches tall, and in pole or climbing varieties, which grow as vines 5 to 8 feet high. Some gardeners like bush beans for small gardens because they mature in less than sixty days and three or four plants can be grown in every square foot of space (but you can also grow pole beans as a bush, see page 82).

Snap Beans (Bush Varieties)

BLACK VALENTINE (HENDERSON'S BLACK VALENTINE) 60 days. Slender, 6" long hairless green beans with dark seeds. Bushy, long-bearing plants. Tolerant of cold and poor soil. Seed source: BAK • COM • PLA • SEED • TERR

BLUE LAKE 274 54 days. Heavy yields of 6" pods containing white seeds. Good canner or freezer variety, as well as fresh eating. Seed source: BAK • BURP • COO • GUR • HAR • IRI • PAR • SOU • STO

BOBIS D'ALBENGA 56 days. Rare Italian heirloom with variegated pods. This variety performs well in hot conditions. Seed source: ANN • GOU

KENTUCKY WONDER BUSH (COMMODORE) 55 days. Stringless, round fleshy 8" pods. Heavy yields. Seed source: BOU • COM • IRI • SEED • SHU

PROVIDER 60 days. Widely adapted. 6–8" snap green beans. 16–18" tall plants. Seed source: ANN • BOU • HAR • IRI • JOH • PAR • SEED • SHU • SOU • STO

RED SWAN 52–58 days. Dusty red-rose colored, stringless 4–5" long pods. Seed source: SEED

ROYAL BURGUNDY 60 days. 24" upright plants. 6" long purple pods are pencil thin. Beans turn green when cooked. Buckskin-colored seeds. Seed source: ANN • GOU • HEN • JOH • PLA • SHU • STO • TER

Snap Beans (Pole Varieties)

BLUE LAKE 60 days. 6' plants. 6 x ¹/₄" white-seeded green pods. Seed source: BOU • BURP • GUR • JOHN • KIT • NIC • SHU • STO • TER • THO

COSSE VIOLETTA 80 days. Round, deep purple pods. Plants have beautiful purple flowers. Seed source: ANN

GRANDMA NELLIE'S YELLOW MUSHROOM 70 days. When cooked these beans taste like mushrooms. Light yellow pods are best picked at 5" long. Seed source: SOU

KENTUCKY WONDER (OLD HOMESTEAD) 70 days. 6–8' vines bear 6–8" long silvery green stringless pods. Brown seeds. Seed source: ANN • BAK • BURG • BURP • COM • GUR • IRI • KIT • NIC • PAR • SEED • SHU • SOU • STO • TER

LAZY HOUSEWIFE 75–80 days. Straight 5–6" long pods with shiny white seeds. No destringing required. Seed source: SEED • TERR

PURPLE PODDED POLE 68 days. Plants climb to 6' tall. Stringless 5–7" long red-purple pods that blanch to light green. This is a French heirloom. Seed source: JOHN • SEED • SHU

RATTLESNAKE 73 days. Especially good for sandy soil. Heavy producer in hot, humid growing areas. Round purple-streaked 7" pods contain buff-colored seeds splashed with brown. Stringless. Seed source: ANN • BAK • BOU • GUR • SEED • SHU • SOU • TERR

SULTAN'S GOLDEN CRESCENT 75 days. Almost extinct. Distinct curled yellow snap beans that are stringless and tender. Seed source: SEED

Snap Beans, Wax Beans (Bush Varieties)

DRAGON'S TONGUE 55–62 days. Dutch wax bean that is a French heirloom. Bush habit. Flat, stringless, 6–8" long cream-colored pods with vivid purple stripes that disappear when blanched. Stringless, wide, crisp pods. Seed source: ANN • IRI • SHU • TERR

PENCIL POD GOLDEN WAX 50–65 days. 15–20" bush habit. Stringless, 5–7" long pods. Has good wax bean flavor. Seed source: SEED

Snap Beans, French Filet (Bush Varieties)

MAXIBEL 60 days. 11–16" tall plant produces very straight, dark-green 7" pods and have mottled purple seeds. Seed source: GOU • JOH • JOHN • PAR • SHU • TER

VELOUR 55 days. Bush plant. Straight 5^1/$_2$" long pods are royal deep purple in color, and are slender, smooth, and round. Changes to green when cooked. Beige seeds. Seed source: JOH • TER

Flat Podded Italian Beans (Bush Varieties)

JADE 60 days. 18–22" upright plant produces 5–7" long, pencil-straight dark green pods. Seed source: PAR • TER

ROMA II 59 days. 20" tall plants produce large 6", medium-green, smooth, flat beans with white seeds. Seed source: ANN • BAK • BURP • GUR • HAR • JOHN • PAR • SHU • SOU • STO • TER

ROMANO 60 days. Heavy yields of 6" stringless flat pods. Seed source: BURP

ROMANO GOLD 55–60 days. Has the taste of Romano-type bean. 20" tall plants produce 4–5" long creamy yellow flat pods with white seeds. Seed source: TER

ROMANO PURPIAT 60 days. A purple Romano bean. 24" tall plants. Deep violet stems, lilac-colored blossoms, and purple 5" long flat pods. Turns jade-green when cooked. Seed source: TER

Flat Podded Italian Beans (Pole Varieties)

GOLD OF BACAU 60–70 days. 6–10" long, flattened golden Romano-type beans. Pods are stringless, tender, and sweet. Seed source: SEED

GOLD MARIE 75 days. Glowing yellow/chartreuse beans ripen to golden Romanos. Vigorous vines. 6" long flattened pods with white seeds. Seed source: SEED

ROMANO 60 days. Unique flavor. 6" long green, stringless beans on 8' vines. Seed source: ANN • BOU • BURP • SHU • TERR

STORTINO DI TRENTO 75 days. Rare Italian bean. Anellino type "Shrimp Beans" with speckled pods that have bicolored seeds. Seed source: GOU

Soybeans (Bush Varieties)

BEER FRIEND 85 days. 1$\frac{1}{2}$–3' lush green plant. 2–3" pods contain 3–4 buff-colored seeds. Seed source: KIT • NIC • TER

Fava Beans (Pole Varieties)

A caution about fava beans: Some people have an allergic reaction to them.

D'AQUADULCE A TRES LONGUE CROSS 85 days. French variety. 3' tall plant. Cold tolerant. This is a multipurpose bean. Use as salad greens, has edible flowers, the very young green pods you can shell like edamame (soybeans) or use as a dry bean. Seed source: BAK • BOU • STO

NEGRETA 70 days. Italian variety. 3' tall plant, 9–10" pods filled with 6–7 bright green seeds when mature. Seed source: TER

Lima Beans (Bush Varieties)

FORDHOOK 242 72 days. All-American Selections Winner. Dense foliage are heat- and drought-resistant. Thick 4" pods contain 3–5 large, flat greenish white seeds with a nut-like flavor. Seed source: ANN • BURG • BURP • GUR • HAR • JOH • PAR • SOU • STO

HENDERSON BUSH 72 days. Bushy 2' tall plants. 3–4 small creamy white seeds per pod. Widely adapted. Use fresh, canned, or frozen. Seed source: ANN • COM • SEED • SHU • SOU • TERR

Lima Beans (Pole Varieties)

CHRISTMAS POLE (GIANT BUTTER, FLORIDA SPECKLED, GIANT CALICO) 90 days. 7–9' tall vines bear 6" pods with large speckled beans in pod. Seed source: ANN • BAK • BOU • BURP • JOHN • SEED • SHU • SOU

KING OF THE GARDEN 88 days. 4–7" x 1¼" pods contain 5–6 creamy white seeds with honey-like flavor. Seed source: ANN • BAK • BOU • SHU • SOU • STO

Shell Beans (Bush Varieties)

BLACK COCO 95 days. 22–24" tall plant. 5" long pods. Black bean when dry. This is a good soup bean. Seed source: TER

BLACK TURTLE BEAN 95 days. 22–24" tall bushes. Plump, beautiful black beans for soups or refries. Seed source: ANN • BOU • JOHN • SHU • SOU

CANNELLI WHITE KIDNEY (WHITE KIDNEY BEAN) 100 days. 24" upright plant. Classic Italian white shelling bean with large kidney-shaped seeds. Seed source: SHU

HIDATSA RED (HIDATSA INDIAN RED) 80–100 days. Dark red seeds reminiscent of kidney beans. Sprawling bush plants climb to 3' if supported. Seed source: ANN • SEED

JACOB'S CATTLE (TROUT BEAN, COACH DOG BEAN, DALMATIAN BEAN) 86 days. Old New England bean. White and maroon mottled beans are a staple for baking and soups. Early bush variety. Seed source: ANN • BAK • IRI • SEED • SHU • SOU • TERR

Shell Beans (Pole Varieties)

MISSOURI WONDER 70 days. Cornfield type. Vines produce pods even under stress. Dry beans look like pintos. Grown in cornfields as stalks support them. Seed source: BAK

SPECKLED CRANBERRY 60–90 days. Triple purpose bean. Snap at 60 days, green shell at 80 days, and dry bean at full maturity. Stringless, 7–9" pods. Pole habit. Seed source: ANN • SEED

TURKEY CRAW 80–100 days. Stringless, 6" pods have brown seeds with tan flecks and brown eye rings. Use as snap or dry bean. Pole habit. Seed source: SEED

Typical Problems

My vines don't produce well. Sometimes the bean ends shrivel up. They are probably not getting enough water. Beans need considerable water and shouldn't ever dry out while growing. When there isn't enough moisture in the soil, the bean ends will sometimes shrivel up. Also, you may not be picking the young beans as they mature; old pods left on the vine will cut the production of new ones.

My beans didn't come up at all. You probably planted before the soil warmed up. Bean seeds won't germinate in cold soil, nor will they come up well if the soil has crusted over. A sprouting bean seed must push the small stem and leaves through the soil; if the ground is too hard at the surface, it can't do this. (This generally isn't a problem in a postage stamp garden because you made it nice and loose and grainy before planting.)

Beans can also get in trouble if they are not well fertilized. If you give them a little supplement of fish emulsion, or other organic fertilizer, that should do the trick.

Harvesting

Snap beans: Snap beans are ready for harvesting about two weeks after they bloom. Pick when the slender, crisp pods are nearly full size but the seeds are still small. Pull the pods from the plants gently to avoid uprooting bush beans or pulling vines away from their support. Discard beans that have large seeds or swollen or limp pods. Keep plants well picked to ensure a continuous harvest and an increased yield.

Bean pods that become lumpy are no longer prime snap beans. You can let them dry and use them as dried beans. When shelled out, these are called "shelly beans," and they are delicious.

Lima beans: The large white or speckled lima beans are at their peak flavor when the beans are fully formed in the pods. Harvest lima bean pods when they swell yet remain green and show three or four beans per pod. To test, simply shell several pods that feel full. If the beans are large and uniform, they are ready to eat. This test will not work for baby limas.

Shell beans: Pick fresh beans when the seeds are fully formed and plump, but still soft. Or permit them to dry fully on the vine and harvest them when 90 percent of the leaves have yellowed and/or fallen off and the pods are dry. Dry beans fully. Shell pods individually. Store in airtight containers.

Storage

Snap beans: Freeze only the small tender beans. Remove their ends, cut them into small lengths, blanch in boiling water for 1 1/2 minutes, cool, place in containers, and freeze.

Growing Tips

Protecting beans: Radishes planted around beans enhance the flavor of the beans and help repel bean beetles. Radishes are ready every twenty-four to thirty days; reseed every ten days or so.

Bush pole beans: To miraculously turn pole bean vines into bush-like plants, pinch off the growing tips every time they exceed 12 inches. This keeps them at easy picking height and doubles the crop over comparable bush beans.

Lima bean early harvest: You can gain a couple of weeks on the season by sprouting lima bean seeds on a windowsill inside wet paper towels. When they start to sprout, set them outside with the sprout tips showing above the soil. Stick the sprouting seeds in the ground the minute the soil warms up.

BEETS

Cool-season crop. Rated excellent for postage stamp gardens.

Beets are double-barreled vegetables; that is, you can eat both the roots and the leaves, and both are delicious. Beets are probably an almost perfect vegetable for the postage stamp garden because they don't take up much room and they grow like mad (as many as four hundred beets in a 4 by 4-foot area).

Planting

Beets generally like cool weather, but they're also fairly tolerant of a wide temperature range. Once started, beets need to grow rapidly without stopping, which means that you've got to keep them watered.

In a postage stamp bed you scatter seeds 1 inch apart and $1/2$ inch deep, but be careful with beet seeds because, unlike most other vegetables, they come in clumps of three or more seeds (called seedballs) that produce three or more plants. This means that it's awfully easy to sow too many. Simply thin out the little plants as you go along, and cook the young beet greens. You'll probably also want to divide your beet area into quarters, planting each quarter five to ten days apart to ensure a continuous harvest.

Crop Stretching

Plant beets in any spot where you've taken out another vegetable—corn, for instance.

Recommended Varieties

You have a choice of globe-shaped, semiglobe-shaped, long-rooted, red, white, or golden beets, as well as beets used mostly for their greens.

ALBINO 55 days. Pure white, fairly smooth round beet from Holland. Can be used for making sugar. Seed source: BAK • COM • SEED

BULL'S BLOOD 40–52 days. Has blood-red foliage. Tender roots are sweet and dark with interior stripes. Harvest as baby beets when young. Seed source: ANN • BAK • BOT • BOU • BURP • GUR • IRI • JOH • NIC • SEED • SHU • SOU • STO • TERR

CHIOGGIA (BARBIETOLA DI CHIOGGIA, CANDY STRIPE) 54 days. Italian heirloom that is 2¹/₂" wide and globe shaped. Beautiful when cut (reveals alternating rings of white and red) and served. Seed source: ANN • BAK • BOU • BURP • COM • COO • GOU • IRI • NIC • PAR • SEE • SEED • SOU • TER • TERR

CYLINDRA 60 days. 8" long by 1¹/₂–2" wide. Carrot-shaped beet that is easy to peel. Deep red color. Seed source: ANN • BAK • BOU • BURG • BURP • GOU • IRI • JOH • NIC • SEED • SHU • SOU

GOLDEN 55 days. Golden roots are tender and do not bleed. Sweet beet. Seed source: ANN • BAK • BOU • BURP • COM • COO • IRI • NIC • SEED • STO • TER

LUTZ GREEN LEAF (WINTER KEEPER) 76 days. For a fall crop this beet produces large roots. They keep for months when properly stored in a box of moist sand. All-purpose beet for fresh use or winter storage. Seed source: BAK • GOU • HAR • PLA • SHU • SOU

RUBY QUEEN 64 days. Very short 10" tops. Red interior, round smooth medium-red roots. All-American Selections Winner. Grows well even in poor soils. Seed source: COM • GUR • SHU • STO • TERR

Typical Problems

My beets tasted woody. The plants are not getting enough moisture. As with most other vegetables, you have to keep beets growing full blast until they mature. Lack of water will slow them down and give them a woody taste.

My beets didn't get very big. You sowed too many seeds and forgot to thin. Thin the small plants, leaving only one plant every inch or so.

Harvesting

Pick beets when small, about 2 to 3 inches in diameter. (Just pull up one to see how big they have grown.) Big beets get tough and taste blah when large.

Storage

Beets like lots of moisture and a temperature between 34°F and 42°F. You can store this root vegetable in a damp cellar or possibly in a cool garage, preferably in a container like a garbage can, with rags that you wet down occasionally on top of the vegetables.

For freezing, pick small beets, peel them, blanch in boiling water for $4^1/_2$ to 5 minutes, cool, place in containers, and freeze. Large beets can also be frozen, but they usually lack flavor.

Growing Tips

Redder beets: To produce bright red beets, sprinkle the bed with a light scattering of common salt, about a spoonful per foot. This improves the growth and color of the roots and eliminates white rings.

BROCCOLI

Cool-season crop. Rated good for postage stamp gardens. 🌡 ▨▨▨

You might call broccoli the postage stamp gardener's best friend in the cabbage family. It's big. After all, it can grow 3 or 4 feet high and branch prolifically. Also, it's easy to grow, and once it gets started it just keeps right on producing for a month or two. All you have to do is cut off the terminal head and the side shoots start to develop in small clusters right away. It's also possible to grow some of the other members of the cabbage family in your postage stamp garden, but they tend to be overlarge, and you have to be very selective in handling them.

Planting

Being a cool-weather plant, broccoli can be a problem because it's pretty sensitive to heat. It'll grow like mad, then all of a sudden—during a heat wave— begin to flower. After that, it's all over as a vegetable.

Buy broccoli from your nursery as small plants. This is the standard planting method, because starting from seeds will take you several weeks longer to get a mature vegetable. Four to six plants are about all that a postage stamp garden can handle because they must be spaced 15 inches apart. You can plant them in the spring a couple of weeks before the last frost, then again in midsummer. Midsummer is probably the best time because the weather will have cooled by the time the plants reach maturity.

If you prefer starting from seeds, plant them indoors in peat pots $1/4$ inch deep about five to six weeks before you intend to set the plants outside. (The other indoor planting methods described in chapter 4 can also be used.)

Broccoli, like other members of the cabbage family, is a heavy feeder, so give it some fish emulsion, or other organic fertilizer, at least once before the heads begin to form (apply according to the manufacturer's directions).

Crop Stretching
Replace harvested broccoli with carrots, beets, or radishes.

Recommended Varieties
Most gardeners think of broccoli as the vegetable that kids don't like with the fat green heads. But some broccoli, like broccoli raab (also known as rapini), are non-heading and are grown for their asparagus-like shoots and leaves. Chinese broccoli is also grown for its stalks and leaves.

CALABRESE (ITALIAN GREEN SPROUTING) 58 days. Italian heirloom. Produces 3–6" central head, plus many side shoots. Seed source: ANN • BAK • COM • GOU • IRI • NIC • SEED • SOU • STO

EARLY PURPLE SPROUTING 120 days. English heirloom bred for overwintering. Very frost hardy. Seed source: ANN • BAK • BOU • COM • GOU • NIC

ROMANESCO 75–100 days. A unique-looking plant. Spiraling apple-green, 6" across heads. I love this variety; it's fun to watch grow. Seed source: BAK • BOT • BOU • BURP • COO • SEED

SPIGARELLO 60–70 days. Well-known in Europe, this special broccoli has small, narrow, and bushy leaves. Many small tops will resprout. Leaves are used much like spinach. Seed source: GOU • SEE

WALTHAM 29 74 days. Widely adapted, drought-tolerant variety. 4–8" diameter heads hold for a long time. Low, compact plant. Produces lateral buds for six to eight weeks after harvesting the main head. Seed source: ANN • BAK • GOU • IRI • JOHN • NAT • SOU

Chinese Broccoli

KAILAAN 60–70 days. Grown for its stalks and leaves. Deep green color and has good flavor. Use in stir-fries, soups, sukiyaki, and tempura. Seed source: KIT

TE YOU 50 days. Dark green leaves are smooth with long, thick stems. Heat tolerant and can also withstand cool temperatures. Cool temperatures will slow plant growth so will be smaller in size. Seed source: KIT

Broccoli Raab (Rapini)

BROCCOLETTO (A FOGLIA D'OLIVO) 40–70 days. Italian variety that has olive leaf–shaped leaves. 14–15" tall plant. Thick stemmed. Used for leaf production as well as shoots. If you love Italian cooking, add this to your garden. Seed source: ANN • GOU • TERR

RAPINI 45 days. Non-heading broccoli grown for flavorful, asparagus-like shoots. Seed source: BAK • TERR

SPRING RAAB 40–45 days. Planted in early spring to produce a quick crop of tender shoots that taste like broccoli. Seed source: BAK • BOU • BURP • JOH • NIC

ZAMBONI 45 days. It resembles asparagus more than it does the large domed broccoli. Small, turnip-like leaves and long, tender stems topped with 1" flower bud clusters. 22" tall plant. Excellent side shoot production. Seed source: STO • TER

Typical Problem

My broccoli flowers before the heads are ready to harvest. You're getting too much heat. If you're having trouble with your spring crop, try planting in midsummer for a fall crop. In mild winter areas, where the temperatures generally don't drop below freezing, you can plant broccoli from early fall through late winter.

Harvesting

Broccoli is ready to cut when the tops are hard and green, just before the buds begin to open. You simply cut the stem a few leaves below the main head. The bud shoots that subsequently form in the leaf joints below the cut will never get more than an inch or two across, but they can be harvested and eaten. If your plants are kept picked, your growing season will continue until warm weather arrives—or, in the fall, until frost.

Storage

Broccoli will keep in the refrigerator for five to seven days. It must be chilled quickly. During storage it will lose vitamin C and its stems will become tough. You can preserve broccoli by freezing it. Separate the head into bite-size pieces, and cut the stems into 1-inch pieces. Cook the broccoli pieces in boiling water for three minutes, then plunge them into cold water for three minutes. Drain and store in plastic freezer bags. You can store frozen broccoli for up to a year.

Growing Tips

Fully packed: Broccoli often produces premature, small scattered heads when young plants are subjected to temperatures below 40°F, before or shortly after planting. Solve this by protecting plants in early spring with hot caps or other protective devices.

BRUSSELS SPROUTS

Cool-season crop. Rated fair for postage stamp gardens.

One brussels sprouts plant will keep producing sprouts until you wonder whether it's ever going to stop (one plant will produce seventy-five to a hundred sprouts). Brussels sprouts are a member of the cabbage family and are an erect plant that produces ever-growing clusters of sprouts or buds in the axils of the leaves. They're easy to grow—if you live in the right climate.

Planting

Brussels sprouts are a cool-weather plant. They do extremely well if you live in an area of summer fog or in an area where the climate is nice and moist and summer daytime temperatures generally average 65°F or less. They don't do well where the climate is hot and dry.

Because brussels sprouts take quite a lot of space, you probably won't want more than one or two in any single postage stamp garden. Set the plants out in early summer so that they mature in the colder fall weather. If you have mild winters, with above-freezing temperatures, you can also plant them in the fall for winter harvest.

Most gardeners buy young plants from their local nursery. Set the plants 16 inches apart. As the plants mature, remove all excess leaves except those at the top of the plant.

You can grow brussels sprouts from seed if you like, but you should start them indoors, planting your seeds ½ inch deep in peat pots five or six weeks before you intend to set them outdoors.

Crop Stretching

Interchange brussels sprouts with early maturing crops, such as radishes and leaf lettuce.

Recommended Varieties

FALSTAFF 90 days. Purple brussels sprouts that stay purple when cooked. Seed source: ANN

LONG ISLAND IMPROVED (CATSKILL) 100 days. Medium green, 1–1½" round firm sprouts. 20" tall plants. Seed source: ANN • BAK • BOT • BOU • BURG • COM • GOU • IRI • NIC • SEED • SHU • SOU • TERR

MEZZO NANO 110 days. Name means "half tall" or short. Small outer leaves, long 3' stalk with many small compact, tender sprouts. Seed source: SEE • TERR

RUBINE 85 days. 1–1½" purple-red sprouts. 24" tall plants. Seed source: TER

Typical Problems

Practically none, other than the weather restrictions already noted on page 87.

Harvesting

When the sprouts are firm and deep green, snap or trim them from the stalk. They have the best flavor when they are 1 to 1½ inches in diameter. Pick the lowest sprouts each time you pick, and break off any leaves left below the "sprout." Don't remove the top leaves.

Storage

For freezing, first wash the brussels sprouts and then soak them for a half hour in salted water (1 teaspoon of salt per quart of water). Place them in clear water and bring just to a boil, then drain, chill rapidly, and freeze. High-quality fresh sprouts will store for approximately three to four weeks at 32°F.

Growing Tips

Sweeter sprouts: Brussels sprouts get sweeter after a frost. An excellent vegetable to extend your growing season.

CABBAGE

Cool-season crop. Rated marginal for postage stamp gardens. 🌡️ ▓

Cabbage often turns out to be a big show-off. It comes in green, red, and purple varieties, smooth leaves and crinkled, and is a great conversation piece if you grow ornamental cabbage in a prominent spot. The only complaint that I have about cabbage is that it takes an awful lot of space for what you get out of it. If you insist on cabbage, you might try planting a variety that is smaller.

Planting

Cabbage is a cool-weather plant, so you want to time your plantings so that the plants reach maturity before or after the hot summer months. Put the plants out in the early spring or in late summer.

Most gardeners buy small seedlings from a nursery rather than start from seeds. The seedlings should be set 12 inches apart in your postage stamp bed. If you want to start cabbage from seed, sow the seeds ½ inch deep in flats or peat pots about six to eight weeks before you intend to set the plants outdoors.

New cabbage plants should never be set where other cabbages or any cabbage relatives have been grown in the past two or three years. This precaution is necessary in order to reduce the risk of being plagued by common cabbage diseases.

Crop Stretching

You can follow beans with a planting of cabbage. Also you can make successive plantings of cabbage to stretch the season.

Recommended Varieties

COPENHAGEN MARKET 63–100 days. Danish heirloom. Solid, 6–8" diameter heads weigh 3–4 pounds. Split resistant. Does well in a wide range of climates. Seed source: ANN • BOT • BOU • COM • GOU • SEED • SHU

EARLY JERSEY WAKEFIELD 64 days. Pointed head. Dark green, sweet conical heads average 5" diameter and 2–3 pounds. Small core and good wrapper leaves. Seed source: ANN • BAK • COM • NIC • SEED • SHU • SOU • TERR

MAMMOTH RED ROCK 90 days. Deep red hearts. Great for pickling. 8" diameter heads weigh 7 pounds. Seed source: ANN • BAK • COM • SHU • TERR

PERFECTION DRUMHEAD 95 days. Finely crinkled savoyed leaves are mild and sweet. Compact short-stemmed plants. Seed source: BAK • COM

PREMIUM LATE FLAT DUTCH (DRUMHEAD, SUREHEAD) 100 days. Large, broad, flat heads weigh 10–14 pounds. Measures 7 x 14". Good keeper. Seed source: ANN • BURG • COM • SEED • SHU • SOU

Typical Problem

My cabbage heads split badly. Cabbage needs a steady supply of water. Any time that the watering becomes irregular, growth becomes irregular—slowing down, resuming, slowing down again. This causes the cabbage to crack. Therefore, you should make sure that you keep your cabbages steadily supplied with water. If you haven't, however, you can try a reverse trick. You can delay growth and halt cracking by holding off on the water when cracking begins, or you can twist the plant to break off some of the roots and thereby slow the growth process.

Harvesting

Pick cabbage heads as soon as the heads feel solid. If you let them mature on the plant, the core gradually lengthens until it bursts through the top and uncurls into a long stalk. When cutting the heads from the stems, leave two or three of the wrapper leaves (outside leaves) on the heads to protect against bruising.

Storage

Cabbage stores best with a moderate amount of moisture and a temperature between 48°F and 62°F. Cabbage does not freeze well.

Growing Tips

Cut-and-come-again: You can easily turn your cabbage plants into a vegetable factory. When you remove the head, cut squarely across the stem leaving four or more leaves. Then cut a shallow slit across the top of the stump. The cabbage plant will produce up to five smaller cabbage heads within six weeks after cutting the first head.

CARROTS

Cool-season crop. Rated excellent for postage stamp gardens. 🌡 ■■■■

When the ancient Greeks and Romans used carrots for medicine but wouldn't eat them for food, they really goofed because carrots supply more food in our gardens over a longer period of time than practically anything else. They're also super-packed with vitamins—A, B$_{12}$, small amounts of B$_2$, and C—as well as sugar and iron.

Carrots, like beets, need to grow fast. So make sure that they are given plenty of water and never let them dry out.

Planting
Carrots are more tolerant of garden mistakes than almost any other plant that I can think of. They are generally considered a cool-season crop—best for spring and fall—but they do pretty well in summer, maturing sixty-five to seventy-five days after initial planting.

For a season-long crop, divide your planting area into quarters, and then scatter seeds in each quarter ten days apart. Cover the seeds with $^1/_2$ inch of soil or planting mix. When the tops show, thin the plants to 1 inch apart; a couple of weeks later, thin to 2 inches apart. The tender young carrots are delicious, cooked or raw.

Crop Stretching
As you pull out a few heads of cabbage or broccoli, plant a few carrots in the same space.

Recommended Varieties
Carrots range in size from 2 inches to 9 inches. With carrots you can go wild and plant almost any shape you desire, from very small and almost round to long and slender. The color ranges from orange, yellow, red, and purple to white.

ATOMIC RED 5–85 days. 11" long by 1$^1/_2$" diameter. Red all the way through. Seed source: BAK • GOU • HAR • IRI • JOH • JOHN • KIT • NIC • SHU

BAMBINA 60 days. Baby carrot with slender, cylindrical blunt roots and very small core. Smooth, deep-orange skin. Adaptable to a variety of soils. Good container variety. Seed source: TERR

CHANTENAY RED CORE (ROUGE DEMI-LONGUE DE CHANTENAY) 70 days. 5^1/$_2$–6" long by 2^1/$_2$" at the shoulders. An all-purpose deep-orange carrot. Good winter keeper. Seed source: ANN • BAK • BOU • COM • GOU • IRI • NIC • PLA • SHU • SOU • TERR

COSMIC PURPLE 58 days. Purple-skinned, 7" long roots. Orange and yellow flesh. Spicier flavor than regular carrots. Seed source: BAK • BOT • GOU • IRI • KIT • SHU • SOU

DANVERS HALF LONG 75 days. 6–8" long and 2" thick, dark orange and sweet. Holds quality in storage. Seed source: ANN • BURP • GOU • GUR • IRI • SHU

IMPERATOR (TENDERSWEET) 74 days. All-American Selections Winner. Requires a loose, deep soil. 7–9" orange-red roots are coreless and have semi-blunt ends and narrow shoulders. Seed source: SHU • SOU

JAUNE OBTUSE DE DOUBS 70 days. Bright lemon-yellow carrot from France. Big, thick carrot with sweet taste. Seed source: ANN • BAK • COM • GOU

LUNAR WHITE 75 days. This is a selection Belgian White. 8" long and white. Has small core. Seed source: ANN • BAK • GOU • KIT • NIC

PARMEX 60 days. Small-cored, round, smooth 1–1^1/$_2$" carrot. Thin to 1–2" apart. Great for containers too. Seed source: JOHN • NIC

ROTHILD 72 days. A European variety that makes an excellent juicer. High carotene content. Intense reddish color. Has good storing ability. Suitable for clay soils. Seed source: GOU

SCARLET NANTES 70 days. Bright orange, 6–8" long, slim-tapered roots. Stores well. Seed source: ANN • BOT • BOU • GUR • HAR • IRI • NIC • PAR • SEED • SHU • SOU • THO

WHITE SATIN 68 days. Pure white roots are crisp and sweet. 8" long and adaptable to difficult growing conditions. Seed source: JOH

YELLOWSTONE 72 days. This is a Danvers type. Rich butter yellow color. Smooth 8" roots. Seed source: IRI • JOHN • NIC • SEE • SHU • THO

YELLOW SUN 75 days. Kuroda type. Golden yellow 6–7" roots with broad shoulders and a well-filled blunt tip. Seed source: JOH • TERR

Typical Problem

My carrots just don't germinate well. I'll get a few in a clump in one area and none in another. Carrot germination can be a problem. Some of this problem is due to the seeds drying out. To reduce evaporation, some gardeners recommend placing a black plastic sheet over the carrot bed immediately after sowing, then removing it as the seedlings start to break through. You must watch carefully, however, in order to make sure you remove the plastic before it stunts the seedlings.

Harvesting

Pick carrots when they're relatively small. Big carrots produce woody cores. For real flavor, plant a few more than you need, then thin them when they're big enough to eat.

Storage

Carrots like lots of moisture and a temperature between 34°F and 42°F. You can store this root vegetable in a damp cellar or possibly in a cool garage, preferably in a container like a garbage can, with rags that you wet down occasionally on top of the vegetables.

Carrots store well in the ground; dig them up as you need them. You can also keep carrots between layers of dry sand in a box that you put in a frost-proof shed (cut off the tops and pack them evenly) or store them outside covered with straw.

For freezing, small carrots are best, but you can cut the big ones into small pieces. Blanch the carrots in boiling water for about three minutes, cool quickly, pack in containers, and freeze.

Growing Tips

Sprout them fast: To ensure uniform carrot germination, try covering your carrot seed bed with a sheet of clear plastic. Carrots are a cool-weather crop but won't germinate well in early spring when the soil temperature is below 40°F. Clear plastic heats up the soil and maintains moisture. Uncover the seed bed on warm sunny days to keep the soil temperature from exceeding 95°F.

Pot magic: To take the guesswork out of growing carrots, try starting in clay or plastic pots. Fit several 4- to 6-inch pots with a good potting mix to within 1 inch of the rim. Sow ten to twelve seeds evenly over the surface. When each plant has two or three fernlike leaves, thin back to six to eight evenly spaced carrots per pot. When the plants reach 6 to 9 inches high, remove the entire root mass from the pot and plant, intact, in the garden. Ten pots planted close together (postage stamp style) yields about seventy carrots.

CAULIFLOWER

Cool-season crop. Rated marginal for postage stamp gardens.

Cauliflower can be a bit finicky about the weather. In the area where I live, it can be cool for a period during the spring, then suddenly hot; under these conditions, cauliflower just doesn't do very well. But if you live in an area of cool or gradually warming springs or cool summers, your cauliflower should do fine. Cauliflower comes in colors other than white, and it's fun to grow the many different colored ones.

Planting

If you live where the spring is fairly cool, but frost-free, you can set out the plants in early spring. If summers are very warm where you live, then you may want to grow your cauliflower in the fall—just set out the plants in late July or early August.

You can grow cauliflower indoors from seed in flats if you like, but it generally takes about fifty days before the plants are ready to set out—an awfully long time. For this reason you should probably buy seedlings from a nursery. Plant them $2^1/2$ feet apart.

When the cauliflower begins to head, you must "blanch" the buds—that is, keep them from turning green—by shielding the head from the sun. You do this by pulling a few outer leaves over the head completely, gathering the tops of these leaves together, and tying them together loosely with string or a rubber band. For purple-headed cauliflower, blanching them is unnecessary.

Crop Stretching

If you plant cauliflower in an intensive postage stamp bed, be sure to grow something else between the plants—radishes or lettuce, for instance. Both radishes and lettuce will be ready to harvest before the cauliflower is large enough to need the space. When the radishes or lettuce come out, plant bush beans. Your cauliflower will be harvested out of the way before your beans are ready to harvest. This way you'll use all the space efficiently.

Recommended Varieties

ALL THE YEAR ROUND 70 days. Warm-weather variety. Large, tight, white head surrounded by leaves. Seed source: BOU

EARLY SNOWBALL 50 days. Head is denser than other early snowballs. Good wrapper leaves cover the white beading on top called curds. Seed source: SEED • SOU

MARCHES GREEN 75 days. Lime-green cauliflower but with rounded head. Italian heirloom. Seed source: GOU

PRECOCE DI JESI 74 days. Old Italian variety. Snowball shape, but has yellowish color. Originally from Venice. Seed source: ANN • GOU • SEE

SAN GIUSEPPE 78 days. Italian heirloom that is Romanesco, with lime-green spiraled heads. Rich, nutty taste. Seed source: ANN • GOU

SICILIAN VIOLET 68 days. Heirloom from Sicily. Purple-headed cauliflower. Seed source: ANN • GOU • JOH

Typical Problem

My cauliflower heads are always small. You probably have a watering problem. It's important that you don't halt the growth of cauliflower at any time. This can happen if you water irregularly or don't water for long periods of time. You must water consistently and fairly deeply, and in very hot weather a gentle overhead misting is beneficial, too.

Harvesting

Pick cauliflower as soon as the heads fill out; otherwise, they will lose quality.

Storage

To freeze cauliflower, break the buds into small pieces, blanch them in boiling water for three minutes, cool, place in containers, and freeze.

Growing Tips

Blanching made easy: To blanch cauliflower easily, place aluminum foil over the heads when they are about the size of a softball. Start with a square of aluminum foil approximately 14 by 14 inches and crinkle it up. Unfold and loosely place the foil over the head, allowing as much air space as possible. Tuck the edges around the head. At harvest time your heads will be nice and white.

Healthy cauliflower: Select seedlings with about four green leaves, a short straight stem, and plenty of root. Reject seedlings with a bluish tinge, because they will produce only small curds. Seedlings with six or more leaves have grown too old too quickly and will die.

CORN

Warm-season crop. Rated fair for postage stamp gardens. ▮ ▩▩

What we call corn today is a far cry from the maize that the Pilgrims found the Indians growing when they first arrived in America. The reason: corn loves to crossbreed and unlike some other plants, every time you cross one kind of corn with another you get something different—something in between. As a result, over the past 150 years corn hybridizers have developed countless varieties, and today you have a huge choice: You can plant tall varieties, short varieties, whites, yellows, blacks, popcorn, early varieties, late varieties, sweet, super sweet, and even super sweeter.

Planting

Corn is a heat lover, so plant the seeds or seedlings after the ground has warmed up. It also needs plenty of water throughout the growing season, and it's a heavy feeder. Generally, postage stamp soil has enough nutrients to carry corn through a full season, but just to make sure, you can give one feeding of fish emulsion, or any organic fertilizer, when the plants are about 15 inches tall (apply according to the manufacturer's instructions).

Corn isn't terribly good in a postage stamp garden because it takes up a lot of space from ten weeks to three months or more. If you like corn that much, however, you can make up a special 4 by 4-foot bed for corn and plant seedlings in it 8 inches apart. (If you use seeds, plant them 1 inch deep, 8 inches apart.) If possible, you might distribute about three of these 4 by 4-foot squares around the yard, planting each square a couple of weeks apart for a continuous crop. Each square will yield about seventy-two ears.

The 4 by 4-foot beds are good because corn is a wind pollinator, and small blocks like these are better than a long row. The reason: Corn is a member of the grass family; the tassels contain the male parts, and the silks that come out of the ears are part of the female flowers. Wind-borne pollen from the tassels of one plant falls on the silks of another plant, and each silk that receives pollen produces a mature kernel. Because the pollen can't float very far, the plants must be fairly close together to pollinate one another.

Crop Stretching

Fast-maturing crops, such as radishes and lettuce, can be planted between your corn, and they'll be harvested before the corn gets tall. Corn and pole beans can be planted at the same time, close together, and the bean vines will then twine up the corn stalks and use them for vertical support.

Recommended Varieties

Sweet corn can be yellow, white, or bicolored and it is cooked at the peak of its sweetness. You'll generally want to plant either a white variety or a yellow one or both, but not both in the same bed, because if pollen from white corn lands on the silks of yellow (or vice versa), you'll get a crazy mixed-up ear with a muddle of whites and yellows.

The older heirloom varieties are well worth trying, but never plant heirloom varieties anywhere near the hybridized corn, as you don't want them to cross-pollinate. Baby corn is picked when very small and it is usually pickled and served in salads or as a garnish. Growing, harvesting, and popping your own popcorn is a dream come true for kids and fun for the whole family.

Sweet Corn

BLACK MEXICAN (MEXICAN SWEET, BLACK IROQUOIS) 78 days. The kernels are white at the mild stage, but turn bluish black in the late milk stage. 7½ by 1½" ears with 8 rows of kernels. Seed source: SHU • SOU

BLUE JADE 70–80 days. 3' stalks bear 3–6 ears with sweet steel-blue kernels that turn jade-blue when boiled. Can be grown in containers. Seed source: SEED

COUNTRY GENTLEMAN 90 days. Irregular pattern of creamy white, slender kernels. Shoepeg type, which has small, narrow tightly packed kernels in an uneven pattern. It is called shoepeg because in the "old" days it resembled the wooden peg that attached soles to shoes. 8' stalks with three 7–8" ears per stalk. Long season corn. Seed source: ANN • BAK • BOU • COM • GOU • SEED • SHU • TER

GOLDEN BANTAM 73 days. 5' stalks. 5$\frac{1}{2}$–6" ears with 8 rows of broad yellow kernels. Seed source: ANN • BAK • BOU • BURP • COM • IRI • NIC • PLA • SHU • SOU • TER

STOWELL'S EVERGREEN 80–100 days. 8–10' stalks, 8" ears with 16–18 rows of creamy white kernels. Seed source: ANN • COM • GOU • SEED • SHU • SOU • TER • TERR

Baby Corn

BABY CORN 65 days. Not a sweet corn, but excellent for pickling. Seed source: COO • NIC

CHIRES BABY SWEET 75 days. 3–5' stalks that bear 8–12 ears per stalk, 2–3" ears. Harvest soon after silks emerge to stimulate more ears to form. Seed source: SEED • TERR

Popcorn

CHEROKEE LONG EAR SMALL 100 days. Rainbow-colored kernels. 6–8' stalks, 5–6" ears. This corn was brought over the Trail of Tears. Seed source: SOU • TERR

DAKOTA BLACK 90 days. 6' stalks. 4$\frac{1}{2}$" ears with 15 rows of maroon-black kernels. Seed source: BAK • SOU

JAPANESE HULLESS 110 days. 5–6' stalks produce 3–6 stubby, 4" ears. Seed source: BOU • SHU

STRAWBERRY 98 days. 4' stalks, 3 ears per stalk. Strawberry-shaped 2" long by 1$\frac{1}{2}$" wide ears. Very large kernels. Seed source: ANN • BAK • BURG • COM • GOU • NIC • PLA • SEED • SOU • THO

TOM THUMB (HULLESS, DWARF RICE, SQUIRREL TOOTH) 85–90 days. 3$\frac{1}{2}$' stalks with 1–2 ears up to 4" long. Good for coastal or short season areas. Seed source: ANN • IRI • SEED

Typical Problems

I just didn't get very many ears from my few plants. Corn is a wind pollinator, so it's best to plant a lot together rather than just a few plants.

The lower leaves of my corn turned yellow. This doesn't happen often if you've made up your postage stamp soil correctly, because this condition indicates a nitrogen deficiency. You might give the plants a feed of fish emulsion, or other organic fertilizer.

When I husk the ears to cook them, quite often some of the kernels have been eaten by a fairly large worm. This is the corn earworm. We'll take this up in chapter 8 when we talk about pests in the garden.

Harvesting

Corn is one of the hardest vegetables to pick properly. To determine when the ears are ready, look for brown, dry silks and a round, blunt tip to the cob. If the husk fits tight to the cob, the corn is ready. If the ear is loose or soft, allow the kernels to fill out for another day or two. As a final test for sweet corn, pull back the husks of one ear and pop one of the kernels 2 inches from the top of the ear with your thumbnail. If the fluid is clear and watery, wait another day. If the fluid is milky, pick immediately. If the fluid is gummy or starchy, you've waited too long. Corn reaches a peak of sweetness, then holds it only two to five days. After that, the sugar starts to turn to starch. Remove the ear with a sharp downward pull and a quick twisting wrist action.

Storage

The minute you pick corn the sugar in the ear starts to turn to starch. Thus, if you're really looking for top flavor, you've got to pop it in boiling water and eat it almost immediately.

For freezing, pick slightly immature yellow corn. If you're freezing corn on the cob, blanch in boiling water for six to eight minutes, cool, put in freezer bags, and freeze. If you're going to cut the kernels off the cob, blanch the cob first for 1 1/2 minutes, then cut the kernels off the cob, cool them, package, and freeze.

Growing Tips

Baby corn: If your mouth waters for those "baby" 3-inch ears of corn used in Chinese cooking and as pickled appetizer goodies, don't bother to plant special varieties, although you can find such varieties in seed catalogs. Just place the corn seeds close together (6 inches or so), then harvest the tiny ears when the silks start to emerge from the husks. At this point the cobs will be about 3 inches long with perfect, but barely developed, kernels.

CUCUMBERS

Warm-season crop. Rated good to excellent for postage stamp gardens. ▮ ▩ ▩ ▩ ▩

Here's a vegetable that undoubtedly is a contender for best actor on the vegetable circuit. Cucumbers have a thousand faces, and if you grow enough different kinds, you'll eventually come up with every shape imaginable. Some are warty, some are smooth, some are prickly, others aren't; they're crooked, straight, balloon-shaped, cigar-shaped, blackjack-shaped, peanut-shaped, and more. Moreover, they're big or small or anything in between. In short, cucumbers really perform in your garden. After all, who wouldn't love a vegetable that is such a big ham.

Cucumber vines are one of those crazy mixed-up plants that drive some of us to fits of frustration. They're what botanists call monoecious; that is, all male flower parts are in one flower, and all female parts are in another (though every plant has both male and female flowers). The first ten to twenty flowers that are produced on any plant are males. Even after that, there are ten to twenty male flowers for every female. The cucumbers themselves come only from the female flowers; thus, we have these plants producing all those nonproductive flowers before they really get down to the business of making vegetables.

Planting

Cucumbers are heat lovers, so wait until the ground has warmed up before planting. Seeds should be planted 1 inch deep and about 4 inches apart if the vines are going to be trained in the air. To get a head start, you can sow the seeds 1/2 inch deep in peat pots or flats two to four weeks before outdoor planting and then transfer the seedlings into your postage stamp bed.

Crop Stretching

Cucumbers ordinarily take up a lot of space. In fact, they'll run all over the ground if you let them. That's something that you just can't afford in a good postage stamp garden. So you've got to take to the air if you want to grow cucumbers effectively in a small area. There are a lot of ways to go:

1 Run a fence of chicken wire between two 6-foot posts, and let the vines grow up the wires. Generally, the north side of the garden is best for this so that the vines won't shade other plants. Allow the main stem of each plant to grow as high as possible; pinch back some of the lateral shoots, but let some shoots grow into branches. Train the branches on

the fence, using plastic tape. You can grow the plants about 4 inches apart along the fence. (See tomato illustration, page 149.)

2   Sink a 6-foot post (preferably a 4 x 4) in your garden, and on it space small 18-inch crossbars up and down the sides. Plant four seeds or seedlings around the post. As the vines grow, tie them to the crossbars. (See illustration at right.)

3   You can also use several types of trellises: rectangular trellises 2 or 3 feet high and 2 or 3 feet wide, X-shaped trellises about 3 by 3 feet, and so on. Buy a ready-made trellis from a local nursery or make one of your own.

   If you pick the cucumbers when they're fairly small (under 6 inches), you won't have to support them. If they get too big, however, they'll drop off or drag down the vine unless you support them with cloth slings, strips of pantyhose, or strings. (See melon illustration, page 115.)

Recommended Varieties

With cucumbers you have a choice of those for eating raw (salad cucumbers) and those for pickling, as well as midget varieties and some in rather unusual shapes, colors, and sizes. If you have trouble with burping, or feel gassy when eating cucumbers, you might want to plant the burpless type. These usually don't cause a problem eaten raw. Asian cucumbers tend to be long, light in color, and a little bitter, and either straight or curled. However, there are some Asian cucumbers that come in green, white, and brownish colors, and can be short, fat, and weigh several pounds.

Salad Cucumbers

ARMENIAN 55 days. Eastern European heirloom 24" long, twisting white fruits. Burpless with easily digested skin. Seed sources: BOT • BOU • BURP • GOU • IRI • JOH • JOHN • KIT • NIC • SEED • TER

CRYSTAL APPLE 75 days. Small 3" oval, bright, creamy white about the size of an apple. Likely to have originated in China. You can eat skin and all. Seed source: BAK • SEED

LEMON 58–70 days. I love growing these, but don't particularly like eating them because they are very seedy. 3–4' compact plants. Size and shape of a lemon. Crunchy white flesh and easy to digest. Seed source: BAK • BOT • BOU • BURP • COM • COO • GOU • IRI • JOH • JOHN • NIC • PLA • SEED • SHU • SOU • TER • TERR • THO

MARKETMORE 76 days. 8" long, non-bitter cucumber. Dark green with white spines. Seed source: BAK • BOU • HAR • IRI • JOH • SHU • SOU • STO

MINIATURE WHITE 50–55 days. 3" long yellow-white color, lightly spined, bitter-free cucumber. Slightly compact habit, which is great for postage stamp gardens and containers. Seed source: SEE • TER

POONA KHEERA 60 days. Golden-brown netted skin at maturity. 4" long and 2" diameter. Starts out white, then turns yellow and brown. Seed source: BAK • SEED • SOU

SPACEMASTER 52–75 days. 2–3' in height. 7^1/$_2$" long, green cucumbers. Widely adapted to growing areas. Ideal for the postage stamp garden and containers. Seed source: BOT • BURP • NIC • SHU • SOU

STRAIGHT EIGHT 52–75 days. All-American Selections Winner. Dark green, 8 x 2" cylinder with blunt ends. Vigorous plants. Seed source: ANN • BOT • BOU • BURG • BURP • GUR • IRI • NIC • SHU • SOU

WHITE WONDER 35–60 days. Ivory white at all growing stages. Crisp, very firm 6–7" long fruits with rounded ends. 2–3" diameter. Nearly white flesh. Seed source: BAK • BURG • COM • GOU • JOHN • KIT • NIC • SEE • SHU • SOU

Pickling Cucumbers

BOSTON PICKLING 58 days. Medium-green, blunt-shaped fruit. Seed source: ANN • BOU • COO • SHU • SOU • TERR

BUSH PICKLE 45–50 days. 24–30" plants. Jade green, straight, and cylindrical fruit. Best picked when 5" long. Good variety for postage stamp gardens and containers. Seed source: TER

DE BOURBONNE 50 days. Old French heirloom used to make the 2" long cornichon pickles. High-yielding vines. Seed source: BAK

MEXICAN SOUR GHERKIN (CUCAMELON, MOUSE MELON) 75 days. 1" cukettes have a tangy, citrus twist. Seed source: ANN • BAK • GOU • JOHN • NIC • SEED • TER • TERR • TOT

WEST INDIA GHERKIN (BUR CUCUMBER) 60–65 days. Very small oval shape. Full of seeds. From Jamaican colonists. Seed source: BAK • COM • SEED • TERR

Asian Cucumbers

CHINESE YELLOW 65 days. A very rare Chinese heirloom that matures to a beautiful, 10" long yellow-orange. The young fruit is green. Very mild, great for slicing or for pickles. Seed source: BAK

SUYO LONG 61 days. From northern China. 18" long, dark green with white spines. Almost seedless and is burpless. Never bitter. Heat tolerant. Seed source: BAK • COO • IRI • JOH • TERR

Typical Problems

My cucumbers taste terribly bitter. Some gardeners say that this is due to uneven watering; others believe it is due to temperature fluctuations of more than 20°F daily. If you're having considerable trouble getting a good-tasting cucumber, there are bitter-free cucumbers you might want to try.

The plants just stopped producing new fruit all of a sudden. You probably left some of the cucumbers to mature on the vines. This can stop a cucumber plant from setting new fruit. Pick cucumbers as soon as they reach usable size.

Harvesting

Pick cucumbers when they're young, before the seeds get large and tough.

Storage

Use slicing cucumbers fresh. Pickling cucumbers can be pickled.

Growing Tips

Compost ring: For cucumber salads all summer long, try planting a few cucumbers in a compost ring. Bend a section of wire that has small mesh openings, such as chicken wire, 4 feet wide and 10 feet long into a cylinder and fasten the wire where the ends meet. Locate in full sun. Fill the ring with leaves, grass clippings, wood chips, sawdust, and other organic matter, alternating with a few shovelfuls of soil and a handful of blood meal. Near the compost ring, mound two hills opposite each other outside the ring, and plant two to four seeds in each hill. As the plants come up, remove all but the two healthiest ones from each hill. Train the remaining plants to climb the wire. Add grass clippings and other plant waste to the heap during the growing season.

EGGPLANT

Warm-season crop. Rated fair for postage stamp gardens. ▮ ▦ ▦

Here's a garden show-off that is widely grown in the warm regions of the Mediterranean and in India. Eggplant grows on treelike bushes about 2 to 3 feet tall, and most varieties produce beautiful shiny, plumpish, purple-black fruit. Actually, eggplant fruit comes in other shapes and sizes and in colors ranging from purple to yellow to white. The plants are often grown as ornamentals in a garden.

Planting

Eggplant is not the best plant for postage stamp gardens because it takes up so much space, but if you love it, you can grow one or two. You can plant a few in your flower beds, or you can put a few in a 4 by 4-foot framed bed.

Because of the long period of time required to develop eggplants from seeds, most gardeners buy seedlings from nurseries. In your postage stamp bed set the young plants 25 inches apart, well after the soil has warmed up in the spring.

If you grow from seeds, you need a lot of patience, for the seeds sometimes take three weeks or more to germinate and another eight to ten weeks before they're ready to be set out. If this is what you decide to do, though, simply sow the seeds $1/3$ to $1/2$ inch deep in peat pots, and transplant the complete unit— seedling, soil, and pot.

Eggplant is a heat lover and needs to grow steadily and unchecked throughout the summer. This means regular watering. Eggplants are also heavy feeders, and it helps if you give them some fish emulsion, or other organic fertilizer, about every six weeks.

Crop Stretching

Grow radishes, lettuce, and similar fast-maturing vegetables in the space around eggplants. They are harvested long before the eggplants mature.

Extending the season: To keep from losing eggplant at the first frost, lay a wide strip of black plastic over each row or cage at night. It protects the fruit and extends the season as much as three weeks.

Recommended Varieties

Eggplant is a staple in many countries and comes in a vast range of colors and shapes. The standard, large, purple-black teardrop-shaped eggplant we see in the grocery stores is the one most of us grew up eating. Italian eggplant tends to be teardrop-shaped and come in shades of purple, violet, or stripes of both colors. The French eggplant is much like the Italian—it can be round or long, and black, purple, or purple striped. Asian eggplants come in any shape and size you can imagine and in just as many colors, although they are often more slender than standard eggplants and have thinner skin.

Standard, Italian, and French Eggplants

BIANCA SFUMATA DI ROSA (ROTONDA BIANCA SFUMATA DI ROSA) 75–120 days. Italian variety. White to white blush, classic egg shape. Seed source: ANN • BAK • GOU • SEE

BLACK BEAUTY 73 days. Uniformly large-fruited eggplant 1–3 pounds. Very deep purple-black. 18–24" plants. Seed source: ANN • BAK • BOT • BOU • BURG • BURP • COM • COO • GOU • IRI • PAR • SHU • STO

LISTADA DE GANDIA 75 days. French heirloom. 5–6" egg-shaped fruits. Purple with irregular white stripes. Drought-tolerant, sets fruit well under high heat. Best in long warm growing areas. No need to peel before cooking. Seed source: ANN • BAK • JOHN • SEED • SOU

LONG PURPLE (VIOLETTE LONGUE HATIVE) 70–80 days. 22–38" tall plants, 4 or more 8 x 2$^1/_2$" fruit per plant. This is a French heirloom. Seed source: BAK • BOT • BOU • COM • GOU • IRI • SOU • TERR

ROSA BIANCA 70–90 days. Italian heirloom with rose-pink fruits with white shading. No bitterness. Seed source: BAK • BOU • GUR • JOH • JOHN • SEED • SOU • TERR

Asian Eggplants

DEWAKO ONE BITE 50–60 days. Japanese variety that is purple-black, firm, small fruit excellent for pickling. Seed source: KIT

EARLY BLACK EGG 65 days. Japanese variety. Small, egg-shaped 5" fruit. Does well in cool, short season areas. Seed source: SOU

KAMO 65 days. Japanese variety. Round with a flat bottom, purple-black skin with purple calyx (bottom of stem next to fruit) and weighs up to $^1/_2$ pound. Seed source: ANN • GOU • KIT

LAO PURPLE STRIPE 90 days. Laotian variety. Ping-pong–size pale lavender with deep purple stripes. Seed source: BAK

PING TUNG LONG (PINGTUNG LONG) 65 days. An heirloom from Pingung, Taiwan. Slender, long, shiny dark lavender skin. Hardy variety. Seed source: BAK • JOHN • KIT • NIC • SEED • SOU

THAI GREEN (THAI LONG GREEN) 70–80 days. Thai heirloom. Light-green, elongated, 2$\frac{1}{2}$ ounces, 1$\frac{1}{2}$" x 10" long. 2' tall plants. Seed source: BAK • SEED • SOU

Other Eggplants

APPLEGREEN 62–70 days. Apple-green color, 3 x 2$\frac{1}{2}$" fruits with skin that doesn't require peeling. Grows in cool growing areas. Seed source: BAK • SEED • SOU

CASPER 70 days. Ivory-white eggplant, 5–6" long. Flesh is white with mushroom-like flavor. Seed source: SEED • TER

LITTLE GREEN 75 days. Brilliant, neon-green fruits. Russian variety. Does well in cooler summer climates. Seed source: BAK

TURKISH ITALIAN ORANGE 74–80 days. Miniature orange-red 2-ounce fruits that look like tomatoes. 4' plants are spineless. Harvest before the fruits turn red, when fruits are green-striped and bite-size. Seed source: BAK • GOU • JOHN • SOU • STO

UDUMALPET 80–90 days. This variety is from India. 3" long pear-shaped light green streaked with purple. Seed source: ANN • BAK • SEED

Typical Problem

I planted a few plants in the spring, and they just sat there and did nothing. You probably planted before it was warm enough. You can protect your small plants by putting a cut-off jug over them or a wall-o-water (an accordion-like plastic circle with open vertical channels to hold water), or by covering them with hot caps bought at a local nursery or through seed catalogs.

Harvesting

Pick your eggplants before they start to lose their glossy shine; after that, they'll be tough. Be sure to keep picking the fruits as they become ready so that the plants will continue to bear.

Storage

Eggplant can't be stored more than a few days in the refrigerator.

Growing Tips

Large fruit: For bushy, fully packed plants that produce a number of larger fruits, pinch out the growing tips when the plants are 6 inches high. This encourages several branches to form. After a number of fruits have started to form, clip out several branches. This encourages the plants to produce larger and few fruits.

ENDIVE see *Lettuce* (page 108)

KALE

Cool-season crop. Rated good for postage stamp gardens.

Other members of the cabbage family may be a little hard to grow, but not kale if you grow it in the right season. Kale is a great flower bed crop, too, because the leaves are so beautiful. They're burled and fringed and range from dark green to bluish purple.

Planting

Kale is a cool-weather plant like other cabbage crops and does best under cool conditions. If your summers are cool, with average daytime temperatures of 75°F or less, you will have no problem. Otherwise, sow your seeds in midsummer so that the plants grow in the cool days of fall. If your frost-free days begin early in the spring, sow seeds for a late spring or early summer crop.

Sow the seeds ¹/₂ inch deep, about 16 inches apart. To keep kale coming along well, you should generally give it a feeding of fish emulsion, or other organic fertilizer, about midseason.

Crop Stretching

You can stretch your harvest by planting kale in place of any crop that matures by midsummer—early corn, for instance.

Recommended Varieties

BLACK TUSCAN (NERO DI TOSCANA, TOSCANO, PALMIZIO SENZA TESTA, BLACK PALM CABBAGE, DINOSAUR) 50–60 days. Italian curly kale. Dark and meaty 2–3' evergreen-colored leaves. Hardy. Seed source: ANN • BOU • COO • GOU • JOHN • SEE • TER • TERR • THO

DWARF BLUE SCOTCH 55 days. Hardy 15" plant spreads 2', producing blue-green, finely curled leaves. Light frost improves flavor. Seed source: ANN • BOT • NIC • PLA • SEED

RUSSIAN RED (RAGGED JACK) 50–60 days. 2–5' plant. Hardy and delicate purple-red oak-type leaves. Can overwinter. Seed source: ANN • BAK • COO • IRI • JOH • NIC • PLA • SEED • SHU • SOU • TERR

TOSCANO (TUSCAN) 65 days. An Italian heirloom. Unique heavily savoyed extra-dark green leaves. Tolerant of hot and cold weather. Seed source: BOT • JOH

WILD GARDEN KALE MIX 50–60 days. Gene pool of Russian/Siberian types. Colors are green through purple, leaf edges are from single to triple cuts. Seed source: BOU • NIC • TER

Typical Problem
My kale isn't doing very well by mid-spring. Kale is a cool-weather crop, remember. It generally does best as a fall crop and doesn't tolerate heat very well.

Harvesting
You can cut the outer leaves as they mature or cut the entire plant. Generally, the inside leaves are more flavorful and tender than the outer ones.

Storage
Kale can be stored in the refrigerator for up to a week.

Growing Tips
More kale: To make kale really produce, just harvest the loose crowns in the spring, on leaf and spear varieties. Remove the leaves from the top down. Without crowns or leaves, side shoots will develop; just pick these like broccoli.

LETTUCE AND ENDIVE

Cool-season crop. Rated excellent for postage stamp gardens.

What an incredible vegetable lettuce is! You can grow lettuce almost without effort, tuck it in anywhere, take your choice of color or type, and spend hours at the seed racks looking at varieties that you've never seen before.

Lettuce, of course, is well-known as the dieter's friend. It is chock-full of vitamins A and B and yet contains almost no calories. What more could you ask for?

Endive makes a great lettuce substitute, but it's actually a member of the chicory family. You'll find it a little lacier than most lettuce and slightly bitter. Grow it just as you would lettuce.

Planting

You can start lettuce from either seeds or plants (the plants can be purchased from a nursery). If you want head lettuce as soon as possible in the spring, start seeds indoors in a pot ($^1/_4$ to $^1/_2$ inch deep) about two weeks before the last frost. When all danger of frost has passed, start setting the plants out in the garden. At the same time, you can plant more seeds in the garden bed itself ($^1/_4$ to $^1/_2$ inch deep) for a later crop.

Set head lettuce about 10 inches apart, butterhead 4 or 5 inches apart. The spacing for leaf lettuce and romaine can vary. If you intend to pick the outer leaves over a period of time (letting the core of the plant continue to grow), then plant the lettuce 10 inches apart. If you intend to pick the entire plant at once, 4 inches is okay—you'll get more that way.

When summers are hot, plant lettuce in partial shade or give it protection with a lath house or gauze on a frame. Lettuce, remember, is a cool-season crop. In hot areas, the longer days and warmer nights of summer encourage flowering (bolting to seed). You can correct this problem somewhat by planting varieties that are slow to bolt.

Endive is more heat- and cold-resistant than lettuce, and many gardeners find that they do best by planting it in the summer for fall or early winter harvesting.

Crop Stretching

You can plant loose-leaf lettuce where you intend to grow corn, then harvest it before the corn has grown very large.

Recommended Varieties

Basically, there are five main types of lettuce: head lettuce (also known as iceberg or crisphead), butterhead (also known as Boston or Bibb lettuce), loose head (French Crisp, Batavia), romaine (also called cos lettuce), and loose-leaf lettuce. Here are a few varieties of each you might like to try. Gardeners also have a choice of growing a multitude of different lettuce blends that come prepackaged and ready to plant. I like these blends because they give salads an interesting visual and textural appearance. Endive comes in two types, curled and not curled. The curled type has very frilly, lacy, thin leaves. It adds a slightly bitter piquancy to salads. Non-curly endive is planted in the spring, then dug up and forced to grow in a cool, dark place to form a head.

Head Lettuce

ANUENUE 45–60 days. Hawaiian variety that holds up well in heat. Name means "rainbow" in Hawaiian. Bright glossy green leaves. Heat tolerant and bolt resistant. Can grow in all seasons. Seed source: BOU • NIC • SOU

ICEBERG 85 days. Light green outer leaves are crinkled and fringed, the inner leaves are silvery white. Seed source: BAK • BURP • COM • IRI

RED ICEBERG 50 days. Red, almost chocolate-colored iceberg. Medium-size heads are tight and hold for a long time. Seed source: JOH • SEED • TER

REINE DES GLACES (QUEEN OF THE ICE, ICE QUEEN) 65–70 days. French heirloom that thrives in cold. Emerald-green, lacey leaves with serrated edges. Stays crisp in heat. Seed source: BOU • GOU • JOHN • SEED • TER • TERR

SUMMERTIME 70 days. Heat-tolerant crisphead, never bitter and slow to bolt. Seed source: JOHN • NIC • SHU • TER

Butterhead

BEN SHEMEN 60–70 days. Butterhead from Israel. Large, dark green compact heads are very sweet and heat-resistant. Seed source: BOU

BUNTE FORELLENSCHLUSS 40–55 days. Butterhead companion to Forellenschluss Romaine. *Bunte* means "colorful" in German. Apple-green leaves splashed with maroon and forms 8–10" heads. Seed source: SEED

BUTTERCRUNCH (BUTTER KING) 48–75 days. All-American Selections Winner. Green leaves and a small tight head. Slow to bolt. Seed source: ANN • BOT • BOU • BURG • BURP • COO • GUR • HAR • IRI • JOH • NIC • PAR • SHU • SOU • STO • TER • TERR • THO

CONTINUITY (MERVEILLE DES 4 SAISONS, FOUR SEASONS, MARVEL OF 4 SEASONS, MERVEILLE DES QUATRE SAISONS) 54–56 days. Deep burgundy leaves outside, creamy green leaves inside. Compact 12–16" heads. Seed source: ANN • BAK • BOT • BOU • GOU • JOHN • SEED • TER

DRUNKEN WOMAN FRIZZY HEADED 55 days. I love the name of this lettuce, but haven't tried it. Unique butterhead forms a savoyed head. 8" plants have mint-green leaves tinged in mahogany red. Seed source: TER

MATINA 53–73 days. Small butterhead for individual servings. Bright glossy green outer leaves. Seed source: JOHN • NIC • SEED • TER

SPECKLES (AMISH SPECKLED) 50–55 days. An Amish heirloom that has bright red speckles on olive-green butterhead leaves. Blanched yellow-green heart. Seed source: BOT • IRI • SEED • SOU • TER

TOM THUMB 34 days. Little butterhead that produces heads about the size of a baseball. Dark green outer leaves, creamy yellow interior. Excellent variety for postage stamp gardens and containers. Seed source: BAK • BOT • NIC • SOU • TER • TERR • THO

Loose Head, French Crisp, Batavia

ARIANNA BATAVIAN 50 days. French beauty with thick, shapely mint-green leaves adorning tall, open rose-shaped heads. Widely adapted, tolerant to heat. Seed source: JOHN

VULCAN 52 days. Full head size loose-leaf lettuce. Red, slightly ruffled, frilled leaves are a vivid, candy–apple red over a light green background. Seed source: JOH

Romaine

FORELLENSCHLUSS (FLASHY TROUT'S BACK, SPECKLED TROUT) 58–60 days. Austrian lettuce. Green leaves with maroon markings. Thick midribs. Grows quickly in cold weather, but bolts in heat. Seed source: ANN • BAK • BOU • COO • GOU • JOH • JOHN • SEED • SOU • TER

LITTLE GEM 33–50 days. Heads are about 4" across and 4–6" tall. Miniature green romaine just right for small-space gardens. Seed source: ANN • BAK • BOT • BOU • COO • GOU • IRI • JOHN • NIC • TER

OUTREDGEOUS 52–65 days. 10" tall red lettuce with thick glossy, slightly ruffled leaves. Seed source: BAK • IRI • JOH • JOHN • TER

PARRIS ISLAND 68 days. 10–12" tall, slightly ruffled green head with creamy white hearts. Seed source: ANN • BAK • BOT • GOU • IRI • JOH • NIC • SOU

ROUGE D'HIVER (RED WINTER) 60–62 days. French heirloom has red and green leaves with deep red tips. Forms semi-open romaine. The best color comes in cooler weather. Seed source: ANN • BAK • BOT • COM • IRI • JOHN • SEED • SOU

Loose Leaf

AMISH DEER TONGUE 50 days. An Amish heirloom that is medium green and has triangular leaves that form loose upright head. Seed source: ANN • BAK • SEED

BLACK SEEDED SIMPSON 45 days. Fast-growing, pale green leaves. Seed source: ANN • BAK • BOT • BURP • COM • COO • GUR • HAR • IRI • JOH • NIC • PLA • SHU • SOU • TERR

LOLLO ROSSA (LOLLO ROSSO) 53–60 days. Italian variety. Red-fringed green leaves. Seed source: ANN • BAK • BOT • COO • GOU • JOH • JOHN • SEED

MULTY 50 days. Dutch-bred lettuce has identically formed hand-size leaves that can be cut at one level height for easy harvest and washing. Has finely serrated, frilled and shiny leaves and comes in a variety of either green, burgundy red, or yellowish green. Seed source: JOHN

RED SALAD BOWL 55 days. Big, wine-red leaves. Excellent fall variety. Seed source: ANN • BOT • COO • GOU • HAR • IRI • JOH • JOHN • SEED • SHU • SOU • STO

SALAD BOWL 50 days. Frilly, deeply cut green leaves, large frame with lime-green rosette. Seed source: ANN • BOU • GUR • JOH • NIC • SOU • TER • TERR

TANGO 50–60 days. Frilly, deeply cut dark green lettuce that looks like endive. Widely adapted. Seed source: ANN • BAK • JOH • JOHN • SEED • TER

Mixed Salad Blends

BABY LEAF MIX 40 days. Collection of mini greens that includes green and red oak leaf, Tango, red Lolla Rossa, and green romaine. Cut at 4–5". Seed source: BURP • JOHN

GARDEN HEIRLOOM LETTUCE BLEND 50–55 days. Contains Redder Oaks, Devil's Tongue, and Speckles. Seed source: TER

HARRIS' MESCLUN MIX 40 days. Includes New Red Fire, Black Seeded Simpson, and oak leaf lettuce, Green Boy and Red Giant mustards, Early Mizuna Asian greens, Red Russian kale, and spinach. Seed source: HAR

LONDON SPRING LETTUCE MIX 50–70 days. Bright bold colors of Red Sails, Flashy Trout's Back, Outredgeous, Hyper Red Rumple, and Bullet. Seed source: TER

SEED SAVERS EXCHANGE LETTUCE MIX 40–45 days. Australian Yellow Leaf, Forellenschluss, Pablo, Red Velvet, and four more varieties. Seed source: SEED

TERROIR SEEDS LETTUCE BLEND 45–65 days. Blend of Landis Winter, Sweet Valentine, Yugoslavian Red, Buttercrunch, oak leaf, Salad Bowl, St. Anne's, Tom Thumb, and Cimarron. Seed source: TERR

WILD GARDEN LETTUCE 50–70 days. Literally dozens of varieties, including selections of lettuce that remain unnamed and not available anywhere else other than this mix. Seed source: SOU • TER

WILD GARDEN PUNGENT MIX 30–40 days. Spicy mustard greens. Gold, green, red-striped, and solid purple colors. Leaves can be smooth, glossy, or savoyed, while edges range from plain to toothed or frilly. Sweet to pungent. Seed source: TERR

Endive (Curled)

FRISÉE ENDIVE 60 days. Triple-cut curly heirloom from France. Feathery, fine-branched pale leaves. Big heads and blanched hearts. Seed source: BOU • TERR

RHODOS 65 days. Extra-frilly leaves are smooth and finely ribbed. Tightly massed plants, hearts are naturally blanched to creamy white. Seed source: JOH • TER

Endive (Not Curled)

BELGIAN ENDIVE (WITLOOF) 160 days. White to pale yellow, torpedo-shaped romaine-like heads. Seed source: BOU

FULL HEART BATAVIAN 85 days. Upright, broad, smooth dark green leaves. Yellow centers. 12" plants. Seed source: BAK • SOU • STO

Typical Problems

My lettuce keeps going to seed before it's big enough to eat. Your lettuce is getting too much heat. You can solve this problem in any of several ways: (1) plant earlier in the spring, before hot weather sets in, or in late summer; (2) shade your garden with lath or gauze; or (3) plant one of the varieties that are slow to bolt.

I always get poor heads and sometimes no heads at all. You probably didn't thin out your plants enough. Postage stamp beds let you plant closer than conventional gardens, but you must still thin a little to space out your heads.

My lettuce turns brown at the tips. This is tip burn, due to hot weather. Again, you can prevent this by shading your garden.

Harvesting

Head lettuce should be picked when the heads are nice and crisp. But in general, the leaves of all types of lettuce remain edible at almost all stages; pick them as you need them.

Most postage stamp gardeners like to pick loose-leaf lettuce a leaf or two at a time. This lettuce is cut-and-come-again: cut it and it will grow back. If you intend to pick it leaf-by-leaf, be sure to allow enough spacing (as mentioned previously); otherwise, you're likely to wind up with bitter leaves.

Storage

Place lettuce in a plastic bag and store in the refrigerator for up to eight days.

Growing Tips

Summer lettuce: Try planting in shaded ground beneath pole beans or cucumbers. As soon as the little sprouts poke through the warm soil, tuck mulch around them to keep the roots cool. Keep well watered.

Bigger lettuce heads: As your head lettuce starts to grow, pick the outer leaves a few at a time just as you would leaf lettuce. This doesn't affect the heading, because the heads grow from the center out. Removing the outer leaves, however, makes the plant smaller in comparison with the root structure. This gives the roots time to gain the strength needed to produce stronger, larger tops.

Blanching endive: You generally need to "blanch" endive to lessen its bitterness and improve its flavor. Two or three weeks before you intend to start picking your endive, simply draw the outer leaves over the heart and center leaves until they come together at the top, then tie the bunched leaves together with string or a rubber band. Make sure the center leaves are dry when tied; otherwise, they may rot.

MELONS

Warm-season crop. Rated fair to good for postage stamp gardens. 🌡 ▨▨▨

Melons take a lot of space because they're determined to wander just about anywhere they please. Each vine stem may creep 6 to 10 feet or more, and each plant will have several stems. Nevertheless, cantaloupes (also called muskmelons), watermelons, and other melons are the sentimental favorites of a lot of people. If grown vertically, though, they can be incorporated into a postage stamp garden. Watermelons are a little more difficult, because their fruit is too large to be supported vertically, with the exception of the midget varieties.

Planting

Melons are hot weather plants and can be planted about two weeks after the last frost. Plant seeds or seedlings 24 inches apart and train them up posts or other supports. (If you don't train them into the air, you'll be obliged to plant them 4 to 10 feet apart, because they'll spread out all over the place.)

Crop Stretching

There's no reason at all why you can't grow cantaloupe and other small melons in quantity in a small portion of any good postage stamp garden. All you have to do is grow the vines in the air and support the fruit with cloth slings. (See illustrations at right.) There are several ways:

1 Sink a 6-foot post (preferably a 4 x 4) into the ground and stagger small crossbars on both sides up to the top. Tie the vines as they reach the crossbars. (See illustration, page 101.)

2 Put a construction-wire fence on one side of the garden and tie the vines and fruit to it. Construction wire can be bought at a home center or hardware store in different size rolls (see illustration, top right).

3 Use a construction-wire island. Just form a circle of wire, about 2 feet in diameter, and train three melon plants up the wire (see illustration, bottom right).

Recommended Varieties

The muskmelon species (*Cucumis melo*) contains many of the most popular melons found in grocery stores, including cantaloupe, charentais, crenshaw, casaba, and honeydew. If you like growing different types of melons and want something more unusual that you can't get in the grocery store, try a specialty melon. Asian melons have very unique flavors. Some are bitter and used in Asian savory recipes, while others are sweet and used in desserts. Full-size watermelons are not recommended for the postage stamp garden, but the small varieties listed here are suitable if you grow them vertically.

Cantaloupe

AMISH 80–90 days. Amish heirloom. Oval fruits are 9" long and weigh 4–7 pounds. Sweet orange flesh with full muskmelon flavor. Thick rind. Produces good crops under almost any conditions. Seed source: SEE • SHU

EDEN'S GEM (ROCKY FORD, ROCKY FORD GREEN FLESHED) 89 days. Green flesh. $5^1/_2$ x 4", 2–3 pounds. Heavily netted and slightly ribbed. Seed source: ANN • BAK • COO • GOU • IRI • JOH • SEED • SHU • SOU

EDISTO • 47 90 days. Deep salmon-colored flesh. $4^1/_2$ pounds. Excellent variety for hot, humid conditions. Seed source: BAK • SOU

HALE'S BEST JUMBO 80 days. Deep salmon flesh, sweet and aromatic. 3–4 pounds. $7^1/_2$ x 6" with deep green skin and golden netting. Drought-resistant. Seed source: ANN • BOT • BURP • GOU • IRI • PAR • SHU • SOU

HA 'OGEN (ISRAEL, HA'OGEN) 75–80 days. Identified with Kibbutz Ha 'Ogen in Israel. Name means "the anchor." Round, 3–4 pounds. Spicy green flesh. Yellow-orange rind with shallow green sutures. Seed source: BOU • SEED

HEARTS OF GOLD (HOODOO) 85 days. Orange-fleshed muskmelon dating back to 1890. 2–3 pounds. Heavily netted. Seed source: BAK • BOT • GOU • IRI • SEED • SHU

JENNY LIND (SHIPPER'S DELIGHT, JERSEY BUTTON) 80 days. 1840s heirloom. 1–2 pounds, turban-shaped melon. Light green flesh. Seed source: ANN • BAK • SEED • SHU

NOIR DES CARMES 75 days. A true French heirloom. Rich black-green skin when immature, ripens to orange mottled with green. Orange flesh. Tends to split when ripe. 3–6 pounds. Deeply ribbed with smooth skin. Seed source: BAK • SEED

SWEET GRANITE 65–80 days. Oblong, sweet, orange flesh. Rind has light netting. 2–3 pounds. Well suited for far northern, coastal, and mountain climates. Fruits keep 1–2 days after slipping from the vine. Seed source: JOH • SEED

Charentais, Crenshaw, Casaba, Honeydew

CHARENTAIS 75–90 days. French heirloom from Poitou-Charentes region. Smooth round melons mature to a creamy gray with faint ribs. 2–3 pounds. Orange flesh. Seed source: BAK • BOU • COO • GOU • JOHN • NIC • SEED

CRANE (EEL RIVER) 85 days. Crenshaw. California heirloom. Melons have pale orange flesh. Green-skinned with orange spots when ripe. 3–5 pounds. Seed source: BAK • BOU • NIC • SEED

GOLDEN BEAUTY 90 days. Casaba melon. 1850s heirloom that probably originated in Asia Minor near the town of Kasaba, Turkey. Wrinkled skin matures to a golden yellow. 7–8 pounds. White flesh has a spicy flavor. Excellent variety for hot, dry regions. Seed source: BAK • GOU • TERR

GREEN HONEYDEW 98–115 days. Round to oval with sweet, thick green flesh. Rind is creamy white to pale greenish yellow. 6–8 pounds. Good keeper. Seed source: ANN • COO • JOHN • SHU

ORANGE FLESH HONEYDEW 90 days. Light yellow-green smooth skin. Pale orange flesh. Seed source: GOU

Specialty Melons

AMARILLO ORO 100 days. Pre-1870 heirloom. Golden-yellow, oblong fruit can grow up to 15 pounds. Creamy white flesh. Seed source: BAK

BANANA 90 days. Banana-shaped, smooth, yellow rind, spicy sweet salmon-colored flesh. 16–24" long, 5–8 pounds. 1885 heirloom. Seed source: BAK • COO • SEED • SHU

BATEEKH SAMARRA 95 days. Oblong fruits are brownish-green and netted outside. Lime-green flesh has an unusual, delicious, sweet-tart flavor with a hint of citrus taste. The name means "old melon from Samarra." Known to have been grown in Iraq for one thousand years. Seed source: BAK

COLLECTIVE FARM WOMAN 80–85 days. Heirloom from the Ukraine. Melons ripen to a yellowish gold. White flesh has high sugar content. Tolerates cool summers. Seed source: BAK • SEED

JAKE'S (SNAKE IN THE SHED) 100 days. Unique-looking heirloom. Rind is tan with orange and gray spots. Yellow-orange flesh. Pueblo Indians say it looks like a melon they once grew. Seed source: BAK

NOIR DES CARMES 80 days. A rare heirloom from France known as "Black Rock." The rind is nearly black in color, while the flesh is orange, thick, flavorful, and perfumed. Deeply ribbed with smooth skin. 3-6 pounds. Source: BAK

SLEEPING BEAUTY 85 days. Yellow-orange flesh. Compact vines. Smooth, round, 1/2-pound fruits are light green before ripening. The name comes from the tendency of the fruits to nestle together in groups. Seed source: SOU

TIGGER 90 days. Vibrant yellow with brilliant fire-red stripes. Very fragrant. White flesh gets sweeter in dry climates. 1 pound. Grows well in dry climates. Seed source: BAK • SEED • SOU • TER

Asian Melons

SAKATA'S SWEET 85 days. 3–4" round melons are sweet and have a high sugar content. Has edible skins. Light, golden rind. Japanese variety. Seed source: BAK • SEED

THAI GOLDEN ROUND 81–90 days. 6-pound fruit looks like glowing orange pumpkins. Green flesh is sweet with a tropical taste. Seed source: BAK

Watermelon

BLACKTAIL MOUNTAIN 65 days. Small, icebox type. Great for short season areas. Round, dark green rind with faint stripes. 6–10 pounds. Orange-red flesh. Small brown seeds. Does well in hot, humid climates. Seed source: IRI • SEED • SOU

GOLDEN MIDGET 65–82 days. 3 pounds. Widely adapted. Sweet red flesh. Thin tough green rind turns golden orange when ready. 7–8" oval melon. Small vine. Perfect for postage stamp gardens. Seed source: ANN • BAK • COM • IRI • SEED

WHITE WONDER 80 days. White-fleshed watermelons were common in the 1800s. 3–8 pounds. Has fruity flavor. Seed source: BAK • SOU

Typical Problems

My melons taste bitter. Usually this bitterness occurs when there is cold, wet weather during the ripening period. Melons need warm weather to be at their best. Or the problem could be uneven watering. Never let the soil dry out completely. Ideally, you should water deeply, then don't water again until the soil has dried out to about 8 inches from the top.

I have blossom drop and no fruit setting. Like the blossoms on cucumber vines, the first blossoms on melon vines are male. These will naturally drop. You should simply be patient until the female flowers come along, and then you'll have small fruit developing.

Harvesting

Cantaloupes are ready to eat when the stems pull off easily—usually with a slight touch of the thumb. If they don't pull off easily, they should stay on the vine. You can also tell when they're ready because the skin begins to look like a corky net and the stem cracks a little all the way around.

Honeydew and casaba melons are ripe when the rinds have turned completely yellow.

For testing watermelons, there's nothing like thumping them with your knuckles. They have a *bonggg* . . . sound (that is, a dull rather than a sharp sound). This is a great test for early morning, but once the watermelons get hot late in the day, it's pretty hard to tell whether or not they're good and ripe because the *bong* gives way to a dull thud.

Another test is to look at the discolored spots where the melons touch the ground. If they're ready, these spots have turned from white to a pale yellow. If the stem slips easily from the vine, the melon is ready.

Storage

Melons can be stored uncut at room temperature for a week or two, but once cut, keep them refrigerated.

Growing Tips

More melons: To turn your vines into a melon factory, pinch out the growing tip when the main stem has produced five large leaves. Nip out subsequent side shoots when the growing tip develops three leaves. This stops the plant from producing leafy growth and forces more fruit production. When the plants are growing vigorously, keep them well watered and give them a liquid organic food as the first young fruits reach walnut size.

MUSTARD GREENS

Cool-season crop. Rated good for postage stamp gardens. 🌡 ▦ ▦ ▦

Mustard greens have long been a Southern favorite, and yet they've never really caught on in other regions of the country. There's no reason, however, why everybody can't enjoy this versatile vegetable. They're great as cooked greens and tremendous in salads. In addition (an important consideration for most gardeners), they grow to maturity fast.

Planting
In virtually every climate, you can take out several crops of greens every year. Sow seeds early in the spring, then again in late summer. If you live in an area of mild winters, plant again in the fall. Sow seeds 1/2 inch deep and 2 inches apart, and later thin the plants to 4 inches apart. (Be sure to cook up the tender thinned greens. They're delicious.) Make sure that the plants get a continuous supply of water throughout the season.

Crop Stretching
Plant mustard greens in succession. Divide your mustard greens section into four subsections, planting each subsection three weeks apart.

You can also plant greens among tomato seedlings; the greens will be ready for harvesting before the tomato vines have grown large enough to shade them out.

Recommended Varieties
The standard mustard greens so popular in the South grow large, thick leaves. Asian mustard greens are grown for their thinner, often spicy leaves.

Standard Mustard Greens

GREEN WAVE (TENDERGREEN) 35–50 days. Upright plant habit grows to 2' and has a dark green curled leaf. Bolt resistant. 16–22" spread. Oblong, thick, smooth glossy leaves with pale green midribs. Seed source: BOU • BURP • JOH • JOHN • NIC • SHU • TER

RED GIANT 40 days. Can be enjoyed at any stage of growth. Seed source: BOT

SOUTHERN GIANT CURLED 35–60 days. Large thick, bright green with crumpled frilled edges. Peppery flavor. Cold-tolerant and slow to bolt. Seed source: ANN · BOT · BOU · COO · GOU · HAR · PAR · SHU · SOU · STO

Asian Mustard Greens

IKA HIJIKI (SEAWEED ON LAND) 30 days. Considered to be one of the healthiest greens eaten in Japan. Green stick leaves are 2" long. Seed source: KIT

MIBUNA EARLY 21–40 days. Traditional Japanese heirloom. Dense cluster of long, narrow, rounded, dark green leaves. Leaves have mild mustard flavor. Cold-tolerant. Seed source: ANN · KIT · NIC · PAR · TERR

MIZUNA 35 days. Japanese heirloom. Hundreds of tender, juicy stemmed serrated leaves. Tolerant to cold and rain. Seed source: ANN · IRI · JOH · NIC

MIZUNA EARLY (KYONA, KYOTO) 40–50 days. Japanese mustard has long slender stems and dark green, serrated leaves. Both cold- and heat-tolerant and slow to bolt. This is a cut and come again variety. Keep cutting and it regrows. Seed source: JOH · KIT · SOU · TER

SMALL GAI CHOY 34–48 days. Very vigorous and productive Chinese non-heading type. Medium green leaves have good flavor. Tolerant of heat and may bolt to seed in spring and cold weather. Seed source: KIT

TSA TSAI ROUND (SZECHUAN, SICHUAN VEGETABLE) 120 days. Popular and unique mustard variety from southwest China. It is also known as swollen stem mustard or pressed stem mustard because the stem enlarges into thick tuber-like bumps just below the stems. Stem will grow 4–6" in diameter and weigh up to 1/2 pound. Cool-season crop. Seed source: KIT

Typical Problem

My mustard greens keep going to flower very early. Mustard greens are a cool-weather crop. If you keep having trouble with spring plantings, try planting in August for fall use.

Harvesting

Pick the leaves just before they mature. Be sure to keep the plants cut back by trimming the leaves down to the base for regrowth, to hold off flowering. After flowering, the leaves become tough and bitter.

Storage

Mustard greens can be cut and stored in the refrigerator for a few days.

Growing Tips

As the daily temperatures begin to rise above 85°F, mustard leaves become inedible. In hot areas, grow mustard only in the cool weather (under 65°F) of early spring and fall.

OKRA

Warm-season crop. Rated fair for postage stamp gardens. 🌡 ▦ ▦

If you're from the South, you probably know and love okra, but for some reason, people in the rest of the country often ignore okra, at least as a garden vegetable. If you'd like a delicious vegetable that will add flavor and body to soups and stews, you've got to include this one.

Unfortunately, the standard okra plant is too big to be a really good vegetable in postage stamp gardens. But there are several dwarf varieties that you can use to give you all the okra you'll need.

Planting

This is a warm-weather plant with about the same requirements as corn. Plant only after the ground has warmed up. Soak the seeds overnight before planting, then plant them $1/2$ to $1^1/2$ inches deep, about 8 inches apart. Thin the seedlings to 15 inches apart.

Give okra a feeding of fish emulsion, or any organic fertilizer, at least once, six to eight weeks after planting.

Crop Stretching

Stick okra in odd corners of flower beds to use extra space that would ordinarily not be productive for vegetables.

Recommended Varieties

BURMESE 58 days. From Burma. 18" tall plant continues to bear until frost. Leaves are 16" across. 9–12" slightly curved, spineless pods. Pods mature from light green to creamy yellow-green. Pods are less slimy than others. Best picked at 10" long. Seed source: BAK • SOU

CAJUN JEWEL 53 days. 2¼–4' tall spineless plants. 7" long pods by 1" diameter. Seed source: SOU

PENTA DRAGON 60 days. 25" tall dwarf plant from Asia. Pods are pentagonal, deep green, spineless, almost free of fluting. Seed source: ANN • GOU

VIDRINES MIDGET COWHORN 60–70 days. Dwarf cowhorn okra (pods look like they have horns) from St. Landry Parish, Louisiana. 3' plants produce 15" pods, which appear white but are actually a creamy, pale green. Seed source: BAK

Typical Problems

The buds keep dropping off, and no pods come. This usually results from a lack of adequate moisture. Make sure that you water regularly during the growing season.

I planted my okra early in the spring, and the plants didn't do well for a long time. Okra is a warm-season crop. Don't plant until the soil has warmed.

Harvesting

Pick the pods young, before they become too large—within a few days after the flower petals have fallen. It's best to harvest when they are young and tender with half-grown, immature seeds. If left on the plant, they become hard and unpalatable and they will also cause the plants to cease producing.

Storage

Use fresh or as pickles. To freeze okra, cut the stems off the pods, blanch the pods in boiling water for two to three minutes, cool, place in containers, and freeze.

Growing Tips

Cut, don't pull: Instead of straining to pull off okra pods, just cut with scissors.

ONIONS

Cool-season crop. Rated excellent for postage stamp gardens. 🌡 ▦▦▦▦

Onions comprise a happy family of vegetables for gardeners and cooks. They're grown the world over and used as seasoning for meats, vegetables, and salads and as vegetables alone. Although they're mainly a cool-weather crop, they'll do fine in moderately warm weather.

Planting

Onions can be grown from seeds, seedlings, or sets (small bulbs or roots). Seeds should be scattered about 1 inch apart and covered with $1/2$ inch of soil. As the plants rise, harvest the small onions so that the remaining plants are spaced about 2 or 3 inches apart, then let the mature bulbs develop. Seedlings, purchased from a nursery, should be planted 1 inch apart and then thinned to 2 to 3 inches apart as they grow larger.

Sets, which are tiny bulbs, are probably the best way to grow onions, because they're a good size and easy to handle. Some varieties, however, can't be grown from sets but must be grown from seeds; generally, in fact, the variety of onions that you'll find available as sets is pretty limited. In any case, plant sets 1 to 2 inches apart, then harvest green onions until the plants are spaced 2 to 3 inches apart, letting the remaining bulbs develop to maturity.

Seeds, seedlings, and sets should all be planted in early spring. In areas of mild winters, they can be planted all winter long.

Onions need lots of moisture, especially during bulb formation (tops grow during cool weather, bulbs during warmer weather). A good general rule is to never allow the soil to dry out. Onions are also heavy feeders, but they do pretty well in postage stamp soil without extra feeding.

Crop Stretching

Plant green onions between tomatoes, corn, eggplant, or other large plants, and harvest them before the later crops get big.

Recommended Varieties

The two most popular kinds of onions are ordinary (dry bulb) onions and green onions (also known as bunching onions or scallions).

Dry Bulb Onions

AILSA CRAIG 110–140 days. Spanish onion. Very large 2 pounds plus. Globe-shaped, straw-yellow skin. Long day type. Seed source: ANN • BAK • BOU • IRI • JOH • SEED • SHU • STO • TER • TERR

BORRETTANA (CIPIOLLINI) 105 days. Italian heirloom "cipollini" onion with classic button shape and translucent yellow color. Use as classic pickling onion. Long to intermediate day type. Seed source: ANN • GOU • IRI • JOH • NIC • SEE • SEED • TER • TERR

LONG RED FLORENCE 100–120 days. Italian heirloom. Long bottle-shaped bulbs, attractive color. Mild and sweet. Best used for fresh eating. Long day type. Seed source: BAK • SEE • SEED

SOUTHPORT WHITE GLOBE 65–120 days. Medium-size globe, fine-grained flesh, snowy white with pungent flavor. Good keeper. Seed source: BOU • COM

WALLA WALLA 100–125 days. Big juicy onion that can grow up to 3 pounds. Not a storage type. Long day type. Seed source: ANN • BOU • BURG • BURP • GOU • GUR • IRI • JOH • NIC • PAR • STO • TER • TERR • THO

YELLOW SWEET SPANISH 110 days. Large, dark yellow globe-shaped bulbs. Creamy white flesh is mild. Thick necks dry well before harvest. Use fresh. Long day type. Seed source: GOU • HAR • IRI • SHU • SOU • TERR

Green Onions

EVERGREEN HARDY WHITE 60 days. Perennial onion in fall or spring. Forms long, slender onions with tender shoots. Divide clumps second year to produce new crop. Seed source: ANN • JOH • NIC • SOU

RED WELSH 70–90 days. Super hardy bunching onion. Thick green stems and hollow leaves possess a sharp onion flavor. Perennial that never forms bulbs. Seed source: BAK • BOU

Typical Problem
My onions didn't get very big. You probably let the soil dry out during bulb enlargement. Make sure that you water regularly.

Harvesting

When the tops of ordinary bulb onions begin to dry and yellow, bend them over to a nearly horizontal position on the ground or break them off. This will divert all growing energy to the bulbs. When all the tops are dead, dig the bulbs up and let them dry on top of the ground for a few days before storage.

Green onions can be harvested as needed, but you should recognize that they don't keep long after harvesting, even with refrigeration.

Storage

Bulb onions can be stored on trays of wire netting, tied with string and braided, or placed on wooden shelves. Store them indefinitely in a dry, frost-proof area where air circulates freely.

Growing Tips

When onions flower: Sometimes onions planted from sets form flowers and fail to produce mature bulbs. Avoid this by selecting and planting smaller onion sets. When flowers appear, break off the flower buds and use these poorer onions first.

PEAS

Cool-season crop. Rated good to excellent for postage stamp gardens. 🌡 ▨▨▨▨

Peas are nearly always a star performer in the garden. They come up right away, bloom fast, and produce lots of food within sixty to eighty days. Peas are a cool-season crop, thriving in soil and air filled with cool moisture. Although they'll continue growing and producing when the days become somewhat warmer and longer, they do not do well in hot, dry weather.

Planting

Pea plants grow only from seeds planted directly in the bed where they're going to remain. Plant the seeds in the spring as soon as the ground can be worked, sowing 2 inches deep, 2 inches apart. Use successive plantings, five to ten days apart, for a continuous crop.

Crop Stretching

Peas grow either as bushes or as vines. The vines can—and should—be trained in the air, and you can do this a number of ways:

1 Place a chicken wire fence along the north side of your garden, and train your vines on it.

2 Sink a 4-foot post (preferably a 2 x 2) in the ground with a 1-foot cross nailed to the top. Run pea vines (about twelve plants) up strings stretched from the ground to the cross. You can station several of these crosses around the garden. (See illustration, page 75.)

3 Make a construction-wire island: Form a circle of wire about 2 feet in diameter and 5 feet high and plant and train pea vines inside it. When harvest time comes, you can pick the pods through the wires.

Recommended Varieties

The common green peas, called snap peas, shelling peas, garden peas, or English peas, are grown for their edible seeds; they grow as vines or bushes. Peas grown for their flat, edible pods, popular in Asian cooking, are known as Chinese snow peas or sugar peas and grow as vines. A cross between the snap and the snow pea are sugar snap peas, which have plump, edible pods.

Snap Peas

ALDERMAN POLE (TALL TELEPHONE) 70–78 days. 1881 English heirloom. Robust 5' vines bear pointed, easy-shelling pods. Seed source: BAK • BOU • GOU • NIC • SHU • TER • TERR • THO

GREEN ARROW (GREEN SHAFT) 70 days. English heirloom. 24–28" tall plants. 4–5" pods with 9–11 peas per pod. Double set pods at top of plant. Seed source: ANN • BOT • HAR • IRI • NIC • PAR • SEED • SHU • SOU • TER • THO

LITTLE MARVEL 60 days. Bush 18" plants. 1908 heirloom. Heavy yields. Seed source: ANN • BAK • COM • GUR • HAR • SHU • SOU

WANDO 68 days. Somewhat heat-resistant. Medium-size peas. Seed source: ANN • BAK • BOT • BURG • HAR • IRI • PLA • SHU • SOU

Snow Peas

DWARF GRAY SUGAR 60 days. 1773 heirloom. 30" vines have pink and purple flowers that can be used in salads with the peas. Seed source: ANN · BOU · COM · JOH · KIT · SEED

MAMMOTH MELTING SUGAR 70 days. 4' vines produce large, sweet 4¹/₂" pods. Pick before peas inside grow large. Seed source: ANN · BAK · IRI · KIT · SHU · SOU

OREGON SUGAR POD II 60 days. Large, thick 4¹/₂" pods. Bush plants. Seed source: ANN · BAK · BOT · BURP · HAR · IRI · KIT · NIC · SHU · TER

Sugar Snap Peas

AMISH SNAP PEA 60 days. Heirloom snap pea. Sweet flavor with tender pods and stringless when picked young. Climbing pea vine. Seed source: ANN

Typical Problems

My vines are lush and bushy but produce few peas. To start them producing, simply pinch back the growing tips of the various stems, thereby thinning out the vine a little.

My pea pods are hard when I pick them. You're letting them stay on the vines too long. Pick them regularly.

My peas aren't growing well; the tips of the leaves seem to be dying. Peas need a lot of water when the weather is warm and the atmosphere dry. If the days are extremely hot, there's not much you can do; you must grow peas in cool weather.

Harvesting

Pick off all the pods as they mature in order to keep the plants producing vigorously. It is best to harvest only in the morning; this seems to preserve their flavor. Edible podded peas should be picked when the pods are still flat and the peas barely there. Pick regular peas while they are firm but still succulent. Hold the vine in one hand while picking peas with the other to prevent pulling the vine from the ground.

Storage

After picking snap peas, shell them and store them in the refrigerator as soon as possible.

For freezing snap peas, shell them, blanch the seeds in boiling water for about three minutes, cool, place in containers, and freeze.

Growing Tips

Pollinating peas: When peas produce a profusion of blossoms but no pods, it means the pollen isn't being transferred from the male parts to the female parts of the flower. Peas are self-pollinating, but once in a while they get lazy and need a little help. Just shake them a couple of times a day for about a week, then get ready for a bumper crop.

Pre-sprouting peas: To ensure that peas will come up fast, pre-sprout them by laying a paper towel on a waterproof surface. Scatter peas evenly over it and cover with another paper towel. Dampen this pea sandwich, roll it up, and put it in a plastic bag in a warm room. A few days later, unroll and remove pre-germinated seeds. Plant outdoors. They'll grow even in cold soil.

PEPPERS

Warm-season crop. Rated excellent for postage stamp gardens. 🌡️ ▧▧▧▧

Pepper plants are very pretty. It's not the flowers that make them so attractive, however; it's the fruit and foliage, and they make great ornamentals.

Pepper originally came to the attention of the Western world when explorers landing in the New World tasted the native chile and mistook it for the spice "pepper," one of the trading spices from the Orient. The New World "pepper," however, tasted only vaguely like the East Indian pepper that they were looking for. In fact, the various sweet and hot peppers native to the New World are related to the tomato and eggplant.

Planting

Peppers are classified as hot-weather plants; thus, they like temperatures above 60°F. On the other hand, they also like temperatures below 90°F. Anywhere out of this temperature range, from 60°F to 90°F, seems to keep the fruit from setting.

You can start peppers either from seeds or from plants purchased from your local nursery. If you're going to use seeds, you should start them indoors in peat pots—two to four seeds, $1/2$ inch deep, in each pot—about ten weeks before you intend to set the plants out. In your garden bed, space the seedlings 14 inches apart.

Peppers need lots of regular watering. They are also heavy feeders and should be fed fish emulsion, or any organic fertilizer, about the time that the first blossoms open.

Crop Stretching

Extending the season: To keep from losing peppers at the first frost, lay a wide strip of black plastic over each row or cage at night. It protects the fruit and extends the season as much as three weeks.

Recommended Varieties

There are a lot of different kinds of peppers—all shapes and sizes and colors— but generally the most common can be divided into two classes: sweet and hot (sometimes known as chile peppers). The most familiar sweet pepper shape is the classic bell pepper, but it also comes in long tapering and even round variet- ies. Chile peppers are known for their heat and this heat is classified by Scoville units, which range from almost nothing to 1,000,000 in some Asian peppers. As a general rule, the smaller the pepper the hotter it is. Be careful when han- dling any chile pepper—gloves are recommended and always avoid touching your eyes after handling chiles.

Sweet Peppers (Bell)

CALIFORNIA WONDER 70–75 days. Green bell pepper is 4–4$1/2$", thick flesh, blocky emerald green fruit. Good stuffer. Seed source: ANN • BAK • BOT • BURG • BURP • COM • COO • NIC • PAR • SHU • SOU • STO • TER • THE

CHOCOLATE BEAUTY 70–75 days. Shiny green bell peppers ripen to choco- late brown. Sweet flavor when fully ripe. Seed source: SEED • TERR • THE

ORANGE BELL 100 days. Super sweet, brilliant orange, blocky 4" fruit. Thick flesh. Magnificent pepper. Seed source: ANN • BAK • JOHN • SEED • SOU • THE

PURPLE BEAUTY 75 days. Very colorful. Compact 17" bush plant. Mild, sweet bell. 4-lobed, thick walls. Ripens to radiant purple-red color. Seed source: BAK • GOU • JOHN • SEED • SOU

QUADRATO D'ASTI ROSSO 80 days. Thick, brilliant red flesh is very sweet. Popular in Italy. Good all-round pepper eaten raw, stuffed, or fried. Italian heirloom. Seed source: ANN • BAK • GOU • JOHN

RED CHERRY (CHERRY SWEET) 70 days. Pre-1800 heirloom. Shaped like bonbons, dark crimson red 1¹/₂" x 1" fruits. Bushy 20" tall plants. Great for pickling, canning, or stuffing. Seed source: SOU

RED MINI BELL (BABY BELL) 60 days. Tiny version of bell peppers. Red, 1¹/₂" tall and wide peppers. Thick flesh and very sweet. 2' tall plant is ideal for small-space gardens. Seed source: BAK • GOU • SEED • TER • THE

Sweet Peppers (Tapering)

CORNO DI TORO ROSSO (CORNO DE TORO RED, BULL'S HORN) 75–90 days. Long, thin, deep glowing red sweet pepper. Italian heirloom. 6–8" long and 2" diameter. Seed source: ANN • BAK • BOU • GOU • JOHN • SHU • SOU • THE • TOT

DOUX D'ESPAGNE (SPANISH MAMMOTH) 85–90 days. Pre-1860 heirloom. 6–7" long cone-shaped peppers that are used for frying or salads. Seed source: BAK • THE

GOLDEN TREASURE 80 days. Italian heirloom. 9" long peppers ripen from green to shiny yellow. Sweet, medium flesh. Used for roasting, frying, or eating fresh off the plant. Seed source: ANN • SEED • THE

JIMMY NARDELLO 75–90 days. 1887 southern Italy heirloom. Long, thin-skinned frying pepper dries easily. Rich flavor. Ripens to a deep red. 6–9" long. Seed source: BAK • BOU • NIC • SEED • SOU • TER • THE • TOT

SWEET BANANA (LONG SWEET BANANA) 72 days. Tapered 6–7" long fruit goes from light green to orange to red in color. All-American Selections Winner. Seed source: BOU • BURG • BURP • GOU • GUR • NIC • SHU • SOU • STO • TOT

TEQUILA SUNRISE 77 days. 1" x 5" thick-fleshed peppers that grow upright on small plants. Turns from green to orange. Seed source: BAK • SEED • SOU • TERR • THE

Hot Peppers

ANAHEIM 80 days. Mildly hot flavor. Very large chile pepper. Long, slender fruit. Seed source: BAK • BOU • BURG • COM • SOU • TERR • THE • TOT

ANCHO POBLANO 90 days. Slightly spicy cooking pepper used in Mexican cooking. Use while green or allow to ripen to a deep brick-red color. Seed source: BOT • BOU • BURP • JOHN • TERR

BHUT JOLOKIA (GHOST PEPPER, NAGA MORICH) 100–120 days. Hottest pepper ever, so plant this variety only if you can take the 1,000,000 Scoville units of heat. 4' plants. Thin-skinned, wrinkled, pointed 2–3" long fruit. Seed source: BAK • THE • TOT

CARIBBEAN RED HABANERO 90 days. Twice as spicy as the common orange habanero. Rich, smoky citrus flavor. 2" lantern-shaped fruit. Heavy producer. Seed source: BAK • BOU • STO • TOT

CAYENNE LONG THIN 90 days. 2' plants. Heirloom. Fiery, red-hot seasoning pepper. 3–4" long and 3/4" thick. Peppers turn from green to red when ripe. Seed source: ANN • BAK • BOU • IRI • SOU • TERR • THE • TOT

FISH PEPPER 80 days. An African-American heirloom. Used in fish and shellfish cookery. Colors include green, orange, brown, white, and red. Spicy and hot. 2' tall plants have white and green mottled leaves. 2" long peppers. Seed source: ANN • BAK • JOHN • SEED • SOU • THE • TOT

HABANERO 90 days. One of the hottest peppers of all. 12" tall plants. 2" x 1" thin-walled peppers start out green and ripen to a pink-orange. Seed source: ANN • BOT • HAR • IRI • JOH • NIC • PAR • SOU • STO • TER • THE • TOT

HUNGARIAN HOT WAX (HOT BANANA) 60–70 days. Hungarian heirloom. Long, banana-shaped, medium spicy, 1 1/2" x 6–7" long. Use fresh, canned, or pickled. Seed source: ANN • BAK • BOT • GOU • HAR • IRI • JOH • JOHN • SHU • SOU • STO • THE • TOT

JALAPEÑO 60 days. Hot cone-shaped fruit with distinctive meaty flavor. When smoked they become chipotles. Use green or red. 24" tall plants. Will produce in cooler conditions. Seed source: ANN • BOU • GOU • IRI • NIC • SOU • THE

MCMAHON'S TEXAS BIRD 90 days. 12" tall plants. Seeds given to southwest Texas by Thomas Jefferson. When strung up fruit looks like cranberries. Ideal for postage stamp gardens and containers. Seed source: SEED

MEXICO SERRANO 85 days. 30" bush-like plant. Heavy crops of very red or green peppers shaped like miniature jalapeños. The standard serrano in Mexico. Seed source: GOU

PEPPERONCINI ITALIAN 50 days. Also known as Tuscan peppers. Trim, upright 30" bushes are loaded with slender, slightly wrinkled green to red peppers. Pick when 2–4" long. Seed source: ANN • NIC • TERR

TABASCO 85–90 days. Famous Louisiana 1848 heirloom. Main ingredient in Tabasco Pepper Sauce. Very hot with delicious flavor. 4' tall plants. Thin 1¹/₂" peppers ripen from green to orange, then red. Needs a warm summer. Seed source: ANN • BAK • BOT • COM • GOU • JOHN • NIC • THE • TOT

Asian Hot Peppers

BIRD'S EYE CHILI 69–80 days. From Sri Lanka and is a hot 55,000–80,000 Scoville units. Smooth, tapered 1" long peppers. Seed source: KIT • THE

KOREAN DARK GREEN 112 days. Korean heirloom. 2' tall plants have dark green foliage and produce 3–4" slender peppers that are green to red in color. Very spicy and hot and used in Korean dishes. Seed source: BAK

ORANGE THAI 80–90 days. 2¹/₃" cayenne-type peppers. Can dry and use for seasoning. Fruits turn from green to orange. Seed source: SEED

SHISHITO 60–80 days. Old Japanese variety. 3" long, slightly wrinkled fruit used for making tempura and in other traditional recipes. Emerald green color, mildly flavored with a hint of spice. Seed source: BAK • KIT • TERR

THAI RED CHILE 90 days. Hot heirloom from Thailand. Small, pointed fruit is easy to dry. Bright red. Pungent heat. 1–3" long peppers. 16" compact plants. Seed source: BAK • KIT

Typical Problem

The blossom dropped off, and I stopped getting fruit. This could be the result of a couple of things. The night temperatures may have become too hot or too cold; if so, there's not much you can do. Or you may not be picking the ripe peppers regularly; pepper plants usually won't continue producing more blossoms when the plants have all the fruit they can handle.

Harvesting

Pick bell peppers when they are firm and crisp. Most people believe that they have a better flavor when picked green, not red, unless they are a red variety. Let hot peppers completely ripen on the vine.

Storage

For freezing, first dice or slice them and then freeze for one hour on an uncovered cookie sheet. Then put the pieces in small bags and return to the freezer.

Growing Tips

Increasing pepper production: To double and triple pepper production, plant only the stockiest of seedlings with well-developed root systems. Leggy, already blossoming seedlings will not produce like the younger, fuller plants. When they begin to produce, pick off the first pepper—the "crown set." This encourages a higher production of big fruits over the entire season.

Night temperatures: Spring-planted peppers sometimes just sit there with the leaves turning yellow. The reason: Peppers need nighttime temperatures above 55°F to grow properly. To solve this, wait until the weather turns warm before popping your peppers into the ground.

Helping hand: If peppers are slow setting fruit in hot weather, fill a squirt bottle with water and spray the plants. Then give a dose of liquid fish fertilizer, or any organic fertilizer, every seven to ten days when the first fruits start to swell. This helps produce larger, heavier crops.

RADISHES

Cool-season crop. Rated excellent for postage stamp gardens.

The radish is a quick-maturing, here-today-and-gone-tomorrow plant. Some varieties of radish mature in as few as twenty-two days; others average about a month—which is fast for most vegetables. They're also ridiculously easy to grow; give anyone a package of radish seeds and you make them an instant gardener. Kids love to plant radishes.

Planting

Just pop your radish seeds into the ground as soon as it can be worked; after that, sow more seeds every week or so to ensure a continuous crop. It is best to plant only what you can eat in a week or so; that way, you won't get overloaded with radishes. Because radishes are a cool-weather crop, halt the sowing in early summer and then resume about a month before the first frost. The seeds should be scattered about 1 inch apart, $1/2$ inch deep.

Crop Stretching

Radishes can be sown early in places where you will be planting such later crops as corn and tomatoes. Because of the speed with which radishes grow, you can plant them between any vegetables that require a 4- or 5-inch spacing; the radishes will be harvested before the main crops get very big.

Plant radishes with carrots. Mix carrot and radish seeds together and scatter across the bed. The radishes will come up quickly. Harvest them before the carrots need their first thinning.

Recommended Varieties

There are two main kinds of radishes: the standard ones (though of many shapes and hues), which are small and quick maturing, and the winter ones, which are usually large and require cool weather at the end of their growing season. Usually these are the Asian varieties. The winter varieties should be sown in midsummer. Although both the skin and the flesh of ordinary radishes are edible, the skin of winter radishes should be peeled to reveal the edible white flesh.

Standard Radishes

BUNNY TAIL (SMALL WHITE TIP, ROSSO TONDO A PICCOLA PUNTA BLANCA) 22 days. Italian heirloom. Small bright red with white rootlets. Mild flavor. Seed source: ANN • GOU

CHERRY BELLE 22 days. All-American Selections Winner. Round, bright cherry red roots with white flesh. Seed source: ANN • BOT • BOU • BURP • GOU • GUR • HAR • NIC • SHU • SOU • STO • TER

EASTER EGG 27 days. Round radishes in colors of pink, purple, white, and red. Seed source: BOT • BURG • IRI • JOH • NIC • PAR • SOU • TER • TERR • TOT

FRENCH BREAKFAST (RADISH DEMI-LONG ROSE A BOUT BLANC) 25 days. 1873 heirloom. Mild, spicy flavor. Oval roots have red top and white tip. Seed source: ANN • BAK • BOT • BOU • COM • GOU • GUR • HAR • IRI • JOHN • NIC • SEED • SHU • TER

LONG SCARLET (LONG ITALIAN CANDLE, LUNGO ROSSO, FUOCO, CINCINNATI MARKET) 28 days. Pre-1870s heirloom. Long and slender. Bright red with mild flesh. 6" long. Seed source: BAK • COM • GOU • SEED

WHITE ICICLE (LADY FINGER, LONG WHITE ICICLE, CANDELA DI GHIACCIO) 29 days. Pre-1865 heirloom. Slender 6" ice-white roots. Mild flavor. Seed source: BAK • BOT • GOU • HAR • IRI • JOHN • KIT • SHU • SOU • STO

Winter Radishes

CHINA ROSE (ROSE COLORED CHINESE) 55 days. 1850s heirloom. One of the oldest types of radish. Very hardy fall/winter variety. Roots are 5" long and rose colored. Seed source: BAK • COM • KIT • SHU • SOU

CHINESE RED MEAT 50–60 days. Historic China heirloom. 4" round roots with white and green skin, but have a rose-red center. Must be grown in cool weather. Seed source: BAK • BOT • BOU • BURG • BURP • GOU • JOH • KIT • NIC • TOT

MISATO ROSE 60 days. 3–4" roots are recommended for fall sowing. Skin is light pink to green, but the flesh is bright pink, spicy, and sweet. Large dark green leaves set this variety apart. Seed source: BAK • NIC • SOU

RAT'S TAIL (MONGRI, SNAKE RADISH) 58 days. Asian heirloom. An edible-podded radish that produces loads of tender, large seedpods that are added to salads and stir-fries. These are also good pickled. Seed source: BAK • BOT • BOU • SEED

TOKINASHI (ALL SEASONS, OMNY) 65 days. Japanese heirloom. 18" long, white, mildly pungent. Crunchy texture. Used for cooking, pickles, and eating raw. This daikon is unfazed by heavy clay soils. Seed source: BOU • KIT • NIC • STO

Typical Problems

I get lots of leaves but no radish bottoms. You sowed the seeds too close together. Thin the plants to at least 1 inch apart.

My radishes taste so hot I can hardly eat them. Sometimes this happens when the soil becomes hot and dries out. Keep watering regularly.

Harvesting

Pick radishes when they're still fairly small and young (pull up a couple to see). They'll be tender, succulent, and full of flavor at this stage. Later on they'll be somewhat pithy.

Storage

Radishes are best when fresh picked, but can be refrigerated for a few days.

Growing Tips

Eating seedpods: You can let a few plants go to seed, and then pick the seedpods while they are immature. The pods make a crunchy addition to salads.

Hot radishes: To avoid a very hot radish taste give them plenty of water as they grow.

RHUBARB

Cool-season crop. Rated fair for postage stamp gardens.

If you like big-leaved plants, you'll love this one. It looks almost like a tropical growing in your garden, and it compares favorably with any of the broad-leaved plants grown primarily as ornamentals. Rhubarb, however, is a perennial, like asparagus, and will spread out and take up an awful lot of space. It's therefore not the best thing for postage stamp gardens. That shouldn't rule it out, though, because it'll do very well in its own separate bed or especially in your flower beds, where it'll look tremendous.

Planting

Rhubarb doesn't do well in most subtropical regions of the United States because it needs a winter dormant period, although it can do well in mild winter areas. You should purchase root crowns from your nursery and plant them 12 inches apart in the spring or fall (36 inches apart if you want giant plants). Dig holes and set the plants in so that the tops of the roots stand 3 or 4 inches below ground level; cover with soil. Wait two years after planting before you begin to pull stalks for eating. From then on you'll have ample yield for the next eight or nine years.

Water rhubarb regularly and deep, and give the plants a feeding of fish emulsion, or any organic fertilizer, once or twice a year.

Crop Stretching
Put rhubarb in odd flower bed space not suited for other vegetables.

Recommended Variety

VICTORIA 360 days. Pre-1840 heirloom. Thick, greenish stalks. Start harvesting the second year. Do not eat the leaves—they are toxic. Seed source: BAK • BOU • BURG • BURP • COM • SHU • SOU

Typical Problems
Practically none.

Harvesting
Select the larger outside stalks; grasp them firmly near the base and snap them off. Use only the stalks for eating; discard the dark green leaves, which are poisonous. For freezing rhubarb, wash the stalks, cut them into $3/4$-inch slices, put in containers, and freeze.

Storage
Rhubarb is best used fresh as needed.

Growing Tip
Early rhubarb: To get a jump on the season, force rhubarb during the winter months (cooler climates only), place a 2-foot-high barrel, wooden box, or large pot over the plant, and cover with a lid to keep out the light. Cover the whole thing with grass clippings, straw, dead leaves, or garden compost. The rhubarb in the barrel will produce rhubarb stalks early in the season, well before any exposed rhubarb plants start to grow.

RUTABAGAS see *Turnips* (page 157)

SPINACH

Cool-season crop. Rated fair to good for postage stamp gardens. ▯ ▦ ▦ ▦

Spinach is one of those on-again, off-again vegetables. I live in an area where it may be cool in March and April and 90°F a few weeks later in May. That's what you might call a spinach grower's nightmare, because spinach must have cool weather, or else. Give it long days and hot temperatures, and all of a sudden it's gone to seed.

Planting

Spinach grows best from seeds, set directly in the ground where they're to grow. Sow the seeds in early spring and again in late summer, placing them about $1/2$ inch deep and 2 inches apart. Thin the seedlings to about 6 inches apart. For a long crop, make successive plantings ten days apart.

Spinach is a heavy feeder, so give the plants a feeding of fish emulsion, or any organic fertilizer, about halfway through the season.

Crop Stretching

You can harvest your early spinach in the late spring and then plant beans. Later, when it cools off, you can follow the beans with another planting of spinach for a fall crop.

Recommended Varieties

Spinach is considered a cool-weather vegetable that goes to seed in the heat of the summer. Spinach substitutes like New Zealand spinach and Mountain spinach are not true spinaches, but they look and taste like spinach and are grown in the summer for a continued abundance of greens.

Standard Spinach

BLOOMSDALE LONG STANDING 39–60 days. Pre-1908 American heirloom. Glossy, dark green savoyed leaves. Does better in hot weather than most. Seed source: ANN • BAK • BOU • BURG • BURP • COM • GOU • GUR • IRI • NES • NIC • PLA • SHU • STO • TER

LARGE VIROFLAY 50 days. 1900s heirloom. Very broad dark green, smooth leaves. Seed source: COM

MONSTER OF VIROFLAY 40–50 days. Nineteenth-century French heirloom. Plants grow up to 2" in diameter. Huge, dark green, crisp savoyed leaves have a sweet and complex flavor. Very cold hardy. Seed source: ANN • BOT • BOU • GOU • NIC

STRAWBERRY SPINACH (STRAWBERRY BLITE) 90 days. Plain-leaf variety grown in Europe for centuries. Very showy compact 18" plant. Triangular toothed leaves and tender shoots. Shiny red mulberry-like fruits are edible and added to salads. Self-seeding annual. Seed source: SEED

TYEE 37 days. Big, upright semi-savoyed leaves are held well above ground. Bolt resistant. Seed source: BOT • GUR • HAR • IRI • JOH • SHU • TER

Spinach Substitutes

GREEN MALABAR SPINACH 70 days. Big glossy bright-green leaves, tender 1/2" stems. Will climb 6–10". Seed source: JOHN • TERR

NEW ZEALAND SPINACH 60–70 days. 1700s heirloom. This variety takes the heat of summer and keeps producing. Not frost hardy. Seed source: BAK • BOT • BURP • COM • GOU • JOHN • NES • SEED • SHU • STO

RED ORACH (MOUNTAIN SPINACH) 60 days. Tall, erect hardy annual. Native to Europe. Cultivated in America since the 1800s. Tender, spinach-like leaves. Tolerates heat, cold, and drought, as well as salty and alkaline soils. Seed source: TERR

SPINACH BEET GREENS 60 days. 1869 heirloom. Large soft-green leaves are a great spinach substitute with a sweeter flavor. 2' bushy plants. Withstands heat. Seed source: TERR

Typical Problems

There are very few, if any, problems growing spinach.

Harvesting

To harvest spinach simply cut the leaves and add to a salad or cook.

Storage

Spinach is best used fresh. Spinach can be frozen.

Growing Tip

Cut back: Some gardeners stop spinach flowering by cutting the plant back to the ground when there are just four or five leaves on the plant. As soon as new leaves appear, harvest and cut back again. If you wait too long, hoping the leaves will become nice and big, you end up with less spinach.

SQUASH

Warm-season crop. Rated good for postage stamp gardens.

Summer squash is harvested and cooked in summer while immature and soft-skinned; it will not store for long. Winter squash, which is left on the vines until the shells are thoroughly hardened and the leaves turn brown, stores well for fall and winter use. Postage stamp gardeners prefer summer squash because it grows usually as bushy compact plants, and doesn't take up much space.

Winter squash has runner-type vines that can require lots of space. However, there are bush varieties you could try, or you can grow the vines of winter squash vertically. The heavy fruits must be tied up with cloth supports.

Planting
Squash is extremely easy to grow, but it's a heat lover and shouldn't be set outdoors until nighttime temperatures regularly stay above 55°F.

Use seeds or seedlings purchased from a nursery. Plant seeds 1 inch deep, 18 inches apart. Set seedlings 18 inches apart.

Crop Stretching
Small-fruited winter squash can be trained up in the air on the same kind of structures as those used for cucumbers and melons. Be sure to support the fruit with cloth slings (see page 115).

Recommended Varieties
Among the varieties of summer squash, zucchini is a wonder, because it can be prepared in so many ways: You can stuff it, fry it, bake it in a casserole, cut it up for salads, and even use it in dessert breads. Generally, you'll find two or three zucchini plants are enough because the plants are so prolific. You may find it in bloom one morning, then come back two days later and pick a full-grown zucchini. If you become overrun by zucchini you can always make zucchini bread, freeze it, and give it out at Christmastime. Try some of the other summer varieties for color and texture. Winter squash, while grown in the summer, develops a hard rind that makes it suitable for long winter storage. Winter squash don't produce as many fruit per plant as summer squash.

SUMMER SQUASH

Zucchini

BLACK BEAUTY 50 days. Classic dark-green zucchini. 1920s heirloom. Best picked when young. Seed source: ANN • BAK • BOT • BOU • GOU • IRI • PAR • SEED • SOU • STO • TER • TERR

COSTATA ROMANESCO 52 days. Famous Italian/Roman zucchini. Long, fluted, and ribbed. Medium-green striped skin, rich flavor. When cut, the slices are scalloped. Seed source: ANN • BAK • BOT • BOU • JOH • SOU

GOLDEN 50 days. Slender bright golden-yellow zucchini. Bush plant. Seed source: BAK • GOU • SEED • SHU

RONDE DE NICE (TONDA NIZZA) 50 days. French heirloom. Round, green zucchini. Ideal for stuffing. Great taste. Seed source: BAK • BOT • COO • GOU • IRI • JOHN • SEE • TERR

TATUME 55 days. A must in Mexican cuisine. Old heirloom is picked small and used like zucchini. Round to slightly elongated, flavorful green fruit. Vigorous vining plants. Seed source: BAK • BOT • JOHN • NIC • PAR

VERDE CHIARO D'ITALIA 45 days. Early Italian zucchini with very light streaks on smooth, nearly ribless light green fruit. Good blossom producer for frying. Seed source: GOU

Straightneck

EARLY PROLIFIC 50 days. All-American Selections Winner. Uniform lemon-yellow club-shaped fruit. Firm flesh. Seed source: ANN • BAK • BOT • BURP • GOU • GUR • IRI • JOHN • SHU • SOU

Crookneck

YELLOW 55 days. 1700s heirloom. Yellow, bulb-shaped fruit with a narrow, curved neck. Skin becomes bumpy and warted on large fruit. Best eaten at 6" long. Seed source: ANN • JOH • SOU • TER

Patty Pan

BENNING'S GREEN TINT 50–63 days. Colorful, light green, scallop-shaped fruit. Old favorite. 2–3" diameter. 3–4' bushes yield up to 15 squash. Seed source: ANN • BAK • BOU • JOHN • SOU • TER • TERR

PATISSON PANACHE BLANC ET VERT 60–70 days. Pre-1865 French heirloom. Stunning pure white scallop with deep green radial streaks. Small fruit may not show streaking, and it can be variable. Seed source: BAK • SEED

WINTER SQUASH

Acorn

FORDHOOK ACORN 110 days. 1890 heirloom that is a good producer. 2 pounds each. Creamy tan-colored. Oblong, acorn-shaped fruit. Seed source: BAK • SEED

TABLE QUEEN (DES MOINES, DANISH) 80 days. 1913 or earlier heirloom. Dark green fruit. Small fruits have sweet orange flesh. Seed source: ANN • BAK • BOU • BURG • BURP • GOU • SEED • SOU

Banana Shaped

JUMBO PINK BANANA 105 days. Large, pink, banana-shaped fruit can weigh 10–40 pounds. Fine-flavored dry, sweet orange flesh. Seed source: BAK • BOT • BOU • IRI • SHU • TER

NORTH GEORGIA CANDY ROASTER 100 days. 1900s Appalachian heirloom. Banana-shaped fruits are up to 18" long and 6" wide. Pink with blue tips. Smooth orange flesh. Seed source: SOU

Buttercup

BURGESS 85–95 days. 1925 heirloom. 3–4 pounds. Vining plants. Rich flavor. Seed source: ANN • BOU • BURG • JOH • SEED • SHU • SOU • STO

BUSH BUTTERCUP 95 days. 3–4 pounds, green-skinned with sweet dry, orange flesh. 3–4' compact bush plant. Seed source: BAK

MARINA DI CHIOGGIA 95 days. The heirloom sea pumpkin of Chioggia, Italy. Large turban-shaped fruit are deep blue-green. Rich, sweet, deep yellow-orange flesh. 10 pounds each. Good pie squash. Seed source: GOU

TURK'S CAP (TURBAN, FRENCH) 90 days. French heirloom. Striped in red, orange, green, and white. Thick orange flesh. Seed source: BAK • SEED

Butternut

PENNSYLVANIA DUTCH CROOKNECK 100–110 days. 10–20 pounds. Seeds are contained in the bottom half. Simply cut the long curved neck into rings and bake. Sweet dark orange flesh, excellent for pies or soups. Good keeper. Seed source: SEED

ROGOSA VIOLINA "GIOIA" 100 days. An Italian butternut-type squash that has a violin shape and wrinkled tan skin. The flesh is deep orange and sweet. Bake, roast, stuff, or use for desserts. Seed source: BAK • GOU

WALTHAM 100 days. All-American Selections Winner. An old favorite. Rich, orange-colored flesh and great baked. Seed source: ANN • BAK • BOT • BOU • BURG • BURP • GOU • GUR • HAR • JOH • SEED • SHU • SOU • STO • TER

Hubbard

BLUE HUBBARD 110 days. Huge, teardrop-shaped fruit weighs 15–40 pounds. Fine-grained golden flesh that tastes like hazelnuts. Hard, blue-gray shell helps keep squash in storage. Seed source: ANN • BAK • COM • GOU • HAR • JOH • NIC • SHU • TERR

CHICAGO WARTED 110 days. 1894 heirloom. 13 pounds. Dusky olive-green, deeply wrinkled, and warted. Classic hubbard shape. Fine-grained, sweet orange flesh. Seed source: BAK • SHU • TERR

Cushaw

GREEN STRIPED 95 days. Native American squash, pre-1860s. Big, white fruit with small green stripes. Oblong with crooked necks and bulbous bottoms. Originally from the West Indies earlier than 1700. Seed source: BAK • GOU • SHU • SOU

Asian

CHIRIMEN 100 days. Japanese heirloom was popular during the Edo period (1603–1867). Fruit weighs 5 pounds. Flattened and ribbed and deep greenish black. Bright orange, sweet flesh. Turns more tan during storage. Seed source: BAK • GOU • KIT

RED KURI (HOKKAIDO) 92 days. Japanese winter squash. Red-orange fruit. 5–10 pounds each and has teardrop shape. Golden flesh is smooth, dry, sweet, and rich. Seed source: BAK • JOH • TER

SHISHIGATANI (TOONAS MAKINO) 110 days. Heirloom since the Edo period. Japanese pumpkin kabocha squash is used in *shojin ryori* (Buddhist cuisine). Skin is ribbed and warted, and it turns light brown when ripe. Light yellow flesh. Seed source: GOU • KIT

Other Types of Winter Squash

DELICATA 110 days. 1894 heirloom. High sugar content. 1–3 pounds each. Skin color is yellow-white with green stripes. Seed source: BAK • COM • GOU • IRI • JOH • PLA • SHU • STO • TER

LONG ISLAND CHEESE 105 days. Heirloom favorite on Long Island for pies. Flat, lightly ribbed fruit look like wheels of cheese with buff-colored skin. 6–10 pounds each. Very good keeper. Seed source: ANN • BAK • COM • GOU • SEED • TER

SPAGHETTI SQUASH (VEGETABLE SQUASH) 88–100 days. 1934 heirloom. May have originated in China. I love this squash because there are no carbs or fat. Dieter's best friend. Stringy flesh is used like spaghetti. Oblong, yellow. Seed source: ANN • BAK • BOT • BURG • BURP • GOU • GUR • HAR • IRI • KIT NIC • PAR • SHU • SOU • STO • TER • TERR

SWEET DUMPLING 90 days. Sweet, 1-pound fruit is white with green stripes. Tender, orange flesh. Seed source: BAK • HAR • JOH • JOHN • KIT • SHU • STO

Typical Problem

My zucchini plants start out each year producing some small squash that rot before they get very big. Some female flowers on the plant bloomed before there were male flowers around to pollinate them. These unpollinated flowers result in small fruits that rot. Just wait and you'll get plenty of zucchini that will grow to full size.

Harvesting

Pick summer squash when it's fairly young and small. It's tender and delicious then. Usually, summer squash is too old for eating when the thumbnail doesn't readily pierce the skin with little pressure.

Let winter squash mature fully on the vine until its skin is very hard. Cut them from the vine, leaving a 2- to 3-inch stem on each squash. Cure the squashes in the sun for a week or more.

Storage

Store winter squash in a cool, dry place over the winter. Both summer and winter squash can be frozen, but winter squash must first be peeled. Cut the squash into small pieces, blanch the pieces in boiling water for 1½ minutes, cool, place in containers, and freeze.

Growing Tips

Summer Squash

Playing bee: If mature squash plants produce few fruit, the problem may be a lack of bees. Collect the yellow pollen with an artist's brush and dust the female flowers (the ones with the tiny miniature squash at the base). Put the pollen on the tip of the small fruit above the flower (the stigma).

Baby squash: You don't need a particular variety to create a baby squash delicacy. Simply pick miniature-size squash with the blossoms still on the fruit. Cook and serve whole.

Winter Squash

Squash basics: Before harvesting winter squash for storage, push your thumbnail against the squash as hard as you can. If the outer skin doesn't cut easily, the squash will keep for a long time. If the squash skin cuts easily, it will probably rot in storage. If already picked, cook the squash within a few days.

SWISS CHARD

Cool-season crop. Rated good for postage stamp gardens. 🌡 ▨ ▨ ▨

If you've tried spinach and failed or are just tired of fighting its special weather requirements, then you'll want to grow Swiss chard, for it can take summer temperatures that would make spinach bolt to seed. Chard, a member of the beet family but without the bulbous root, has big crinkly leaves and white stalks that are both delicious. That's a double dividend. The leaves are cooked like spinach or other greens. The stalks are cooked and served like asparagus.

Planting

In cold winter areas, plant seeds in the spring about two or three weeks before the final frost; in areas where winter temperatures stay above 25°F, plant in the fall for harvesting the next year. In fact, in regions of very mild climates you can plant almost any time of the year.

Broadcast the seeds about 4 inches apart across the bed and cover with 1/2 inch of soil. When the seedlings come up, thin to at least 8 inches apart.

Crop Stretching

Plant Swiss chard in spaces that will later contain corn, tomatoes, and other heat lovers.

Recommended Varieties

BRIGHT LIGHTS 60 days. All-American Selections Winner. Light shades of pink, crimson, orange, yellow, gold, purple, and white 20" stems. Light savoyed leaves are burgundy with some green. Seed source: BURP • COO • JOH • JOHN • NIC • SHU • TER • TERR • TOT

FORDHOOK GIANT 60 days. Large, dark green, very savoyed leaves. 8–10" pale green stalks. Seed source: ANN • BAK • BOT • BOU • BURP • COO • JOH • SEED • SHU • TERR

RUBY RED (RHUBARB CHARD) 55–60 days. Crimson stalks have heavily crumpled leaves. Plant grows 20–24" tall. Seed source: ANN • BOT • BOU • COM • HAR • JOHN • NIC • SEED • TERR

Typical Problems

Almost none.

Harvesting

There are two ways to harvest Swiss chard. When the outer leaves are 6 to 10 inches tall, every few days you can cut the outer leaves from the plant while it continues growing. (Don't let old and tough leaves remain on the plant, or the plant will stop producing fresh leaves.) Or you can also cut off the whole plant a couple of inches above the root crown, and the plant will produce new leaves.

Storage

Use chard when fresh.

Growing Tips

Find a permanent home in a flower bed to show off the beauty of colored chard.

TOMATOES

Warm-season crop. Rated excellent for postage stamp gardens. ❚ ▧ ▧ ▧ ▧

Let your imagination go wild when it comes time to think about tomatoes. Tomatoes come in a wide array of sizes and colors. With heirloom tomatoes in particular, the focus is on the flavor and high quality of the fruit, in contrast with some of the varieties that often taste like cardboard when purchased from supermarkets.

Planting

You can start your tomatoes from seeds or buy them as seedlings. Buying seedlings is the easiest way, and the one I use. You'll generally have to grow from seed, however, if you want a wide choice of varieties.

To start from seeds, plant them $1/2$ inch deep in compressed peat pots. Then after the weather has warmed up, plant the pots with the seedlings in your postage stamp beds 18 inches apart. As warm-weather plants, tomato seedlings should not be set out in the garden until nighttime temperatures begin staying above 58°F.

There are a couple of rules that you should follow when transplanting seedlings. If you have a bushy plant (which is preferable to a long lean one), bury it so that half to three-fourths of the stem as well as the root ball is below the soil level; roots will form along the buried stem. For really long-stemmed plants, you still should get half to three-fourths of the stem underground, but you should be careful not to place the root ball too deep. In a shallow hole, put the root ball almost on its side so that the stem is semi-horizontal, or at least not vertical; then you gradually bend the stem so that only the bushy part appears upright above ground level.

Tomatoes generally are deep-rooted, often going 6 feet deep or more. The plants should get plenty of moisture during the growing season. Overwatering, however, can stimulate too much leaf growth and cause blossoms to drop. Too much shade or too much nitrogen fertilizer can also cut down blossoming. Despite these apparent problems, tomatoes can be easy to grow.

If you have tomato diseases around (ask your nursery person), avoid these diseases by looking for letters *V, F,* and *N* on the instructions accompanying your seeds or seedlings. The letters stand for varieties resistant to verticillium, fusarium, and nematode, respectively, which are major tomato diseases.

Tomatoes are heavy feeders; however, in a postage stamp bed it usually isn't necessary to give them an extra feeding during the season. If you find you need to feed them, give them an organic fertilizer once during the growing season.

Crop Stretching

There are several ways to adapt tomato plants to a postage stamp garden:

1   Make a fence of chicken wire stretched between two 5- or 6-foot posts (preferably 2 x 2s). As the plants grow, cut back enough foliage to make each plant easy to tie to the wires, but leave as many stems as possible—say, two to six. This way, you'll get more fruit. (See illustration, below left.)

2   Make a lath framework or trellis for each plant. Pinch off all but two or four main stems and tie them to the frame. (See illustration, below center.)

3   Buy tomato towers from your local nursery.

4   Make a circular tomato cage from a 5-foot length of construction wire. (That's the kind used for concrete reinforcing, with a 6-inch mesh.) Just circle each plant in your garden with the wire, and tie the ends of the wire together. You don't have to cut off any plant stems, but you'll probably have to tie the stems to the wire. This tomato cage will give you an extremely productive bushy tomato factory. (See illustration, below right.)

Recommended Varieties

You've got a lot of choices of tomatoes, from early to late varieties, from small fruit and container varieties. The early varieties set fruit at lower temperatures than later maturing plants; you get tomatoes much earlier in the season. You also have a choice of red, green, black, purple, striped, white, orange, pink, and yellow tomatoes. There are literally hundreds of tomatoes available. Visit www.postagestampvegetablegardening.com to find a comprehensive collection of tomatoes from many sources.

Tomato plants are known to be either determinate or indeterminate. Determinate varieties are short-vined plants that usually do not need staking. They stop growing and produce tomatoes. Indeterminate varieties are long-vined plants that bear fruit continuously. These varieties should be caged or staked. Of course, there are semi-determinate plants and are so noted next to the variety. They are usually staked.

Early Season Tomatoes

MARMANDE 70 days. French heirloom. Scarlet, lightly ribbed fruit is full of flavor. Medium-large fruit produce even in cool weather. Semi-determinate. Seed source: ANN • BAK • TOT

SIBERIAN 57–60 days. Dwarf sprawling plants. Egg-shaped 2–3" fruits with strong flavor. Determinate. Seed source: ANN • BOT • SEED • TOT

STUPICE 65 days. Czechoslovakia variety. Early variety is good for short season areas. Red, small to medium-size 3–6 ounce fruit. Indeterminate. Seed source: ANN • BAK • BOU • IRI • NIC • SEED • SOU • TER • TERR • TOT

THESSALONIKI 68 days. Baseball-size tomatoes. Greek variety. Red, mild flavor and virtually refuse to rot even when completely ripe. Indeterminate. Seed source: TERR • TOT

Midseason Tomatoes

ACE 75 days. Proven heirloom for vigor and large crops. Round, red, low in acid. Determinate. Seed source: BOT • GOU

BEEFSTEAK 85 days. Popular old standard variety. Deep red and very large. Old-time tomato taste. Indeterminate. Seed source: ANN • BAK • BOT • GUR • TOT

BRANDYWINE RED 85 days. Large-lobed, beefsteak-shaped with thin, pinkish red skin. Not acidic. Best staked or grown on a trellis. 16-ounce tomatoes. Indeterminate. Seed source: BOT • COO • GOU • GUR • IRI • JOHN • NIC • PAR • SEED • SHU • SOU • TER • TERR • TOT

COSTOLUTO GENOVESE 85 days. Nineteenth-century Italian heirloom. Flattened and quite attractive with deep ribbing. Standard for eating and preserving. Determinate. Seed source: BAK • BOU • COO • GOU • JOHN • PAR • TER • TERR • TOT

DELICIOUS 77 days. Weigh over 1 pound. Beefsteak type. Small cavity is almost solid meat. Indeterminate. Seed source: ANN • BAK • BOU • BURG • GOU • GUR • IRI • SHU • SOU • TERR • TOT

PANTANO ROMANESCO 70–80 days. Italian heirloom. Large deep red fruit. Flesh is very rich, flavorful, and juicy. Like most Italian tomatoes, they ripen from the inside out. Indeterminate. Seed source: BAK • GOU

PONDEROSA RED (PONDEROSA SCARLET) 80–90 days. 1891 American heirloom. Meaty 10–24 ounce flattened beefsteak, deep red fruits. Tends to do well in humid areas. Indeterminate. Seed source: SEED • SHU • TOT

TAPPY'S HERITAGE 85 days. Smooth, large, red globe-shaped fruit. Bred from heirloom varieties. 6 ounces. Indeterminate. Seed source: BAK • SOU • TERR

Late Season Tomatoes

RUTGERS 72–100 days. New Jersey heirloom. Good canning variety. Large, red, 8-ounce globes. Large vine. Indeterminate. Seed source: BAK • BOU • BURP • COM • GOU • SOU • TOT

Purple Tomatoes

BLACK KRIM 78 days. Russian heirloom. Very juicy with thin skin and dark green shoulders. Brown-red when ripe. Slight saltiness that enhances taste. 4" fruit. Indeterminate. Seed source: ANN • BOT • BOU • BURP • COO • GOU • GUR • IRI • NIC • SEED • SHU • TERR • TOT

CHEROKEE PURPLE 80 days. Cherokee Indian pre-1890 heirloom. Deep dusky purple-pink color. Very large tomato. Sweet flavor. 10–12 ounces. Indeterminate. Seed source: ANN • BAK • BOT • BOU • COO • GOU • IRI • NIC • PAR • PLA • SEED • SHU • SOU • STO • TER • THE • TOT

TRUE BLACK BRANDYWINE 80–90 days. Pennsylvania Quaker heirloom. Extra-large full of deep earthy, sweet flavor. Some fruits tend to crack. Heavy yielder. Indeterminate. Seed source: BAK

Green Tomatoes

AUNT RUBY'S GERMAN GREEN 85 days. German heirloom by way of Greenville, Tennessee. One of the largest green beefsteaks. Can grow to 1 pound. Brilliant, neon-green flesh with strong, sweet, fruity flavor. Indeterminate. Seed source: ANN • BAK • BOT • BOU • JOHN • SEED • TERR • TOT

EMERALD EVERGREEN (TASTY EVERGREEN, EVERGREEN) 80 days. Heirloom green tomato. Medium-large fruit. Large plant. Lime-green tomatoes have rich, sweet flavor. Indeterminate. Seed source: BAK • COM • GOU • SEED • TOT

Pink Tomatoes

ARKANSAS TRAVELER 80 days. Arkansas heirloom. Medium-size pink tomato with smooth rose color. Tolerate heat and humidity. Crack-resistant. Good flavor. Indeterminate. Seed source: ANN • BAK • BOU • GOU • SOU • TOT

BRANDYWINE 80 days. Popular 1885 heirloom. Large fruit, great flavor. Pink fruit up to 1$^{1}/_{2}$ pounds. Potato-leaf plant. Indeterminate. Seed source: ANN • BAK • BOT • BOU • BURP • COO • NIC • PLA • SEED • SHU • SOU • STO • THO • TOT

GERMAN JOHNSON 80–90 days. Productive plants. Very large 1–2 pound fruit is flavorful and crack-resistant. Indeterminate. Seed source: BAK • COM • GOU • SOU • TOT

MORTGAGE LIFTER (RADIATOR CHARLIE) 79–85 days. 1930s heirloom. Large, smooth, 1-pound deep pink tomato. Rich sweet taste. Crack-free. Indeterminate. Seed source: ANN • BAK • BOU • BURG • BURP • COO • GOU • GUR • NIC • SEED • SHU • SOU • TER • TERR • TOT

OXHEART 88 days. 1925 heirloom. Meaty, extra-large tomato weighing 1–2 pounds. Firm flesh with few seeds and mild flavor. Indeterminate. Seed source: BAK • COM • SHU • SOU • TOT

TAPPY'S FINEST 77 days. West Virginia heirloom. Slightly irregular fruits are a bit flattened, weigh 14–16 ounces, and sometimes up to 2 pounds. Very meaty with small core. Excellent processing tomato. Makes great tomato juice. Indeterminate. Seed source: SOU

Yellow Tomatoes

AZOYCHKA 80 days. Russian heirloom. Glowing lemon-yellow color, round, flat, and weigh 6–8 ounces. Sweet, rich, citrusy taste. Indeterminate. Seed source: ANN • BAK • GOU • TOT

GOLDEN PONDEROSA 78 days. West Virginia heirloom. Large core, yellow-gold fruits weigh over 1 pound. Mild-flavored, sub-acid fruits. Indeterminate. Seed source: SOU • TOT

YELLOW BRANDYWINE 76–90 days. Indiana heirloom. Same flavor as Pink Brandywine. Large, slightly ribbed beefsteaks are sweet and tangy. Fruits keep well. Large potato-leaf foliage. Indeterminate. Seed source: ANN • SOU • TOT

Orange Tomatoes

AMANA ORANGE 75–80 days. Iowa heirloom. Big, 1-pound glowing orange beefsteaks. Very attractive full, intensely flavored tomato. Indeterminate. Seed source: ANN • BAK • GOU • TOT

GOLDEN JUBILEE 70–80 days. Fine, sweet, mild-flavored good-size tomato. An old standard variety. Indeterminate. Seed source: BAK • SEED • THE • TOT

KELLOGG'S BREAKFAST 80–85 days. West Virginia heirloom. Orange beefsteak. Sweet, complex, bold flavor. 1–2 pounds each. Good acid/sugar balance. Indeterminate. Seed source: ANN • BAK • GOU • PAR • SEED • TER • TOT

NEBRASKA WEDDING 85–90 days. 4" round fruits with glowing orange skin. Nebraska heirloom seeds were given, and still are, to brides as a wedding gift. 36" tall plants. Determinate. Seed source: ANN • SEED • TERR • TOT

PERSIMMON 80–90 days. 12 ounces or more. Rose-orange hue. Sweet flavor. Ripens from the blossom end up. Indeterminate. Seed source: GOU • JOHN • SOU • TER • TERR • TOT

White Tomatoes

GREAT WHITE 80–85 days. Large, 1-pound creamy white tomato. Has a tropical flavor. Smoother than most beefsteaks. Indeterminate. Seed source: BAK • GOU • TOT

WHITE QUEEN 75 days. 1882 heirloom. 4–8 ounces. Creamy white color. Intensely sweet. Indeterminate. Seed source: ANN • BAK • TERR

WHITE SNOWBALL 85 days. Skin and flesh are creamy white. Non-acid. 5 ounces each, firm and mild flavored. Indeterminate. Seed source: SHU

WHITE WAX 75 days. Creamy white Pennsylvania Mennonite heirloom. Has waxy appearance. Sweet flavor. Heavy yields. Indeterminate. Seed source: COM

Striped Tomatoes

ANANAS NOIRE (BLACK PINEAPPLE) 85 days. From Belgium. 1¹/₂ pounds, multicolored smooth fruit, green, yellow, and purple mix. Flesh is bright green with deep red streaks. Superb flavor being both sweet and smoky with a hint of citrus. Indeterminate. Seed source: BAK • JOHN • TER • TOT

BIG RAINBOW 85 days. Huge fruit up to 2 pounds. Sweet tasting. Very striking when sliced, the yellow fruit have neon-red streaking through the flesh. Indeterminate. Seed source: BAK • BURP • COO • GUR • JOHN • PAR • SOU

GREEN ZEBRA 75 days. Chartreuse with deep lime-green stripes. Flesh is bright green, sweet with a sharp bite. 3-ounce tomatoes, 2¹/₂" diameter. Semi-determinate. Seed source: ANN • BAK • GOU • GUR • IRI • NIC • SEED • STO • TER • TOT

PINEAPPLE 75–95 days. Up to 2 pounds each. Yellow fruit has red marbling through the flesh. Very sweet and mild. Indeterminate. Seed source: ANN • BAK • BOU • NIC • PAR • STO • TER • TERR • TOT

WILLIAM'S STRIPED 85–90 days. Kentucky heirloom. 1 pound or more. Beautiful exterior and interior of red and yellow colors. Indeterminate. Seed source: BAK

Paste Tomatoes

AMISH PASTE 80 days. Wisconsin Amish heirloom. Giant, blocky, Roma-type tomatoes have delicious red flesh. 6–8 ounces. Indeterminate. Seed source: ANN • BAK • BOU • COO • GOU • IRI • NIC • SEED • SHU • SOU • TERR • TOT

MARTINO'S ROMA 75 days. Italian heirloom. Puckered foliage. Heavy set of mild 2–3 ounce fruits. Fruit tends to fall off the vine when fully ripe. Indeterminate. Seed source: ANN • SEED • TOT

PRINCIPE BORGHESE 70–80 days. Italian heirloom. 1–2 ounces, grape-shaped fruit. Very dry and have few seeds. These are the famous Italian tomatoes used for sun-drying. 1–2" tomatoes. Determinate. Seed source: BAK • BOT • BOU • GOU • GUR • SEED • SOU • TER

ROMA 76 days. Thick flesh, good paste tomato. Good yields. Determinate. Seed source: BAK • BOT • BOU • BURG • BURP • GOU • GUR • HAR • NIC • SHU • SOU • STO • TOT

SAN MARZANO 80 days. Italian heirloom. Long, blocky 4-ounce, 3" meaty tomatoes. Intense flavor yields a perfect paste. Few seeds. Also great for canning and drying. Indeterminate. Seed source: ANN • BOT • COO • GOU • HAR • NIC • SOU • STO • TERR • TOT

STRIPED ROMAN (SPECKLED ROMAN) 80–90 days. Long, pointed, red fruit have wavy orange stripes. Meaty flesh with excellent flavor. Has very few seeds. Indeterminate. Seed source: BAK • BOT • SEED • TER • TERR • TOT

YELLOW BELL 60 days. Tennessee heirloom. Yellow sauce tomato, 5–12 fruits per cluster. Roma-shaped, 3" x 1$^{1}/_{2}$". Ripens from green to creamy yellow to yellow. Survives cool, wet conditions. Sweet and rich flavor. Indeterminate. Seed source: SOU

Small Tomatoes (Cherry, Grape, Pear)

BLACK CHERRY 75 days. Dusky purple-brown and look like grapes. Large vines. Unique and delicious variety. Indeterminate. Seed source: BAK • GOU • TERR • THE

CHOCOLATE CHERRY 70 days. Small, 1" oval fruits are deep burgundy color. Color develops best in sun and heat. Sweet taste. Indeterminate. Seed source: BOU • GUR • PAR • SHU • TER • TOT

GARDEN PEACH 75 days. 100-year-old heirloom. Small, 2-ounce fruit with slightly fuzzy yellow skin with a pink blush. Soft-skinned. Long storing ability. Indeterminate. Seed source: GOU • GUR • TERR • TOT

GREEN GRAPE 70–80 days. Rich, sweet, and zingy. Lime-green inside and chartreuse-yellow skin. Size of a large grape. Strong bushy plant. Borne in clusters of 4–12 fruits. Semi-determinate. Seed source: BAK • GOU • IRI • SEED • SOU • TOT

LEMON DROP 70–90 days. $^{3}/_{4}$" elongated tomatoes. $^{3}/_{8}$" diameter. Sweet, wild tomato from South America. Indeterminate. Seed source: COO • IRI • SEED • TOT

RED CURRANT 76 days. 1885 heirloom. Very small, the size of a pea, borne in clusters. Indeterminate. Seed source: COM • GOU • SOU • STO • TER • TOT

RIESENTRAUBE RED 76–85 days. German heirloom offered in the 1800s in Philadelphia. Sweet, red, 1", 1-ounce fruit grows in clusters. Name means "Giant Bunch of Grapes." Large plants. Indeterminate. Seed source: BAK • SEED • SOU • TERR • TOT

SNOW WHITE 74 days. Small, ivory-colored cherry tomato. Indeterminate. Seed source: BAK

TIGERELLA 55–75 days. 2" round fruits are bright red with orange stripes. Popular variety from England. High yields even in cool summers. Indeterminate. Seed source: BAK • THO

YELLOW PEAR 78 days. Pre-1800 heirloom. Very sweet, 1$^{1}/_{2}$" yellow, pear-shaped fruit. Mild flavor. Very productive plants. Indeterminate. Seed source: BAK • BOU • BURP • COM • GOU • IRI • NIC • PLA • SOU • TER • TERR • THE • TOT

Typical Problems

I planted in the spring, and the plants took forever to start growing. Remember that tomatoes are a warm-season plant. They'll just sit there looking unhappy if you put them out while it's still too cold. Nighttime temperatures should be above 58°F. In fact, tomatoes grow best in a fairly narrow temperature range—70°F to 75°F at night and 80°F to 90°F during the day.

My tomato blossoms keep dropping off instead of producing fruit. This happens when the night temperatures go much below 58°F. The problem corrects itself when the nights become warmer. Excess heat can cause the same problem.

My tomato plants look great; they're nice and bushy, but they're just not producing any tomatoes. This could happen because they're getting too much shade or too much water or because it's too hot at night. Try pinching off the terminal shoots and cutting down on the water that you're giving your plants.

Harvesting

Tomatoes are best harvested when they have reached their full color, but they may also be picked when showing only a tinge of red, then stored in a warm dark place to ripen.

Storage

Tomatoes should never be stored in the refrigerator.

Tomato puree can be frozen. Make an X across the top of the tomatoes with a sharp knife, douse the tomatoes in boiling water for a few seconds, then plunge into an ice water bath. You can then skin them easily; remove the seeds if you wish. Then puree the skinned tomatoes in a blender, package the puree, and freeze.

Too many tomatoes left at the end of the season? Make tomato sauce. Remove the skins by dunking in boiling water, then quickly in ice water. Dice or slice the tomatoes and fill your slow cooker. Add fresh basil, oregano, and any other herb you wish and cook overnight. You can either freeze or can the tomato sauce.

Growing Tips

Improving fruit set: To improve the fruit set of your tomatoes, try giving individual tomato flower clusters a daily vibration with a battery-operated toothbrush. This scatters pollen from top to bottom. You can also give your tomato plants a vigorous shaking. The best time to shake and vibrate is midday, when it is warm and the humidity is low.

Extending the season: To keep from losing tomatoes at the first frost, lay a wide strip of black plastic over each row or cage at night. It protects the fruit and extends the season as much as three weeks.

TURNIPS AND RUTABAGAS

Cool-season crops. Rated good for postage stamp gardens. 🌡 ▪ ▪ ▪

Turnips and rutabagas aren't grown nearly as often in gardens as are other kinds of root crops, such as carrots and beets, but they really have their own distinctive flavor and a very enthusiastic group of fans. The roots of both plants look alike, both having purplish tops, but turnips have white flesh and are about 2 inches across, and rutabagas have either white or yellow flesh and are 4 to 5 inches across. Also the leaves of turnips are edible as cooked greens; the leaves of rutabagas are not.

Planting

Turnips and rutabagas are both cool-season vegetables and should be planted as early in the spring as the ground can be worked. Sow the seeds ¹⁄₈ to ¹⁄₄ inch deep, about 1 inch apart; in stages, thin the resultant seedlings to 2 inches apart for turnips, 6 inches apart for rutabagas.

Turnips can also be planted in spring and midsummer in the cooler northern parts of the country. Where winters are frost-free and mild, they can be planted in the fall. Turnips mature in about thirty-five to sixty days, rutabagas in about ninety.

Make sure that turnips and rutabagas receive a steady supply of water to maturity.

Crop Stretching

Plant turnips and rutabagas between cabbages.

Recommended Varieties

Turnips

BOULE D'OR (GOLDEN BALL, ORANGE JELLY) 65 days. 150-year-old French heirloom. Yellow flesh is sweeter and milder than white varieties. Fine flavor. Seed source: BAK • BOU • GOU • TER • TERR

MILAN (DE MILAN ROUGE, VIOLA DI MILANO) 35–45 days. Buttery flavored baby turnip. Sweet and tender. Bright red-blushed shoulders. Favorite in Europe. Seed source: ANN • GOU • JOHN

PURPLE TOP WHITE GLOBE 45–65 days. Pre-1880s heirloom. Purple-white skin. Easy to grow. Nearly round, 5" across. Harvest at 2–3". Seed source: ANN • BAK • BOT • BOU • GUR • HAR • IRI • KIT • NIC • SHU • SOU • TER • TERR

SNOWBALL 35–40 days. English heirloom. Fine white roots have mild flavor. Good baby turnip. Seed source: BAK • COM • GOU

Rutabagas

AMERICAN PURPLE TOP (GOLDEN NECKLESS) 95 days. Pre-1920 heirloom. Mild and sweet, great cooked or raw. Bright yellow flesh is top quality. Dull reddish color above ground. Seed source: ANN • BAK • BOT • COM • HAR • IRI • JOH • JOHN • NIC • SHU • SOU

JOAN 90 days. Uniform purple top, round roots with yellow flesh. Sweet and milder than other types. Hard frost improves the flavor. Seed source: ANN • IRI • NIC

Typical Problems
Practically none.

Harvesting
Harvest turnip roots when they are 2 to 4 inches in diameter and before they get pithy. For turnip greens, harvest the leaves when they are young and tender. Harvest rutabagas when the roots are about 3 to 5 inches in diameter.

Storage
Turnips and rutabagas like lots of moisture and a temperature between 34°F and 42°F. You can store these root vegetables in a damp cellar or possibly in a cool garage, preferably in a container like a garbage can, with rags that you wet down occasionally on top of the vegetables.

For freezing turnips and rutabagas, peel the roots, cut them into cubes, and blanch them in boiling water for one to two minutes. Then cool them, place them in containers, and freeze.

Growing Tip
Seed saving: Rutabagas will cross with turnips, Chinese cabbage, and Asian mustard, so isolate any varieties you want to set seed and save.

Herbs

Herbs are fun to grow, are great for kitchen use, and have beneficial effects in the garden, which we'll discuss in chapter 7.

For the kitchen, you can always use herbs fresh; just pick pieces as you need them. You can also dry them for storage, but they should be dried quickly and in the dark, in order to preserve their best flavor. You do this by spreading them on a cookie sheet and placing them in the oven for two to three hours at the lowest possible heat setting. The oven door should be left slightly ajar (but without the light on). Store the dried herbs in glass or metal containers that can be closed tightly to preserve the flavor.

Buy the plants or seeds from nurseries, seed catalogs, and garden centers.

BASIL

Most Italian cooks would be lost without sweet basil to flavor pasta and other Italian dishes. It's also great for almost any other kind of cooking. The plant is an annual with light green foliage that grows 1 to 2 feet high. It also comes in a bush form and purple.

Basil will make an attractive plant set in a sunny corner of your flower beds or stuck into a few odd corners of your postage stamp garden. Simply sow the seeds about 2 inches apart after the last frost. To harvest basil, cut the stems regularly—the more you cut, the more they grow. When the plants flower, cut them about 6 inches from the ground, dry them, and then strip the leaves and flowers and store these in jars.

CHIVES

Chives are a gourmet's delight. You can buy pots of chives from a nursery and separate them. Plant a clump in your postage stamp garden, or stuff them in an odd corner of a flower bed. (They prefer full sun but will tolerate filtered shade.) When you want some leaves, just clip off what you need. Chives can grow for two years or more without having to be resown. It often reseeds itself.

DILL

Dill is used in pickling; its slightly bitter taste and unusual fragrance are fascinating. Sometimes the "weeds," or stems, are used to flavor salads (especially green salads) and fish and lamb dishes. Dill is good in cottage cheese or with eggs. The plant itself grows 4 feet high, with flowers in clusters. Dill is an annual.

Sow dill seeds in spring or late summer in a sunny area, and thin the young plants to about 10 inches apart. Harvest the leaves when you need them. Harvest the seeds from the flower beds when they begin to turn brown.

GARLIC

Garlic is not really an herb but a relative of the onion. It is strong medicine, and many gardeners believe that the plant (and its extracts) can be used to control a wide range of insects (see chapter 8). There are two types available: regular garlic bulbs, which contain a number of small cloves, and elephant garlic. Elephant garlic has the flavor of regular garlic but none of its strong pungency. You can, for instance, slice elephant cloves right into salads. Garlic is an annual.

Plant garlic cloves 1 to 1¹/₂ inches deep, 2 inches apart, base down, in an area of full sun. When you can see the cloves forming in a cut-open bulb, stop watering. Wait until the leaves are mostly dry, or the tops fall over in mid- to late summer, and then dig up the bulbs with a garden fork. The heads should be closed with tight skins. To store, tie the plants in small bunches, and hang them in a cool, dark, well-ventilated location.

MARJORAM

Marjoram is used as a seasoning for zucchini, as a wonderful flavoring for Italian dishes, and as an enrichment for many other foods, too. Sweet marjoram is a bushy plant that grows 1 to 2 feet high. Marjoram is a woody perennial.

Start marjoram seeds indoors in winter; then, after the last frost, set the small plants in sunny areas in your garden. Harvest the leaves and stem tips at any time, and use them fresh (new leaves and stems will appear after the cuttings). Or pick the leaves just before blossoming, dry, and store them.

MINT

Everybody should have a little mint planted around somewhere—to use for iced tea, lamb dishes, and many other foods and drinks. You can grow spearmint, orange mint, peppermint, and many other flavors. The distinctive flavors in all the mints come from the oils produced within the plants. Spearmint is probably the favorite of most gardeners; it grows from 1 to 2 feet high, producing clusters of flowers on spikes. Orange mint grows to about the same height and has a subtle taste and smell comparable to that of oranges. Peppermint grows to 3 feet, producing spikes of tiny purple flowers.

To start mint, plant roots or runners in the spring, or buy a few plants from a nursery. It needs plenty of water and prefers full sun, but will tolerate partial shade. To harvest, simply cut a few sprigs whenever you need them; the more often you cut, the better the plants grow. You can also dry the leaves for storage. Mint is an invasive plant and will take over your garden, so I recommend you plant mint in containers. Mint is a perennial.

OREGANO

Sometimes called wild marjoram, oregano (or origanum) has been an essential seasoning in Latin cooking since ancient times; today it is found in many Italian, Spanish, and Mexican dishes. The plant is a hardy perennial shrub growing 2^1/$_2$ feet tall.

Start oregano from seeds, or buy small plants from a nursery. Because oregano starts slowly, some gardeners like to begin seeds indoors in winter and transplant the seedlings later, after the last frost. To harvest, pick the leaves as you need them. You can also dry the leaves and store them for later use.

PARSLEY

Parsley is an old favorite that can garnish almost anything and is especially good in salads. There are three types: curled, plain leaf, and turnip rooted.

Sow parsley seeds outdoors in spring or summer. Soak the seeds in warm water twenty-four hours before planting to hurry them along, because they're slow to germinate. Sow them 1 to 2 inches apart, and then thin the seedlings to 8 to 10 inches apart. To harvest, pick mature leaves whenever you need them. Parsley is a biennial.

ROSEMARY

Rosemary is a great seasoning for veal, lamb, and fish and is used in many sauces and breadings. It is a perennial evergreen shrub and can grow to 6 feet tall. Fortunately, there's also a dwarf that grows only 2 feet tall. You can use rosemary in your postage stamp garden if you keep it trimmed back; otherwise, plant it in a flower bed in a sunny spot where it won't spread out to crowd your other plants.

You can propagate rosemary from cuttings taken from a growing plant, or you can buy small plants from a nursery. To harvest, just cut off leaves whenever you need them.

SAGE

Sage is good in all kinds of dressings and stuffings, for pork as well as for poultry, and it's often used in making sausage or pâté. The plant is a gray-leaved perennial, growing 1 to 2 feet tall, and there are many varieties.

You can grow sage from cuttings taken from existent plants, you can plant seeds, or you can buy small plants from a nursery. If you use seeds, plant them indoors in the winter and later transplant the seedlings. Give sage full sun. To harvest, pick the leaves during the growing season before blossoming. Cut the plant back to the ground as soon as it has stopped blooming; the plant will renew the next year.

SAVORY

Savory is used in cooking beans, other vegetables, and soups and in preparing seasoned salads. There are two kinds: summer savory and winter savory. Summer savory, which is the most popular, is an annual that grows 18 inches high. Winter savory is a perennial, also growing to about 18 inches.

Start summer savory from seeds planted in the place where you want it to grow. Start winter savory from cuttings taken from existing plants, or buy plants from a nursery. To harvest, take leaves during the growing season. Cut back winter savory to the ground as soon as it stops blooming; it will arise again the next season.

TARRAGON

Tarragon is a seasoning for fish, salad dressings, stews, sauces, vegetables, and many other dishes. A perennial, tarragon grows to about 2 feet. Once started, it's good for about two years.

You can grow tarragon from cuttings taken from existing plants, but most gardeners buy small plants from a nursery. To harvest, cut the leaves during the growing season before blooming. Dry leaves for preserving.

THYME

There are so many thymes available that you hardly know which one to grow first—lemon thyme, caraway thyme, golden thyme, French thyme, and more. As the names imply, lemon thyme has a lemon scent and caraway a caraway scent. All varieties make good seasonings for vegetables and meat sauces. The plants grow 8 to 12 inches tall.

You can sow seeds indoors in the winter and later transplant the seedlings outside, you can start plants from cuttings taken from existing plants, or you can buy small plants from a nursery. Plant thyme in full sun, 8 to 12 inches apart. Replant every three years. To harvest, cut the plants when in full bloom. After blooming, cut the plants back to the ground; they are perennials and will arise again the following year.

Now you're well-informed about which vegetables and herbs can be grown in your garden. As you can see, there's really a wide selection. Eventually, as you get more experience and become an avid gardener, you'll want to try different or unusual varieties that you've never tried before. You can experiment to see just how much you can grow in the space that you have available. That's half the fun of gardening. And that's just the beginning.

CHAPTER 7

Plants That Like Each Other

Today, *ecology* has become a household word. The postage stamp method of gardening is based on ecological principles—maintaining the balance of nature and restoring to the earth what we take from it. An important part of this effort is sometimes called companion planting, which rests on the idea that certain species of plants aid each other by their mere presence together or, conversely, that certain species do poorly when living together.

There is much evidence that plant relationships are extremely important. In the early 1900s, Rudolf Steiner and his followers in Europe developed and explored the companion plant concept. Later, Richard Gregg carried on a great deal of field observation in New York. And still later, E. E. Pfeiffer developed what is called crystallization to determine the relationships between plants.

It is now known from other research that all plants give off chemicals called root diffusates, which affect other plants in various ways. Moreover, the aromas given off by some herbs repel or attract certain types of insects. Many herbs are quite pungent, and their scents can permeate the garden, especially if you occasionally crush a few of their leaves or stems to release the oils. Many gardeners swear that herbs are cure-alls for everything that ails the garden—from bad vibes to crows to insects.

Which ones do what? It can be hard to tell. This is an area where superstition and fact intertwine. Nevertheless, there is a great deal of truth concerning the compatibility of plants, which can help make our gardens healthier and more vigorous; and that, after all, is what we want. In this chapter, I'll give you some of the general beliefs about particular plants, and you can experiment yourself to find out what works best for you in your own garden.

Companion Vegetables

ASPARAGUS Some gardeners find asparagus plants make tomato plants grow profusely. Scientists have indeed isolated a substance, called asparagine, that seems to exert a good influence on tomato plants. Many gardeners like to plant tomatoes in the asparagus bed after they've harvested the asparagus in the spring. In the postage stamp bed, you might want to plant asparagus, tomatoes, marigolds, and beans next to each other. Together these offer protection from a number of insect pests. Parsley and basil also do well with asparagus.

BEANS Beans seem very compatible with many vegetables. Gardeners have found that they do pretty well with beets, carrots, cauliflower, cucumbers, corn, and radishes. Pole beans are stimulated by corn and will use the stalks for support. Bush beans grow well with celery. French beans like potatoes and strawberries. Neither pole nor bush beans (all types) seem to grow well with onions, garlic, or other members of the onion family; planted too close together, beans and onions tend to stunt the growth of one another.

BEETS Beets do well with almost everything in the garden—except pole beans. They do especially well with lettuce, cabbage, onions, and even bush beans.

BROCCOLI Broccoli seems to do well near all the smelly herbs (such as chamomile, dill, sage, and rosemary) and also next to potatoes, beets, and onions. It also prefers to be planted near other members of the cabbage family (such as brussels sprouts, cabbage, and cauliflower). Keep it away from pole beans and strawberries.

BRUSSELS SPROUTS Brussels sprouts grow well with broccoli and all other members of the cabbage family. But never follow brussels sprouts in the same space that other members of this family have just occupied. They do well next to potatoes and Chinese cabbage. They are influenced by aromatic herbs and seem to be stimulated by close planting with sage, rosemary, hyssop, and thyme. They help repel the cabbage butterfly.

CABBAGE You can follow an early cabbage crop with beets, kohlrabi, onions, and radishes. All members of this family grow well with marigolds.

CARROTS Carrots produce a root exudate that has a beneficial effect on peas. Carrots also grow well with chives, leaf lettuce, onions, red radishes, and tomatoes. In short, the carrot is an all-around plant in companionability. However, it doesn't like dill, fennel, or potatoes.

CAULIFLOWER Cauliflower, another member of the cabbage family, has most of the family's usual wants and needs. It is greatly influenced by aromatic herbs such as basil, borage, hyssop, sage, and thyme. Don't grow near strawberries.

CELERY Celery does well with cabbages and cauliflower because it repels the cabbage butterfly. It grows especially well with tomatoes.

CORN Corn has interesting relationships with a lot of plants. It is stimulated by both peas and beans—probably because these two add nitrogen to the soil in usable form. Corn also has a beneficial effect on cucumbers, melons, squash, and other vine crops.

CUCUMBERS Cucumbers are very adaptable in the garden. The plants grow well intermixed with corn or cabbage, and they like nearby companion plantings of such paired vegetables as lettuce and bush beans or lettuce and radishes. Raccoons dislike the odor of cucumbers. If you have a problem with these pests eating your corn, plant cucumbers between the plants. Cucumbers don't care much for the aromatic herbs.

KALE Kale does well planted with its cabbage relative. It also benefits by being planted near aromatic herbs.

LETTUCE Lettuce seems to be a very chummy vegetable. It grows well in combination with beets and cabbage—that is, all three together. It aids onions and is aided by the presence of carrots and radishes. Also interplant it with French marigolds.

MELONS Cantaloupes like to be near corn. If you grow them up supports, they can benefit from marigolds planted underneath.

ONIONS Onions and cabbage do well together. Onions like to grow with beets and seem to benefit when planted near lettuce, tomatoes, and summer savory. Apparently, they inhibit the growth of beans and peas. When planted around rose bushes, they increase the fragrance of the roses.

PEAS Peas are one of those great plants that seem to help almost everything. In particular, they fix nitrogen in the soil so that other plants can use it. They especially like beans, carrots, cucumbers, corn, radishes, and turnips.

Their growth is retarded, however, by onions, garlic, fennel, and strawberries. Rotate the location of your peas every year.

PEPPERS Peppers are relatives of tomatoes and eggplant and can be grown among them without any problems. Onions and carrots do well sown among pepper plants. Basil makes a good companion to peppers and adds flavor to sweet peppers.

POTATOES Potatoes do especially well with peas and can be planted with beans, cabbage, corn, peas, and strawberries. They are especially helped by the nitrogen-fixing ability of peas. Summer savory makes a good companion for potatoes, as do nasturtiums and marigolds. Surprisingly, they don't like cucumbers or tomatoes.

RADISHES Radishes and peas are mutually beneficial, and pole beans are aided by radishes. Nasturtiums give radishes a great flavor, and leaf lettuce makes them tender.

SPINACH Spinach helps maintain soil microorganisms and soil moisture. It also produces an exudate that stimulates other vegetables, such as cabbage.

SQUASH AND PUMPKINS Squash and pumpkins like to grow among corn plants. Winter squash and pumpkins provide a good groundcover for corn, holding the moisture in the soil. Good companions for all squash include beans, mint, and radishes. Nasturtiums protect summer squash (including zucchini) from aphids.

TOMATOES Tomatoes and asparagus are mutually beneficial. Tomatoes also do well grown near cabbage, carrots, celery, onions, and peas. They help shade leaf lettuce in hot weather and benefit from its presence. They grow particularly well around basil and sage. When planted near members of the cabbage family, they help repel cabbage butterflies. They don't do well with potatoes.

TURNIPS AND RUTABAGAS Turnips and rutabagas are mutually helpful. Turnips are also generally helpful to a number of other vegetables, including all members of the cabbage family.

Companion Herbs

BASIL Sweet basil is generally beneficial to many vegetables. It enhances the flavor of summer savory and helps tomatoes grow larger. Basil is often planted near lettuce. It also repels whiteflies and aphids.

BORAGE Borage is a great companion for tomatoes; the two plants seem to stimulate each other. Borage is especially good for strawberries. The one drawback is that it spreads rapidly in the garden.

CHERVIL Chervil helps enhance the flavor of other plants. It is a good companion to carrots and radishes. It likes to be shaded by other plants.

CHIVES Like most other herbs, chives seem generally good for the garden. They especially stimulate the growth of carrots and tomatoes.

CORIANDER Coriander repels aphids when planted among other plants.

DILL Dill, in small quantities, has a beneficial effect. It is especially good with cabbages. When young, it helps carrots, corn, cucumbers, and tomatoes. It repels carrot fly. Mature dill, however, retards carrots and tomatoes.

GARLIC As a member of the onion family, garlic has the same effects as onions.

LEMON BALM Lemon balm can be a good companion for cucumbers and tomatoes.

MARJORAM Some people insist that sweet marjoram is absolutely indispensable in the vegetable garden because it stimulates almost everything. Marjoram and peppers seem to stimulate each other. It also does well planted near sage.

MINT Mint is generally beneficial to the garden and seems to repel many kinds of insects and pests. It helps repel aphids, cabbage butterflies, and whiteflies. Plant it in pots and sink the pots in the ground to keep the roots contained.

OREGANO As a close relative of sweet marjoram, oregano is considered equally helpful in the garden. Oregano and peppers seem to stimulate each other. It also does well planted near sage.

PARSLEY Parsley stimulates tomatoes and corn, especially when grown between the plants. Parsley and carrots encourage each other. It protects against carrot flies.

ROSEMARY Rosemary and sage stimulate one another, and rosemary generally is beneficial to the garden. It is a good companion to beans, carrots, and cabbages. It repels bean beetles, cabbage butterflies, slugs, and snails. It is especially useful because it attracts bees in droves. Do not grow potatoes near rosemary.

SAGE Sage is especially helpful to cabbage, protecting it from some pests and making it tender. Generally, sage is helpful to all plants.

SAVORY Summer savory is beneficial to onions and to beans. It acts as a deterrent to many insect pests.

TARRAGON Some gardeners favor tarragon as much as they do sweet marjoram in insisting that it be planted in every vegetable garden. It is especially helpful to eggplants and peppers.

THYME Thyme seems generally beneficial and can be planted near eggplant and cabbage. Many garden pests (cabbage root flies and whiteflies) are repelled by thyme.

Companion Flowers

GERANIUMS Besides providing wonderful scents in the garden, geraniums help repel white cabbage butterflies. Try them in the corner of a bed near members of the cabbage family.

LUPINES Lupine seems like a strange plant to put in a vegetable garden, but it does well with most vegetables and especially stimulates corn.

MARIGOLDS Every postage stamp garden needs a few marigolds. They are well-known for controlling certain types of destructive nematodes, making marigolds a good companion for all root vegetables. They also help protect cabbage and potatoes. Marigolds also will help reduce the whitefly population attracted to your tomatoes.

NASTURTIUMS Nasturtiums act as a trap crop for aphids, slugs, and snails and are effective in keeping these pests away from cabbage and lettuce. They also repel cucumber beetles and whiteflies. Plant them near squash, tomatoes, and all members of the cabbage family.

PETUNIAS Petunias repel bean beetles, potato beetles, and squash beetles. They are a good companion to beans, potatoes, tomatoes, and all members of the cabbage family.

SUNFLOWERS Every postage stamp garden needs a couple of sunflowers. Two planted close to each other won't take up much space and will be spectacular when mature. They act as a host plant to several beneficial insects, such as predatory wasps, which help keep garden pests under control. They also attract bees to the garden.

CHAPTER 8

Controlling Pests, Diseases, and Critters

What is it about bugs in the garden that causes a normally sane gardener to rush indoors, grab a spray can, and pour clouds of chemical spray all over a garden? This seems to be a form of insect insanity. Now, panic may be justified if the garden is being overrun by hoards of insects, but I've seen gardeners do this when I couldn't find more than two bedraggled bugs in the whole garden.

That kind of vigilance is absolutely unnecessary. There are many factors determining whether or not a particular insect attacks your garden. Weather has a lot to do with it. Insects move from one place to another and are often influenced by temperatures and day lengths (which also affect vegetables, of course); any change can send them out of your garden and off in another direction.

Insect Control Methods

Generally, I don't use chemical insecticides or fungicides in postage stamp gardens because they destroy the balance of nature. For one thing, they kill or scare off organisms and insects that help our garden as well as those that we want to get rid of. Second, using chemicals in our garden means those chemicals will get on or in the vegetables that we grow and eat. What we want to do is keep our gardens vigorous and healthy by resorting to the simplest, safest, easiest methods possible. The postage stamp garden rule is this: Use whatever works, and don't worry too much. There are a lot of ways to do that.

Being Mr. or Mrs. Clean

The first thing that you must do is keep your garden area clean. Get rid of all dead weeds, clean up piles of trash, move any lumber away from the edge of your garden, and don't let fruit, vegetables, or leaves lie on the surface. Simply haul the refuse away. Some organic materials can be put into your compost pile. (However, if you have diseased plants, don't throw them on the compost heap; burn them to keep them from spreading diseases.)

These rules of cleanliness are extremely elementary. Yet they are vitally important if you intend to garden without resorting to a full-scale chemical attack.

Getting Physical with Those Insects

All you really have to do with some insects is simply pluck them off with your fingers or spray them off with a water hose. These methods work well with slow-moving creatures. Insects with wings, of course, may just fly away and laugh at you from another plant—but not always. It's worth trying to eradicate them by knocking or hosing them. If insects do reappear in your garden, in the same or even greater numbers after you've tried simple methods, then you can haul out some bigger guns.

The Soap-and-Water Treatment

So you've tried cleanliness and physical therapy, and they didn't work well enough. Well, don't give up yet. The next thing to try is soap and water, which often does the trick. Simply mix about 1¹/₄ cups of soap flakes (such as Ivory) in 6 gallons of water. Then put the mixture in a spray can or tank and go after your plants. (The diluted soap won't hurt your plants.) You'll be surprised how well this method works.

Or you can use Safer Insecticidal Soap (a commercial product). This popular product is derived from potassium salts and is totally biodegradable and environmentally safe. It is effective against aphids, earwigs, grasshoppers, leafhoppers, spider mites, scales, whiteflies, and others. It can be applied on the day of the harvest. You can also use it as a soil drench to control mealybugs.

Oil Products

Most oil products are effective as a smothering agent and as a repellent. They control adult and egg stages for aphids, beetles, corn earworms, lace bugs, leafminers, mealybugs, and others. When mixed with Safer Insecticidal Soap, its effect is enhanced. There are oil products on the market that don't contain petroleum.

Mother Nature's Insect Predators

I always feel that I've had the last laugh when I turn friendly insects loose in the garden, and they go around gobbling up the pests that have been destroying my beloved vegetables. There are some great predator insects just ready and waiting to go to work for you: lacewing flies (the larvae really go after aphids), ladybugs (they have a greedy appetite for aphids, thrips, tree lice, and the eggs and larvae of many other plant-destroying insects), praying mantises (the young eat aphids, flies, and other small insects; adults consume massive quantities of beetles, caterpillars, grasshoppers, and other damaging garden pests), and trichogramma wasps (they're especially effective on the larvae of the cabbage worm).

Predatory nematodes (*Steinernema carpocapsae*) attack the pupal and larva stages of a number of insects in the ground: cutworms, army worms, June beetle grubs, onion maggots, cabbage root maggots, and others. They can be purchased through suppliers of beneficial insects and through most seed catalogs.

Mechanical Bugaboos

Some pests can be killed off or repelled easily using simple devices placed in your garden. Some gardeners give up and don't bother to do anything to get rid of slugs and snails, for instance. But the solution is so simple that you'll hardly believe it. In researching the slug problem, a prominent scientific institution tried a number of very elaborate methods to eradicate snails and slugs. Finally, after many years of experimentation, they stumbled on an answer: Just put out shallow saucers of beer around the garden at night. Slugs and snails are attracted by the beer and drown in it. Or maybe you're having trouble with earwigs (they're the menacing-looking bugs with big pincers;

you'll never forget them once you've seen one). Try rolling up a newspaper and putting it near the problem plants. Earwigs will hide inside the rolled-up newspaper in droves. Then you can simply burn them.

Companion Plants

Here's our old friend from the last chapter: plants that exert a good influence on other plants (or animals). Some gardeners are enthusiastic about using particular plants or herbs to repel insects; other gardeners aren't so sure. The truth is that although scientific research has proven that some plants do repel pests (marigolds, for instance, repel or kill nematodes, a variety of parasitic worms that live in the soil), it has not verified the claims made for many other plants. Therefore, you will have to experiment yourself and see what works in your garden (see the previous chapter for particulars).

Plant Sprays

Many gardeners believe not only that living plants repel insects but also that their leaves or petals can be liquefied and turned into effective sprays that give your garden strong protection. There are a couple of methods you can try. Choose plants with the most disagreeable odors, such as marigolds, chives, and garlic.

In the first method, you put your garlic (just one garlic clove is enough), petals, and leaves in a pot or pan, add enough water to cover the ingredients, bring the mixture to a boil, and then turn off the heat. Strain off the solid particles, dilute the remaining liquid with four to five parts of water, and stir for five to ten minutes. Now you're ready to spray.

In the second method, drop the garlic clove, petals, and leaves into a blender. Put in enough water to cover, and turn on the blender. Blend until the contents seem fairly liquefied. Strain off the solid particles (if any), add about 2 to 3 teaspoons of the remaining liquid to 1 quart of water, and use the diluted mixture in your sprayer.

The leaves of such companion plants as mint, rosemary, and radishes can similarly be turned into sprays and used against the specific pests that they're supposed to repel.

Or you can try hot pepper wax, a commercial product manufactured from capsaicin, an active ingredient in cayenne pepper that is a lethal stimulant for many soft-bodied insects. Combined with food-grade paraffin wax, it sticks to insects and to plant foliage, killing (within twenty-four hours) aphids, hoppers, leafminers, spider mites, scale, thrips, and whiteflies. This product is 100 percent natural. (Apply with a sprayer.)

Biological Sprays

Today there are spray preparations on the market that contain bacterial organisms that kill certain kinds of insects. One of them, Thuricide (containing *Bacillus thuringiensis,* known as Bt), paralyzes the digestive system of such leaf-chewing worms as caterpillars, cabbage loopers, and tomato hornworms without having any deleterious effect on birds, bees, pets, or humans. There are now a number of variations of Thuricide formulated for specific insects. You will find this preparation available at many nurseries and listed in most of the seed catalogs of companies cited in Appendix B.

Grasshopper Bait infects grasshoppers with a predacious protozoa, *Nosema locustae*. The protozoa spread the disease among themselves by eating sick hoppers and by laying infected eggs. And Milky Spore attacks and kills Japanese beetle grubs in the soil.

Botanical Sprays

There are some extremely effective botanical sprays. Pyrethrum, a contact spray produced from the dried flowers of *Chrysanthemum cinerariifolium*, is a knockdown insecticide. Also, it excites certain insects, flushing them from protected hiding places. It is effective against aphids, army worms, beetles (asparagus, blister, cucumber, Colorado potato, flea, Mexican bean), cabbage loopers, caterpillars, earwigs, fleas, flies, harlequin bugs, fruit flies, leafrollers, leafhoppers, thrips, whiteflies, and more. It can be applied up to the time of harvest.

Rotenone is derived from the *Derris* family of plants grown in the tropics. It is effective against a number of hard-to-kill insects, including cucumber beetles, harlequin bugs, squab bugs, thrips, scales, mites, leafhoppers, flea beetles, Japanese beetles, and more. Rotenone is an insect stomach poison. You can buy pyrethrum and rotenone separately or mixed together.

Some commercial organic sprays that are harmless to humans and animals can be found in seed catalogs and nursery outlets. Here are a few.

BONIDE ALL SEASONS CONCENTRATE PEST CONTROL SPRAY This is used in organic gardening and has paraffinic oil. It is used for scale insects, red spiders, aphids, bud moths, leafrollers, blister mites, whiteflies, and mealybugs.

HOT PEPPER WAX This protects plants from pests by repelling them. It is used for aphids, mites, thrips, whiteflies, leafhoppers, and other insects.

SHARPSHOOTER This is a citric acid that destroys the wax coating of the insect's respiratory system. Biodegradable, it is used for aphids, beetles, caterpillars, cutworms, earwigs, flies, lace bugs, leafhoppers, loopers, mites, moths, snails/slugs, mosquitoes, whiteflies, and more.

SAFER BRAND 3-IN-1 READY-TO-USE GARDEN SPRAY This works as a fungicide, an insecticide, and a miticide. It is an insecticidal soap with a sulfur-based fungicide; it targets and kills aphids, leaf-feeding beetles and caterpillars, earwigs, lace bugs, mealybugs, and mites.

Plant Diseases

Generally, postage stamp gardeners are organic gardeners and don't use chemical preparations to fight plant diseases, blight, and fungi. In a postage stamp garden we keep disease to a minimum without chemical help by resorting chiefly to two procedures: planting disease-resistant varieties of seeds and seedlings and destroying diseased plants whenever they are found in the garden.

Rooting out and burning diseased vegetation is part of the cleanliness that I mentioned earlier. A few of the most common diseases that you may encounter are mildew (appearing as a white or gray, powdery or downy coating on leaves and stems), rust (appearing first as whitish pustules or warts on the underside of leaves, then as powdery red or brown spores carried by the wind), blight and scab (both appearing as spreading yellow, brown, or red spots on leaves, especially shaded lower leaves), and wilt and root rot (both causing decayed roots and revealed by the wilting of foliage).

As for planting disease-resistant seeds and seedlings, currently there is much research under way to produce vegetable varieties that are resistant to major plant diseases. Each year something new reaches the market. For instance, there are cabbage strains resistant to virus yellows; cucumber strains resistant to anthracnose, downy mildew, mosaic, and powdery mildew; and snap beans resistant to mosaic, powdery mildew, and root rot. You can get these and other disease-resistant varieties from seed catalogs or seed racks; the catalog descriptions on package labels will state the diseases to which the varieties are resistant. Heirlooms are not highly resistant to diseases, so use the prescribed method that best fits your gardening practices.

Not recommended are chemical preparations (such as Captan and Phaltan) to combat plant diseases. There are, however, organic products on the market that work well. Safer Garden Fungicide Liquid (an all-natural sulfur fungicide) is used on vegetables. It controls most mites as well as powdery mildew, black spot, scab, brown rot, brown canker, leaf spot, and more. Botanical fungicides (a neem oil derivative) are made from plants that have fungicidal properties. They are effective on the same diseases as the Safer fungicide. Most seeds purchased from seed companies have already been treated with fungicides. You can buy untreated seeds from a lot of these same seed catalogs and specialized organic seed catalogs.

Organic sprays used for plant diseases that are safe for humans and animals can be found in seed catalogs and local nurseries. Below are some suggestions.

ACTINOVATE This is a high concentration of a patented bacterium in a 100 percent water-soluble powder. It effectively suppresses and controls a wide range of soil-borne diseases.

BONIDE COPPER FUNGICIDE QT This is a copper fungicide that controls early and late blight, leaf spot, downy mildew, anthracnose, and other fungal diseases.

LIQUID COPPER FUNGICIDE This is a preventive measure preceding a rain to prevent fungal spores from landing on leaves and establishing themselves.

SAFER 3-IN-1 READY-TO-USE GARDEN SPRAY This is an insecticidal soap with a sulfur-based fungicide. It controls and kills powdery mildew, black spot, leaf spot, and rust.

So that gives you a rundown on what you can do to control insect pests and diseases without making your garden an armed camp. In most cases, postage stamp gardens won't have these problems—not to any serious degree—because your vegetables will be healthy, fast growing, and moderately disease-resistant. If and when you do have trouble, however, it's best to try the easiest remedy first, moving on to the really big artillery, such as sprays, only when they're needed.

Animal Protection

In addition to certain insects and plant diseases, some species of animals can be a nuisance in the garden. These animals include gophers, rabbits, and birds.

Gophers can be driven out of your garden by using a device marketed under the name Klippity Klop (available at many garden centers). It is essentially a small windmill that sets up a vibration in the ground that gophers can't tolerate. My garden was plagued by these pesky little beasts until I took aviary wire and made cages 14 inches around and 12 to 14 inches deep (gophers rarely go below 12 inches) and placed them in the scooped-out hole that was to be planted, then filled the hole in with organic enriched garden soil and planted the vegetable. I've actually seen gophers burrow up to the cage and back off. My vegetables survived. I leave these cages in the ground year after year and scoop out the soil in each cage and replenish it with organic material the next year.

Rabbits can be held off easily. Simply surround your small plot with a chicken wire fence.

Birds are a mixed blessing. They do feed on damaging insects and many gardeners build birdhouses to attract birds into their gardens. On the other hand, some birds will eat tiny seedlings or such fruit as tomatoes, and you may have to drive them off if they get too pesky. One defense is to hang metal foil strips on strings extended 2 or 3 feet over your garden. An extreme measure is to enclose your garden completely—sides and tops—with gauze or chicken wire held up by posts or a frame. Or you can spread floating row covers over the entire bed (available at any garden center). These same row covers are especially good when used for cool-season vegetables in late fall.

WHAT KIND OF CONTROL DO YOU USE FOR WHAT PEST?

VEGETABLE	SYMPTOM	PEST	REMEDY
Asparagus	Shoots channeled; leaves eaten by larvae or beetles	Asparagus beetle	Pick off, hot pepper wax, pyrethrum, rotenone
Beans	Colonies of black sucking insects on leaves	Aphids	Hose off with water, use soap solution, Safer Insecticidal Soap, mineral oil, hot pepper wax, sticky yellow traps, pyrethrum

continued

VEGETABLE	SYMPTOM	PEST	REMEDY
Beans, *continued*	Circular holes eaten in leaves	Bean leaf beetles	Pick off, pyrethrum
	Small plants cut off at soil level at night	Cutworm	Put paper collar around lower stem of plant and extending into soil, beneficial nematodes
	Hopping, running insects that suck sap from leaves	Leafhoppers	Safer Insecticidal Soap, pyrethrum, rotenone
	Lower surface of leaves eaten between veins; skeletonized	Mexican bean beetles	Pick off, pyrethrum, rotenone
	Scaly nymphs on underside of leaves; white adults flutter about when disturbed	Whiteflies	Sticky traps, hose spray, mineral oil, hot pepper wax, pyrethrum
Beets	Leaves eaten, leaving trail of silver slime	Snails and slugs	Put out saucers of beer
Broccoli	Colonies of small green insects on leaves	Aphids	Hose off with water, soap solution, Safer Insecticidal Soap, mineral oil, hot pepper wax, sticky yellow traps, pyrethrum
	Plants sickly; maggots attack underground parts of plant	Cabbage maggots	Wood ash around base of plant
	Holes in leaves eaten by larvae	Cabbage worms and loopers	Pick off, B.T. (*Bacillus thuringiensis*), pyrethrum
	Small plants cut off at soil level at night	Cutworms	Put paper collar around lower stem of plant and extending into soil, beneficial nematodes

VEGETABLE	SYMPTOM	PEST	REMEDY
Brussels sprouts	Colonies of small insects on leaves	Aphids	Hose off with water, soap solution, Safer Insecticidal Soap, mineral oil, hot pepper wax, sticky yellow traps, pyrethrum
	Plants sickly; maggots attack underground parts of plant	Cabbage maggots	Wood ash around base of plant
	Holes eaten in leaves by larvae	Cabbage worm and loopers	Pick off, B.T. (*Bacillus thuringiensis*), pyrethrum
	Small plants cut off at soil level at night	Cutworms	Put paper collar around lower stem of plant and extending into the soil, beneficial nematodes
Cabbage	Colonies of small insects on leaves	Aphids	Hose off with water, soap solution, Safer Insecticidal Soap, mineral oil, hot pepper wax, sticky yellow traps, pyrethrum
	Plants sickly; maggots attack underground parts of plant	Cabbage maggots	Wood ash around base of plant
	Holes eaten in leaves by larvae	Cabbage worms and loopers	Pick off, B.T. (*Bacillus thuringiensis*), pyrethrum
	Small plants cut off at soil level at night	Cutworms	Put paper collar around lower stem of plant and extending into soil, beneficial nematodes
Cauliflower	Colonies of small green insects on leaves	Aphids	Hose off with water, soap solution, Safer Insecticidal Soap, mineral oil, hot pepper wax, sticky yellow traps, pyrethrum
	Plants sickly; maggots attack stems and underground parts of plant	Cabbage maggots	Wood ash around base of plant, beneficial nematodes
	Holes in leaves eaten by larvae	Cabbage worms and loopers	Pick off, B.T. (*Bacillus thuringiensis*), rotenone

continued

VEGETABLE	SYMPTOM	PEST	REMEDY
Corn	Silks cut off at ear; kernels destroyed by fairly large larvae	Corn earworms	Pick off, mineral oil on tips, rotenone
	Ears and stalks funneled by larvae	Corn borers	Pick off, pyrethrum
	Small plants cut off at soil level at night	Cutworms	Put paper collar around lower stem of plant and extending into soil, beneficial nematodes
Cucumber	Colonies of small insects on underside of leaves	Aphids	Hose off with water, soap solution, Safer Insecticidal Soap, mineral oil, hot pepper wax, yellow sticky traps, pyrethrum
	All parts eaten	Cucumber beetles	Pick off, pyrethrum, rotenone
	All parts of vines eaten	Pickleworm	Pick off, B.T. (*Bacillus thuringiensis*), pyrethrum
Eggplant	Plants defoliated (beetles are black striped, larvae are brick red)	Colorado potato beetles	Pick off, mineral oil, pyrethrum, rotenone
	Colonies of small insects on underside of leaves	Aphids	Hose off with water, soap solution, Safer Insecticidal Soap, mineral oil, hot pepper wax, yellow sticky traps, pyrethrum
	Colonies on underside of leaves	Eggplant lace bugs	Hose off with water, rotenone
Kale	Colonies of small insects on underside of leaves	Aphids	Hose off with water, soap solution, Safer Insecticidal Soap, mineral oil, hot pepper wax, yellow sticky traps, pyrethrum
	Small pin-size holes chewed in leaves	Flea beetles	Pick off, sticky yellow traps, pyrethrum, rotenone

VEGETABLE	SYMPTOM	PEST	REMEDY
Lettuce	Colonies of small insects on leaves	Aphids	Hose off with water, soap solution, Safer Insecticidal Soap, mineral oil, hot pepper wax, yellow sticky traps, pyrethrum
	Leaves eaten by pincer bugs	Earwigs	Trap in rolled-up newspapers, Safer Insecticidal Soap, pyrethrum
	Wedge-shaped insects found on leaves; tip of leaves turn brown	Leafhoppers	Safer Insecticidal Soap, hot pepper wax, yellow sticky traps, rotenone
	Leaves eaten, leaving trails of silver slime	Snails and slugs	Put out saucers of beer
Melons	Colonies of small insects on underside of leaves	Aphids	Hose off with water, soap solution, Safer Insecticidal Soap, mineral oil, hot pepper wax, yellow sticky traps, pyrethrum,
	All parts of plant eaten	Cucumber beetles	Pick off, pyrethrum, rotenone
Mustard greens	Colonies of small insects on leaves	Aphids	Hose off with water, soap solution, Safer Insecticidal Soap, mineral oil, hot pepper wax, yellow sticky traps, pyrethrum
	Leaves with holes eaten by larvae	Cabbage worms	Pick off, B.T. (*Bacillus thuringiensis*), rotenone
	Plants sickly; maggots attack root and stem underground	Root maggots	Wood ash around base of plant, beneficial nematodes
Okra	Holes eaten in pods	Corn earworms	Pick off, mineral oil on tips
Onions	Older leaves wither; small yellow insects feed at base of leaves	Onion thrips	Pyrethrum, hot pepper wax, rotenone
	Plants sickly; maggots attack part below ground	Onion maggots	Wood ash around base of plant

continued

VEGETABLE	SYMPTOM	PEST	REMEDY
Peas	Terminals deformed; colonies of small insects on leaves	Pea aphids	Hose off with water, soap solution, Safer Insecticidal Soap, mineral oil, hot pepper wax, yellow sticky traps, pyrethrum
	Beetles feed on blooms; larvae bore through pod and enter young peas	Pea weevils	Pick off, pyrethrum
Peppers	Colonies of small insects on leaves	Aphids	Hose off with water, soap solution, Safer Insecticidal Soap, mineral oil, hot pepper wax, yellow sticky traps, pyrethrum
	Plants defoliated by orange and yellow-bodied beetles	Blister beetles	Pick off, pyrethrum, rotenone
	Small plants cut off at soil level at night	Cutworms	Put paper collar around lower stem of plant extending into soil, beneficial nematodes
	Small pin-size holes chewed in leaves	Flea beetles	Pyrethrum, yellow sticky traps, rotenone
	Leaves and fruit eaten	Pepper weevils	Pick off, pyrethrum, rotenone
Radishes	Plants sickly; maggots attack plants below ground	Root maggots	Wood ash around base of plant, beneficial nematodes
Spinach	Colonies of small insects on leaves	Aphids	Hose off with water, soap solution, Safer Insecticidal Soap, mineral oil, hot pepper wax, yellow sticky traps, pyrethrum
	Larvae tunnel through leaves	Spinach leafminers	Pyrethrum, rotenone

VEGETABLE	SYMPTOM	PEST	REMEDY
Squash	Colonies of small insects underneath the leaves	Aphids	Hose off with water, soap solution, Safer Insecticidal Soap, mineral oil, hot pepper wax, yellow sticky traps, pyrethrum
	All parts eaten	Cucumber beetles	Pick off, pyrethrum, rotenone
	Plants wilted (brownish flat bug)	Squash bug	Pick off, pyrethrum, rotenone
	Sudden wilting of runners; holes in stem near base	Squash vine borer	Locate grub by "sawdust frass" around bored hole in stem, slit stem carefully with sharp knife and remove grub, mound earth over slit and along stem; pyrethrum
Swiss chard	Colonies of small insects on leaves	Aphids	Hose off with water, soap solution, Safer Insecticidal Soap, mineral oil, hot pepper wax, yellow sticky traps, pyrethrum
Tomatoes	Colonies of small insects on leaves	Aphids	Hose off with water, soap solution, Safer Insecticidal Soap, mineral oil, hot pepper wax, yellow sticky traps, pyrethrum
	Small plants cut off at soil level	Cutworms	Put paper collar around lower stem of plant extending into soil, beneficial nematodes
	Many small holes in leaves	Flea beetles	Pyrethrum, beneficial nematodes, yellow sticky traps, rotenone
	Leaves eaten (large green worm with horn)	Tomato hornworm	Pick off, B.T. (*bacillus thuringiensis*), pyrethrum
	Scalelike nymphs attached to underside of leaves	Whiteflies	Pyrethrum, hot pepper wax, mineral oil, yellow sticky traps

How to Compost

For the amateur gardener, the word *composting* is often terrifying. It should not be. A compost pile is simply any collected mixture of vegetation, manure, or other organic materials that is allowed to decay and is then used for fertilizing and soil conditioning. It can be simply an unconfined heap, or it can be an enclosed bin or other container. It usually takes time to make one because it takes time to collect the material and also time for the material to "ripen," but anyone can compost successfully.

Before learning some specific methods of building compost, you should be aware of certain principles governing "traditional" composting. You should know that good old-fashioned composting depends primarily on particle size, on the heat produced, on the moisture of the pile, and on whether or not the pile is turned over periodically. Here are some guidelines:

1   The smaller the particle size, generally the faster the decomposition, because bacteria can then attack more surface area faster. Thus, if the leaves, stems, and other materials are shredded into small pieces before being added to the compost pile, they'll decay quicker and be ready sooner.

2   The bacteria in the pile need nitrogen. If there is too much organic material (carbon) in proportion to the available nitrogen, then the bacteria will not work as fast, and the decomposition will go slowly. The evidence of this will be poor heat production in the compost pile. Generally, you can correct this deficiency by adding nitrogen in the form of fresh manure or blood meal here and there throughout the pile.

3   A compost pile must heat up for effective bacterial action to occur. The degree of heat depends on the size of the pile. If the pile isn't high enough, it will lose heat and bacterial action will slow down. Too high a pile is also bad because it will then be compressed too much, shutting off the air supply to the bacteria.

4   Every pile also needs moisture for decomposition to take place. A moisture content of 40 to 60 percent is about right; more than this can cut down on the oxygen available to the bacteria. You can keep your pile at about the right moisture content by making sure that it remains as damp as a squeezed-out wet sponge. Just put your hand in the pile and feel. (Watch out, however, for it can be really hot—about 130°F to 160°F.) If it doesn't seem moist enough, just add water with a hose until it has the right consistency.

5   A compost pile also needs turning. Using a manure fork or a shovel, turn it so that the top and side materials become the center. This allows air penetration and also brings raw matter to the center, where more action is taking place.

When finished, or "ripe," the materials placed in the compost pile will have been converted into a crumbly brown substance with the fragrance of good earth. It's then ready to use. (The volume of organic materials, by the way, will have decreased considerably. As decomposition proceeds, most piles shrink to about half their original size; a 5-foot pile, for instance, will end up hardly more than $2^1/_2$ feet high. One cubic foot of ripe compost is usually enough to make up 4 square feet of a postage stamp garden.)

I'm now going to show you how to make compost piles with almost no effort. I'll also show you some more complicated ways to make compost. Remember, though, that I'm dedicated to doing things the easy way. After all, Mother Nature doesn't care. Just provide her with the right conditions (no matter how quickly or easily you created them), and she'll work hard for you.

Using a Garbage Can, or Just a Garbage Bag

You can produce an entirely acceptable compost in a garbage can or garbage bag, placed either outdoors or in a corner of your garage. The method isn't governed by all the principles just outlined, and it doesn't have all the refinements of some of those bulky piles out in the garden, but it works, and that's what counts. Now here's how you do it:

1   Buy a galvanized garbage can (a 20- or 30-gallon size) and line it with a plastic bag. Or just buy a dark-colored plastic bag, the kind used to line 20- or 30-gallon garbage cans.

2   Inside, on the bottom of the liner, put a 2-inch layer of soil or peat moss.

3   Add almost any kind of kitchen waste materials—scraps from the table, vegetable and fruit leftovers, orange peels, coffee grounds, tea leaves, eggshells, and so on. Although you can also add garden wastes such as grass clippings and leaves, you should use mostly garbage, because you want a moist, gooey, rotting mixture for quick results.

4   Always close the garbage bag with a twist tie and keep the lid on the garbage can between additions of new material. You want to keep air out.

5   When the can or bag is full, put it out into the hot sun and let it stand covered and untouched for about three weeks. The heat will cook it, and it will then be ready to use.

Some people object to this method, complaining that the compost smells excessively. It does. Unlike most other kinds of composting, this one uses anaerobic bacteria (the kind that don't need air). You don't have to expose the odor, however. Just close the plastic liner with a twist tie and keep the lid on the can.

Another Garbage Can Method

Here is a longer but more customary method of composting (using a garbage can, though, makes it somewhat unusual):

1 Buy a galvanized garbage can (a 20- or 30-gallon size) and punch several small holes in the bottom. Put the can up on a few bricks, and place a pan underneath to catch any liquid that might drain out from the moisture contained in the decaying garbage that you will be adding.

2 Inside, on the bottom of the can, put a 3-inch layer of soil or peat moss.

3 If you like, buy some red worms—the fishing kind—and add them to the soil at the bottom.

4 Add 2 to 3 inches of kitchen garbage, then a 2-inch layer of grass clippings and leaves, another layer of kitchen garbage, a layer of grass clippings and leaves, and so on until the can is full.

5 Put the lid on the can. The compost will be ready in about three or four months. If you start the can in the fall, the compost will be ready to add to your garden by spring. (You don't need to worry about the moisture content of this kind of pile, nor does it need to be turned.)

Using a Barrel

If you have a space problem in your yard or if you simply want to confine your compost pile to a small space, here's a good method:

1   Buy or find a large barrel—the 50- to 55-gallon kind. It can be wooden, or it can be one of those big steel oil drums. Cut the bottom and the top out, and set the barrel anywhere you wish on exposed soil. Make sure that you fashion some kind of tight-fitting lid for the top.

2   Put in a 6-inch layer of kitchen waste, then a 2-inch layer of garden soil, and then a 2-inch layer of leaves, grass clippings, and other garden waste. Repeat the layering as materials become available. You might also want to add red fishing worms to speed up the process. (Fig. 1)

3   When the barrel is full, lift it off the pile, and start a new pile right next to it. The contents of the first pile will more or less stand alone without the support of the barrel. (Fig. 2)

4   Water and turn the compost as necessary. It will be ready for your garden in about four to six months.

FIG. 1

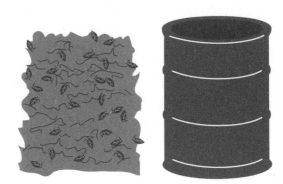

FIG. 2

A Big Conventional Pile

Some gardeners aren't happy unless they're building a big messy compost pile out in the backyard. For these types, here's a method that will keep them happy for almost a quarter of the year.

1   Clear off a 5- or 6-foot square area of ground in the yard.

2   On top of the cleared area, put down a 6-inch layer of fairly coarse material—twigs, brush, a few cornstalks, sunflower stalks, and so on. This provides ventilation underneath the pile.

3   Start building the main body of the heap in layers. Put down a 6-inch layer of vegetation materials—grass clippings, leaves, weeds, vegetable remains, organic garbage, and so on. On top of this greenery, add a 2-inch layer of fresh manure. (You can also add a thin layer of limestone to improve bacterial action and hasten the decomposition.)

4   For every two or three layers of vegetation and manure, add a 1-inch layer of soil. Soil contains bacteria that will help break down the organic material. Now wet down the pile until it is just moist, not saturated.

5   Repeat this procedure until the pile reaches a height of about 5 feet.

6   When finished, add a thin covering of soil to the pile to help seal in the moisture. You must, however, also keep air flowing throughout the pile in order to keep the bacterial action high. Take a stick or thin pole and punch vertical holes into the top of the pile, reaching all the way to the bottom. Make the holes about 2 or 3 feet apart.

7   Always keep the moisture content of the pile at 40 to 60 percent—about the consistency of a squeezed-out wet sponge. Check the moisture by feeling inside the pile with your hand, and add water whenever necessary. Watering may be required every four or five days in hot weather.

8   Except for watering, let the pile sit undisturbed for two to three weeks. Then turn it, putting the material from the top and sides into the middle. Turn it again at three-week intervals. When the inside materials turn brownish and crumble on touch, the compost is ready for your garden. This usually takes three and a half to four months.

SOIL
MANURE
WASTE VEGETATION
SOIL
MANURE
WASTE VEGETATION
SOIL
MANURE
WASTE VEGETATION
SOIL
MANURE
WASTE VEGETATION
COARSE VENTILATING MATERIALS

The University of California Quick Method

In 1954 the University of California's Organic Experimental Farm developed a composting method that's great for impatient types because the compost is ready in just fourteen days. The decomposition is speeded up by shredding the materials and mixing them all together so that the bacteria have many surfaces to work on at once. Here's how it works:

1   Mix together one part fresh manure and two parts other compost ingredients (leaves, grass clippings, cut-up cornstalks, table scraps, and so on). You can obtain fresh manure from a local riding stable or from a nursery. It must be fresh, not processed, manure, however.

2   Using a rotary lawnmower, shred everything completely. (You have to catch everything in a bag, naturally.) Simply put down a small pile of materials, and run the lawnmower over it. Then put down another pile, and repeat the process. Better yet, use a power shredder. In any case, the materials must be shredded into very small particles for this method to work well.

3   Mix everything together, and form the mixture into a 4-foot-high, 4 by 6-foot heap. By the second or third day, the middle of the pile should have begun to heat up to 130°F to 160°F. If it hasn't, add more manure.

4   Turn the heap on the fourth day. Make sure that it's warm and moist. Simply put your hand inside, but be careful because it can be quite hot. If it doesn't feel moist to the touch, about like a squeezed-out wet sponge, add some water.

5   Turn the heap again on the seventh day.

6   Turn it once more on the tenth day. The heap should now have started to cool off, for it's almost ready.

7   It should be ready on the fourteenth day. It won't look like fine humus, but the materials will have broken down into a dark, rich, fairly crumbly substance. You can let it rot further if you wish, or you can use it in your garden right away.

Composting in a Bin

Many gardeners like to put their compost in bins. There's no doubt that it's easier and neater to work with that way. After all, who likes a big, messy pile in the middle of the backyard—or even a little messy pile, for that matter?

You can make a good compost bin with a few boards. Twelve pieces of board—each 12 inches wide, 1 inch thick, and 30 inches long—will work fine. Just take four of the boards and nail them together to make a frame or bottomless box. Using the remaining boards, make two more frames. You then set one frame on the ground and stack the other two on top of it to make a large bin. Now all you do is chop up your waste materials with a lawnmower and throw them in. You then proceed using the composting method that suits you—either the Big Conventional Pile method (page 191) or the University of California Quick Method (opposite).

You can steadily multiply these bins or piles by simply taking off the top frame after the compost has sunk below its level. Place the frame on the ground beside the other two, and start to fill it with new materials for compost. As the compost in the first bin subsides some more, you take the second frame off and put it on your new bin. When finished, your original bottom frame goes on top of your new bin, forming a three-frame compost bin again.

A compost bin actually can be made from almost anything. Just make it about 3 feet high and about 2½ feet square. A neighbor of mine nailed four window screens together with a screen over the top to keep out flies. There are lots of other materials you can use: concrete, blocks, stones, a simple picket fence with slats, chicken wire, and more. Let your imagination soar and see what you can come up with.

Commercial Compost Bins

You can also buy a ready-made compost kit that includes a bin, instructions, and sometimes compost-maker tablets ("starters"). You can get one from most nurseries or purchase from many seed companies listed in Appendix B.

Commercial firms also manufacture a variety of compost bins that work well. Most are made from recycled plastic and range from 10 cubic feet to 27 cubic feet or so. If you are especially concerned about neatness, try one of these.

COMPOST TROUBLESHOOTING

SYMPTOMS	PROBLEM	SOLUTION
The compost has a bad odor	Not enough air	Turn it
The center of the pile is dry	Not enough water	Moisten materials while turning the pile
The compost is damp and and warm in the middle but nowhere else	Too small	Collect more material and mix the old ingredients into a new pile
The heap is damp and sweet smelling but still will not heat up	Lack of nitrogen	Mix in a nitrogen source such as fresh grass clippings, fresh manure, blood meal, or ammonium sulfate

Seed Sources

There are literally hundreds of seed suppliers. I'm including ones that range from small seed suppliers to bigger companies. But you can find these and many more seed companies online. The three-letter or four-letter code for each company corresponds to the source codes used on pages 30–34 and 72–159.

A WORD ABOUT THE SAFE SEED PLEDGE
Many seed suppliers have joined together to take the Safe Seed Pledge, which means that they do not knowingly buy or sell GMO (genetically modified organism) seeds or plants. They wish to support agricultural progress that leads to healthier soils, genetically diverse agricultural ecosystems, and ultimately, people and communities.

ANN · Annie's Heirloom Seeds
www.anniesheirloomseeds.com
P.O. Box 467
Beaver Island, MI 49782
(800) 313-9140
Charming selection of heirloom seed varieties.

BAK · Baker Creek Heirloom Seeds
www.rareseeds.com
2278 Baker Creek Road
Mansfield, MO 65704
(417) 924-8917
Beautiful printed catalog with lots of colored pictures. They also have a California store (Petaluma Seed Bank, 199 Petaluma Blvd. North, Petaluma, CA, 94952). All their seed is non-hybrid, non-GMO, non-treated, and non-patented.

BOT · Botanical Interests
www.botanicalinterests.com
660 Compton Street
Broomfield, CO 80020
(877) 821-4340
Lots of vegetables listed in this interesting magazine-style catalog that contains articles and sidebars with gardening tips.

BOU · Bountiful Gardens
www.bountifulgardens.org
1712-D South Main Street
Willits, CA 95490
(707) 459-6410
Heirloom, untreated, open-pollinated seeds for sustainable growing. Dedicated to ecology. Safe Seed Pledge.

BURG · Burgess Seed and Plant Co.
www.eburgess.com
905 Four Seasons Road
Bloomington, IL 61701
(309) 662-7761
Burgess has been in business since 1912. Their printed catalog has lots of color photos and garden supplies.

BURP · Burpee
www.burpee.com
300 Park Avenue
Warminster, PA 18974
(800) 888-1477
This has been one of the most popular seed companies for gardeners over the years. Their printed catalog has lots of color pictures and garden supplies. They have hybrid and some heirloom varieties.

COM · Comstock, Ferre & Co.
www.comstockferre.com
263 Main Street
Wethersfield, CT 06109
Heirlooms, non-GMO, non-patented, and non-hybrid seeds. Comstock, Ferre & Company is 200 years old. Their catalog is chock-full of color pictures. Comstock seeds are mostly Northern varieties that do well in shorter-season areas.

COO · The Cook's Garden
www.cooksgarden.com
P.O. Box C5030
Warminster, PA 18974
(800) 457 9703
Hybrid and heirloom seeds and organic plants for gourmet gardeners. Color catalog. Perfect for kitchen gardeners. Also has gardening supplies.

GOU · Gourmet Seed International
www.gourmetseed.com
HC 12 Box 510
Tatum, NM 88267
(578) 398-6111
Hybrid and heirloom seeds. Also carries Bavicchi Italian seeds and supplies. Safe Seed Pledge.

GUR • Gurney's Seed & Nursery Co.
www.gurneys.com
P.O. Box 4178
Greendale, IN 47025
(513) 354-1492
You can order a climate zone map, along with hybrid and a few heirloom variety of seeds. Large-format catalog with tons of color vegetable pictures.

HAR • Harris Seeds
www.harrisseeds.com
355 Paul Road
Rochester, NY 14624
(800) 544-7938
Lots of vegetable varieties, hybrid and heirloom, and garden supplies. They provide some untreated and organic seeds.

HEN • Henry Field's Seed & Nursery Co.
www.henryfields.com
P.O. Box 397
Aurora, IN 47001
(513) 354-1495
Catalog has lots of color pictures.

IRI • Irish Eyes Garden Seeds
www.irisheyesgardenseeds.com
5045 Robinson Canyon Road
Ellensburg, WA 98926
(509) 933-7150
Large selection of potatoes, garlic, shallots, onions, and organic vegetable seeds. Safe Seed Alliance and Safe Seed Pledge.

JOH · Johnny's Selected Seeds
www.johnnyseeds.com
P.O. Box 299
Waterville, ME 04903
(877) 564-6697
Their printed catalog is full of color pictures, information, and garden supplies.
Safe Seed Pledge.

JOHN · John Scheepers Kitchen Garden Seeds
www.kitchengardenseeds.com
23 Tulip Drive
P.O. Box 638
Bantam, CT 06750
(860) 567-6086
Chock-full of heirlooms.

KIT · Kitazawa Seed Co.
www.kitazawaseed.com
201 4th Street #206
Oakland, CA 94607
(510) 595-1188
I highly recommend this Asian vegetable seed company. They have been a
California-based business for 94 years. They explain each variety and their
Asian names. Their printed catalog contains tempting Asian vegetable recipes.
No GMO seed.

NAT · Native Seeds / SEARCH
www.nativeseeds.org
3061 N. Campbell Avenue
Tucson, AZ 85719
(520) 622-5561
This is a nonprofit organization that promotes the use of ancient crops by
gathering seeds and working to preserve the knowledge about their uses.
A wonderful resource for Southwest gardeners. Full diversity of arid lands
varieties. Heirloom seeds.

NES · Neseed
Company Code: **NES**
www.neseed.com
3580 Main Street
Hartford, CT 06120
(800) 825-5477
Non-GMO seeds. Organic seed, flower seed, herb seed, Italian gourmet seed and gardening supplies.

NIC · Nichols Garden Nursery
www.nicholsgardennursery.com
1190 Old Salem Road NE
Albany, OR 97321
(800) 422-3985
Lots of garden information, vegetables, and garden supplies. Widely adapted varieties that grow well in the Northwest. Safe Seed Pledge.

PAR · Park Seed Co.
www.parkseed.com
3507 Cokesbury Road
Hodges, SC 29653
(800) 845-3369
Park Seed has been around since 1868. They carry hybrid and some heirloom seeds. Very nice catalog. Has garden supplies.

PLA · Plants of the Southwest
www.plantsofthesouthwest.com
3095 Agua Fria Road
Santa Fe, NM 87507
(800) 788-7333
There are a few vegetable varieties. Wonderful for native Southwest plants.

POT · Potato Garden
www.potatogarden.com
12101 2135 Road
Austin, CO 81410
(877) 313-7783
If you're a potato lover you'll love this company. All potatoes, both heirloom and hybrids.

SEE · Seeds from Italy
www.growitalian.com
P.O. Box 3908
Lawrence, KS 66046
(785) 748-0959
An American distributor of Italian seeds.

SEED · Seed Savers Exchange
www.seedsavers.org
3094 North Winn Road
Decorah, IA 52101
(563) 382-5990
Seed Savers is the company that started collecting and saving heirloom seeds long before the others. They have seed-saving supplies. Beautiful catalog with color pictures and heirloom seed stories. Safe Seed Pledge.

SHU · R.H. Shumway's
www.rhshumway.com
334 W. Stroud Street
Randolph, WI 53956
(800) 342-9461
The catalog of this 142-year-old company is an old-fashioned large illustrated garden guide printed on newsprint paper. It's like stepping back in time visually, but up-to-date in products. Catalog tends to be confusing to read, but fun. Hybrid and some heirloom seeds. Has garden supplies.

SOU · Southern Exposure Seed Exchange
www.southernexposure.com
P.O. Box 460
Mineral, VA 23117
(540) 894-9480
Their mission is to ensure that people retain and control their food supply, that genetic resources are considered, and that gardeners have the option of saving their own seeds. Some hybrid seeds. Lots of heirloom seeds and seed stories. Chock-full of information. Has some garden supplies. Varieties for the Southeast, but these do well in other growing areas as well. Safe Seed Pledge.

STO · Stokes Seeds
www.stokeseeds.com
P.O. Box 548
Buffalo, NY 14240
(800) 396-9238
A seed company since 1881. Hybrid seeds and some heirloom seeds. Their printed catalog has lots of color pictures and garden supplies.

TER · Territorial Seed Company
www.territorialseed.com
P.O. Box 158
Cottage Grove, OR 97424
(800) 626-0866
They have a nice catalog with lots of pictures. Carries hybrid and open-pollinated seeds. Has garden supplies. Northwest varieties that do well in other growing areas, too. Safe Seed Pledge.

TERR · Terroir Seeds
www.underwoodgardens.com
P.O. Box 4995
Chino Valley, AZ 86323
(888) 878-5247
Heirloom and open-pollinated seeds. Nice folks at this company. They have an informative newsletter. Safe Seed Pledge.

THE · The Pepper Gal
www.peppergal.com
P.O. Box 23006
Fort Lauderdale, FL 33307
(954) 537-5540
Specialist in hot, sweet, and ornamental peppers. Some tomatoes and pumpkins included. Some garden supplies.

THO · Thompson & Morgan
www.tmseeds.com
P.O. Box 397
Aurora, IN 47001
(800) 274-7333
Features hybrid and some heirloom seeds. Their catalog has lots of color pictures.

TOM · Tomato Growers Supply Company
www.tomatogrowers.com
P.O. Box 60015
Ft. Myers, FL 33906
(888) 478-7333
They carry a huge variety of tomatoes, peppers, some eggplant, and tomatillos seeds. All varieties are non-GMO and not chemically treated with pesticides or fungicides. They also carry garden supplies and have a beautiful full-color catalog.

TOT · Totally Tomatoes
www.totallytomato.com
334 West Stroud Street
Randolph, WI 53956
(800) 345-5977
They carry more than just tomatoes. A nice selection of other salad vegetables and garden products. Hybrid and heirloom seeds. Their catalog has lots of color photos.

Glossary

ACID SOIL See pH.

ALKALINE SOIL See pH.

ANNUAL Plant that completes its life cycle in one growing season.

BACILLUS THURINGIENSIS See thuricide.

BLANCH (1) To immerse (a vegetable) briefly in boiling water to stop enzyme action and thereby retard further flavor loss and toughening. (2) To blanch (a growing vegetable) by excluding light, as by drawing leaves over a cauliflower head to keep the buds white.

BLOOD MEAL Dried animal blood used for fertilizer; its nitrogen content ranges from 9 to 15 percent.

BOLTING Going to seed, especially prematurely. Some cool-weather plants, such as head lettuce, if exposed to high temperatures (70°F to 80°F), will not form heads but will undergo premature seeding and be useless as vegetables. Young cabbage will bolt at low temperatures (50°F to 55°F).

BONEMEAL Finely ground steamed animal bone used for fertilizer. It contains from 20 to 25 percent phosphoric acid and 1 to 2 percent nitrogen.

BREATHING, SOIL See soil aeration.

CATCH CROPPING Planting quick-maturing vegetables in a plot where slow-maturing main crops have just been harvested. It may be done between planting of main crops, or it may be done toward the end of a season, to utilize the last bit of frost-free time.

CLAY Soil composed of fine particles that tend to compact; it is plastic when wet but hard when dry. It takes water slowly, holds it tightly, drains slowly, and generally restricts water and air circulation.

COMPANION PLANTS Plants that influence each other, either beneficially or detrimentally. The influence may be chemical (odors or other exudates may have an effect), luminescent (a tall sun plant may protect a shade-loving low plant), and so forth.

COMPOST Mixture of loose vegetation, manure, or other once-living wastes that is left to decay through bacterial action and that is used for fertilizing and soil conditioning. Ripe compost is compost that has completed its decomposition and is ready for use.

COTTONSEED MEAL Ground cottonseeds used for fertilizer. It contains from 6 to 9 percent nitrogen, 2 to 3 percent phosphorus, and 2 percent potassium.

CROP ROTATION Growing different crops in a plot or field in successive years, usually in a regular sequence. Its purpose is to balance the drain on soil nutrients and to inhibit the growth of certain plant diseases. For nutrient preservation, for instance, heavy-feeding plants may be succeeded one year by plants that restore fertility to the soil; the following year light feeders may be planted, and the next year heavy feeders may be planted again to begin the cycle anew.

CROP STRETCHING Any mode of vegetable planting that efficiently extends the use of a plot of ground. It may involve intercropping, succession cropping, or catch cropping, or it may involve the use of trellises, poles, or other devices to train plants in the air to save ground space.

CROWN Section of a plant at which the stem and root merge.

CUTTING Section of a stem or root that is cut off and planted in a rooting medium (such as vermiculite or soil) so that it will sprout roots and develop into a plant that is similar in every respect to the parent plant. Nurseries and seed catalogs sell powdered "rooting hormone," which encourages root growth for this purpose (directions for use are given on the package).

DORMANT Passing through a seasonal period of no active growth. Most perennials and other plants go dormant during the winter.

FISH EMULSION Liquid mixture containing discarded soluble fish parts, used as fertilizer. It usually contains 5 to 10 percent nitrogen and lesser amounts of phosphorus and potassium.

FLAT Shallow box in which seeds are planted to produce seedlings, generally indoors.

FRASS Sawdustlike refuse left behind by boring worms or insects. The term less commonly denotes the excrement left by insects.

FROND Leaf of a fern or palm; also, any fernlike leaf.

GERMINATION Sprouting of a new plant from seed.

GRANITE DUST Finely ground granite, used as a fertilizer. It contains about 8 percent potassium and a number of trace elements.

GREENSAND Sea deposit containing silicates of iron, potassium, and other elements, usually mixed with clay or sand. It contains 6 to 8 percent potassium and is used for fertilizer.

GYPSUM Mineral containing the soil nutrients calcium and sulfur and often used as a soil conditioner.

HARDENING OFF Getting an indoor-grown seedling used to outdoor weather by exposing it gradually to the outdoors.

HARDPAN Compacted clayey layer of soil that is impenetrable by roots and moisture. If near the surface, it can be spaded up and mixed with compost, manure, and other elements to make it more open, fertile, and hospitable to plants.

HEAVY FEEDER Any vegetable that absorbs large amounts of soil nutrients in the process of growth. Heavy feeders include cabbage, cauliflower, corn, cucumbers, leafy vegetables, rhubarb, and tomatoes.

HOT CAP Small wax-paper cone that is set over an individual young plant to protect it from springtime cold. It is commercially made; one brand is called HotKap.

HUMUS Black or brown decayed plant and animal matter that forms the organic part of soil.

INTERCROPPING Also called interplanting. Planting quick-maturing and slow-maturing vegetables close together and then harvesting the quick-maturing ones before the slow-maturing ones have become big enough to overshadow or crowd them. Quick-maturing lettuce, for instance, can be seeded between beans.

LEACHING Dissolving nutrients or salts out of soil or fertilizer by the action of water percolating downward.

LEGUME Plant or fruit of a plant that bears edible pods, such as beans and peas. Legumes restore fertility to a soil by taking nitrogen compounds from the air and making them available in the soil.

LIGHT FEEDER Any vegetable that requires small or moderate amounts of nutrients in the process of growth. Root crops are light feeders.

LOAM Soil containing a fertile and well-textured mixture of clay, sand, and humus.

MANURE Livestock dung used as fertilizer. Fresh manure consists of recent excretions that have not decayed; it is generally unsuitable for direct application to soil in which plants are growing, but it is used in composting. Processed or rotted manure is decayed manure that is suitable for direct application as fertilizer.

MICROCLIMATE Sometimes called mini climate. (1) Climate from the surface of the soil to the top foliage of a plant; plants set close together overarch their leaves, creating trapped air beneath with moderate temperatures and less air-flow. (2) Uniform climate of a local site or geographical region.

MULCH Protective covering placed over the soil between plants. It may be peat moss, sawdust, compost, paper, opaque plastic sheeting, and so on. Its purpose is to reduce evaporation, maintain even soil temperature, reduce erosion, and inhibit the sprouting of weeds.

NEMATODE Microscopic parasitic worm that infects plants and animals (phylum *Nematoda*).

NITROGEN One of three most important plant nutrients, the others being phosphorus and potassium. It is particularly essential in the production of leaves and stems. An excess of nitrogen can produce abundant foliage and few flowers and fruit.

NUTRIENT Any of the sixteen elements that, in usable form, are absorbed by plants as nourishment. Plants obtain carbon, hydrogen, and oxygen from water and air, and the other elements from the soil. The main soil elements are nitrogen, phosphorus, and potassium; the trace elements are boron, calcium, chlorine, copper, iron, magnesium, manganese, molybdenum, sulfur, and zinc.

PEAT Prehistoric plant remains that have decayed under airless conditions beneath standing water, such as in a bog. Peat moss, the most common form, is the remains of sphagnum moss. Its nutrient content is low—less than 1 percent nitrogen and less than 0.1 percent phosphorus and potassium; it is also highly acid. Added to the soil, it makes soil finer and more water-absorbent but will also increase its acidity.

PEAT PELLET Small net-enclosed peat wafer that rises to six or seven times its original size with the addition of water. When expanded, it takes seeds, which develop into seedlings. Pellet and seedling together can be sown in the garden.

PEAT POT Tiny molded container made of peat, usually containing its own soil or planting medium. Seeds are planted in the pot, and seedling and pot together are transplanted to the soil outdoors. Pot shapes vary from cubes to truncated cones or pyramids.

PERENNIAL Plant that continues living over a number of years. It may die down to the roots at the end of each season but shoots up afresh every year. In areas of mild winters, the foliage may remain all year.

PH Index of the acidity or alkalinity of a soil. Technically, it refers to the relative concentration of hydrogen ions in the soil. The index ranges from 0 for extreme acidity, to 7 for neutral, to 14 for extreme alkalinity. (The extremes, however, are rarely reached. A pH of 4.0 would be considered strongly acid; 9.0, strongly alkaline.) Soils in areas of heavy rainfall tend to be acid; those in areas of light rainfall tend to be alkaline. Adding peat moss, sawdust, or rotted bark to the soil increases acidity; adding lime increases alkalinity. Vegetables do best in a slightly acid soil, with a pH of 6.5 to 7.0; a safe range is 6.0 to 7.5.

PHOSPHORUS One of the three most important plant nutrients, the others being nitrogen and potassium. It is especially associated with the production of seeds and fruits and with the development of good roots.

PINCHING Snipping off or shortening (shoots or buds) in order to produce a certain plant shape or to increase or decrease blooms or fruits. The snipping is done with finger and thumb. Pinching the terminus of the main stem forces greater side branching. Pinching off the side shoots, conversely, stimulates more growth in the main stem, as well as in other remaining side stems.

POLLINATION Sexual reproduction in plants. Pollen, the fine dust produced by the male stamen of a flower, joins with the ovule of the female pistil of a flower, and the result is a seed to produce the next generation.

POTASH Any potassium or potassium compound used for fertilizer. The potash in wood ash is potassium carbonate.

POTASSIUM One of the three most important plant nutrients, the others being nitrogen and phosphorus. Its special value is to promote the general vigor of a plant and to increase its resistance to disease and cold. It also promotes sturdy roots.

PYRETHRUM Insecticide made from the dried powdered flowers of certain plants of the Chrysanthemum genus. It is especially effective against aphids, leafhoppers, caterpillars, thrips, and leafminers.

ROCK PHOSPHATE Finely ground rock powder containing calcium phosphate. It contains up to 30 percent phosphoric acid. Superphosphate is rock phosphate that has been specially treated to yield phosphorus in various grades—16, 20, or 45 percent. It also contains the nutrients calcium and sulfur.

ROTENONE Insecticide derived from the roots (and sometimes the stems) of certain New World tropical shrubs and vines of the genera *Derris* and *Lonchocarpus*. It is especially effective against beetles, caterpillars, leafminers, thrips, aphids, and leafhoppers.

RYANIA Insecticide made from the ground stems of a tropical South American shrub, *Patrisia pyrifera*. It is used especially against the corn borer.

SAND Tiny, water-worn particles of silicon and other rocks, each usually less than 2 millimeters in diameter. The granules allow free movement of air and water—so free, however, that water flows out readily and leaches out nutrients quickly.

SEEDLING Very young plant, especially one grown from seed.

SET (1) Small bulb, tuber, or root, or a section of a bulb, tuber, or root that is planted. (2) As a verb, often with *out*, to fix (a plant) in the soil, as in *to set out seedlings*.

SOIL AERATION Flow of oxygen and carbon dioxide within the soil, between the ground surface and plant roots and soil microorganisms. Plant roots absorb oxygen and release carbon dioxide (as opposed to plant leaves, which absorb carbon dioxide and release oxygen). Oxygen is also necessary to soil bacteria and fungi to decompose organic matter and produce humus.

SUBSOIL Bed of earthy soil immediately beneath the topsoil. The size of the soil particles may be larger than that of topsoil, sometimes approaching gravel size.

SUCCESSION PLANTING Planting a new crop as soon as the first one is harvested. This harvesting and replanting in the same spot may occur more than once in a season, and it may involve the planting of the same vegetable or of different vegetables.

SUPERPHOSPHATE See rock phosphate.

THINNING Pulling up young plants from a group so that the ones left in the soil have more room to develop properly.

THURICIDE Insecticide containing bacteria (*Bacillus thuringiensis*) that infect and kill several kinds of worms and caterpillars, without being toxic to plants or other animals.

TOPSOIL Surface layer of soil, containing fine rock particles and decayed or decaying organic matter. Its thickness varies from 1 to 2 inches to several feet, depending on the geographic region and past treatment of the soil.

VEGETABLE CLASSIFICATION Categorization of vegetables on the basis of the part of the plant that is used for food. Major root vegetables are beets, carrots, radishes, rutabagas, and turnips. A common stem vegetable is asparagus. Major tuber vegetables are potatoes and yams. Major leaf and leafstalk vegetables are brussels sprouts, cabbage, celery, endive, kale, lettuce, mustard greens, rhubarb, spinach, and Swiss chard. Major bulb vegetables are onions and garlic. The chief immature flowering vegetables are broccoli and cauliflower. Major vegetables that come as fruits (the seed-bearing parts) are beans, corn, cucumbers, eggplant, melons, okra, peas, peppers, squash, and tomatoes.

VERMICULITE Artificial planting medium consisting of inflated mica. It is highly water absorbent and lightweight and is used mainly for growing seeds or plant cuttings. It can also be used to increase the water absorbency of soils.

WOOD ASH Burned residue of wood, used as fertilizer. Its nutrient content varies greatly. Hardwood ash can contain as much as 10 percent potassium; softwood, as little as 2 percent. Exposure to rain can also leach out the nutrients. Wood ash runs high in lime (alkaline) content—sometimes as much as 40 percent lime.

About the Author

Karen Newcomb has contributed to and co-written (with her late husband, Duane) many gardening books, including *The California Vegetable Patch*, *The Complete Vegetable Gardener's Sourcebook*, *The Postage Stamp Garden Book*, *The Postage Stamp Kitchen Garden Book*, *Small Space Big Harvest*, *Growing Vegetables the Big Yield Small Space Way*, *Rx for Your Vegetable Garden*, and *The Backyard Vegetable Factory*. A vegetable gardener all her life, she is a regular online vegetable garden blogger for *Grit* magazine and *Cappers Farmer*. Visit Karen Newcomb's garden website www.postagestampvegetablegardening.com for garden information, vegetable varieties, and more.

Index

In loving memory of my late husband, Duane Newcomb.
A special thank-you to my editor, Lisa Regul.

Originally published in different form as *The Postage Stamp Garden Book* by Adams Media,
Holbrook, MA, in 1999 and by J.P. Tarcher, Los Angeles, CA, in 1975.

Library of Congress Cataloging-in-Publication Data
Newcomb, Karen.
 The postage stamp vegetable garden : grow tons of organic vegetables in tiny spaces and
containers / Karen Newcomb. — First Ten Speed Press edition.
     pages cm
 Other title: Grow tons of organic vegetables in tiny spaces and containers
 "Originally published in different form as The postage stamp garden book by Adams Media,
Holbrook, MA in 1999 and by J.P. Tarcher, Los Angeles, CA in 1975."
1. Vegetable gardening. 2. Organic gardening. 3. Small gardens. I. Title. II. Title: Grow tons
of organic vegetables in tiny spaces and containers.
 SB321.N45 2015
 635—dc23
                    2014027489

Trade Paperback ISBN: 978-1-60774-683-6
eBook ISBN: 978-1-60774-684-3

Printed in the United States of America

Design by Chloe Rawlins
Illustrations by Diana Heom
Front cover photograph by Richard Bloom

10 9 8 7 6 5 4 3 2 1

First Ten Speed Press Edition